PRAIS

WHAT CUSTOMERS LIKE ABOUT YOU

"*What Customers Like About You* makes a powerful case for adding emotional value to your customer service and then demonstrates how to do it."
People Management

"Full of valuable advice . . . Freemantle demolishes several myths and supplies a brilliant chapter on recruitment that alone makes his book a must."
Management Today

"Full of tips on how to instill the crucial mindset into frontline staff. Try the one-hour e-value course on your team."
Director

"Words of wisdom which have wide relevance at a time when customer service is increasingly under attack."
Evening Standard

"Challenges managers to re-evaluate their approach."
The Times

"There are lots of case studies, many of which are inspirational."
Financial Times

"A valuable addition to the bookshelf . . . useful in untangling the behavioural problems associated with customer care."
Professional Manager

"His arguments are strong and clearly presented. This book is full of practical good sense."
Business Life

This book is dedicated to...

...the Freemantle family
*   who seem to be born writers and travelers*

...my late father George who taught me many of the lessons in this book
...my mother Nora who has always loved writing and traveling
...my brother Mike who is also a writer and traveler, his wife Mary and their own family of wandering children, Helen, Dominic, Charlotte and Lizzie
...my "grown-up" children, including Kate who travels much and Tom who is the exception and favors the world of music, together with his wife Nicky and their son (my grandson) Louis George
...my "younger" daughter Ruth-Elena who is displaying an increasing talent as a writer
...my step-daughter Linnet who has traveled to more countries than I can remember.

And finally
...my beautiful wife Mechi who traveled all the way from Venezuela to spend her life with me and travels with me when she can and writes to me when she can't.

WHAT CUSTOMERS LIKE ABOUT YOU

Adding Emotional Value for Service Excellence and Competitive Advantage

DAVID FREEMANTLE

NICHOLAS BREALEY
PUBLISHING

LONDON

This edition first published by
Nicholas Brealey Publishing Limited in 1999

First published in hardback in 1998
Reprinted 1999

36 John Street   1163 E. Ogden Avenue, Suite 705-229
London   Naperville
WC1N 2AT, UK   IL 60563-8535, USA
Tel: +44 (0)171 430 0224   Tel: (888) BREALEY
Fax: +44 (0)171 404 8311   Fax: (630) 428 3442
                    http://www.nbrealey-books.com

© David Freemantle 1998
The right of David Freemantle to be identified as the author of this work has
been asserted in accordance with the Copyright, Designs and
Patents Act 1988.

Library of Congress Cataloging-in-Publication Data

Freemantle, David.
     What customers like about you : adding emotional value for service
excellence and competitive advantage / David Freemantle.
          p.   cm.
     ISBN 1-85788-201-6 (alk. paper)
     1. Customer loyalty. 2. Customer relations. 3. Service
industries. I. Title.
     HF5415.525.F73 1998
     658.8'12--DC21   98-30598
                                                                         CIP

ISBN 1-85788-201-6 (hardback)

British Library Cataloguing in Publication Data
A catalogue record for this book is available from the
British Library.

Printed in Finland by Werner Söderström Oy.

CONTENTS

ACKNOWLEDGEMENTS

Two years ago I set out on my travels to find out why some companies excelled at customer service and others failed, despite their genuine efforts to achieve it. A large number of people around the world contributed to this research in some shape or form. Each one of them "added emotional value" in helping me find the answer – the answer being of course that as customer service "stars" they added emotional value to the service they provide their customers.

These stars who, together with their teams, gave me their time, mostly in face-to-face meetings together with telephone calls and occasionally in writing, are listed in Appendix I. I am incredibly grateful to them all.

I am also grateful to my publisher Nicholas Brealey, who has taken an immense personal interest in this book and helped improve it beyond recognition.

Finally, I am forever grateful to my wife Mechi who provided me with much emotional support and who has helped me learn the lessons of adding emotional value. She epitomizes much of what I advocate in this book.

1

THE IMPORTANCE

OF BEING LIKED

S OMETHING IS GOING WRONG. DESPITE THE EXTENSIVE AND SINCERE efforts of many senior executives to increase profits through better marketing and better customer service, many companies are still failing to deliver the goods.

Ever since Tom Peters' book *In Search of Excellence* was published in 1982 a great deal of attention has been paid to customer service and methods for improving it. I have yet to come across a single company anywhere in the world which does not say that customer service is important. Most companies I know have initiated some form of customer service improvement program.

Yet despite all these initiatives, customer satisfaction levels are falling. A report in the December 1995 issue of *Fortune* stated that in the previous year, overall customer satisfaction ratings in the USA had declined one full percentage point from 74.8 to 73.7 percent.

Another report in the January 1998 issue of the *Harvard Business Review* revealed that "customer satisfaction rates in the United States are at an all-time low, while complaints, boycotts, and other expressions of consumer discontent rise."

In September 1997 the UK National Consumer Council reported that customer service is getting worse – 43 percent of people surveyed had made at least one complaint about service levels in the previous year. The comparable figure from five years previously was only 25 percent.

According to a research report published in November 1996 by the Henley Centre in the UK, this decline in service levels is costing companies billions in lost revenue. The researchers estimated that a 1 percent cut in customer service problems could generate an extra £16 million ($25 million) in profits for a typical medium-sized company over five years.

The same paradox applies to marketing. As companies strive to outmarket their competitors new vogues in marketing techniques are created, vogues which the gurus promulgate and many companies try to emulate. For example, over the last few years "relationship marketing" has become popular. Yet there now seem to be severe doubts about its efficacy. A major article in the *Harvard Business Review* (January 1998) was entitled "Preventing the premature death of relationship marketing". To quote: "ironically, the very things that marketeers are doing to build relationships with customers are often the things that are destroying those relationships".

Business schools have jumped on the bandwagon and have focused on improving customer service and marketing to boost profitability. But despite all this accumulated knowledge and apparent wisdom, over 46 percent of companies named in the Fortune 500 during the 1980s have disappeared from the list. There are daily reports in the financial press of large organizations struggling to survive, of yet another well-known company posting a "profits warning".

Where did these companies go wrong? Many of them were applying the latest theories, systems and practices advocated by the experts. Yet these did not work for them.

The small number of companies which are consistently successful rarely comply with the theories, analyses and practices advocated by business school professors, despite the soundness of their proponents' reasoning and the comprehensive nature of their facts. One only has to look at SouthWest Airlines and Herb Kelleher to conclude that perhaps you have to be "nuts" (in other words, totally irrational) to be successful! Conversely, you might also conclude that we are trying to be too rational in analyzing and determining the routes to success.

In preparation for this book I sought to investigate this paradox, why the application of all of the theories about excellence in customer service rarely led to success. My studies led me to many different companies around the world. I talked with senior executives as well as front-line people. Initially, my intention was to focus on customer service and try to establish why a small number of companies were so good at it while so many others that advocated the importance of service were actually unable to provide it.

As my study progressed, a pattern of attributes emerged that could be related not only to success in customer service but also to marketing and the way the company was managed. In fact, this pattern could be related to success in business in general and the overall attainment of competitive advantage.

THE ONE CRITICAL FACTOR

These attributes derived from one simple factor, a factor which in my view is a critical missing link in all those companies that have consistently pursued business success but failed to achieve it.

The factor simply relates to doing the things your customers like. The degree to which customers like your company and the people who represent it has a critical impact on business success. Simply put, if customers like your company there is a higher probability that they will buy from you than if they do not.

The degree to which customers like your company (and its people) is a function of the *emotional value* you add to the relationship. Of course, the relationship extends beyond the people customers deal with to the product and the brand. Brands such as Harley-Davidson, Virgin and Body Shop have an incredibly high degree of emotional value. This is enhanced by the people who sell and deliver the product. Harley-Davidson enthusiasts like to be served by Harley-Davidson enthusiasts.

To quote Jesper Kunde from his book *Corporate Religion*:

> Emotional values are replacing physical attributes as the fundamental market influencer ... For example it's no coincidence that the Coca-Cola Company has created an emotional universe that human beings all over the world can identify with. It's in Coca-Cola's ESP [emotional selling point] that the real answer lies, which equates to an unconcerned American lifestyle and happy people.

When there is no emotional value in a relationship there is effectively no relationship, at best an incidental and momentary interaction as a customer undertakes a transaction and walks away.

Adding emotional value is at the heart of the debate about people management and customer service. It is all to do with getting people to like each other and what they do for each other. Any organization that fails to address this will inevitably fail in motivating its people and therefore fail in customer service.

LIKEABLE COMPANIES

The companies I studied that tended to be successful also tended to be the most likeable. A natural extension of liking is loving, which can be an incredibly potent force in business. For example, customers of Bank Atlantic in Florida actually loved the bank. People also love restaurant chain TGI Friday's and airline Virgin. They love Prêt-à-Manger, a chain of coffee shops in London, and the Hair Advice Centre, a hairdressing salon in Kings Heath, Birmingham, UK.

> The companies I studied that tended to be successful also tended to be the most likeable

It is not only commercial companies that can be likeable, this extends to the public sector too. We choose local politicians and local councils not just with our votes but with our feet in determining where we live, where we locate our jobs, where we educate our children, and where we perceive the doctors and dentists to be excellent. Effectively, we choose our public servants because we like what they do for us and the community. Successful politicians and public servants add emotional value to the people they serve as much as do the employees in any commercial organization.

FUN AND LIKING

Many, but not all, of the companies I looked at were "fun" companies to deal with. They wanted it to be fun for people to come to work with them and fun for customers to deal with them. Virgin's chairman Richard Branson is the epitome of a "fun" chairman. Another example is Herb Kelleher, who spells out six guidelines for the "Southwest way to a sense of humor":

➤ Think funny
➤ Adopt a playful attitude
➤ Be the first to laugh
➤ Laugh with, not at
➤ Laugh at yourself
➤ Take work seriously, but not yourself.

Another example is Archie Norman's approach at ASDA, a chain of supermarkets in the UK. When he was chief executive he deliberately set out to make it fun to shop and work at ASDA. For example, all managers and employees at the head office in Leeds work in open-plan offices. Any one who wants "thinking time" and no interruptions dons a red cap to signify this and will screw up bits of waste paper to throw at people who still intrude.

Making it fun for and amusing your customers can create immeasurable added emotional value, but it is obviously not applicable in every situation. In many serious business transactions, fun might be out of the question and might in fact devalue the relationship that is being developed.

ADDED EMOTIONAL VALUE AND CUSTOMER CHOICE

The emotional value added in any relationship with a customer is a matter of choice. At a strategic level, companies need to choose and develop the emotional value they add to the brand, while at an operational level front-line employees need to choose the emotional value they add to the transaction. It is a question of choosing and creating the appropriate emotional value for your customers – and customers will choose to trade with those companies where they like the specific type of emotional value being added.

When customers have no choice it doesn't matter whether they like you or not, they will be forced to use your products and services and they will have to put up with whatever they receive. They might well accuse you of exploiting your effective monopoly situation, of being inefficient, disinterested and totally uncaring, but they will have to suffer the inadequacies of your product and service provision because they have no other way of satisfying their basic requirements.

The frequency of this happening across the world is diminishing rapidly, however. With the advent of globalization there is more and more competition across all countries, with a resultant increase in customer choice. For example, no longer do you have to suffer the dreadful service provided by a telephone company with a national monopoly. No longer do you have to wait months for telephone lines to be installed, nor do you have to undertake an urban trek through polluted streets before you find a kiosk where a telephone works.

Given a range of comparable and competitive products to choose from, in future customers will choose the company they like. In the main this means that they will be choosing the *people* they like. In a competitive world it is relatively easy to copy product and price, but it is virtually impossible to copy people and brand. If your company's products and prices are the same as your competitors', then customers will only choose you if they like you more, and that means liking your people and your brand more.

Where there is very little or no personal contact between the customer and the company, the brand is all important in matters of customer choice. However, competitive advantage can be better secured when a customer's emotional attachment to a brand is reinforced by an emotional attachment to the people who sell and deliver the branded product. This is the essence of added emotional value.

ADDED EMOTIONAL VALUE AND CYBERSPACE

The advent of the Internet has led many companies to create a totally new type of relationship with their customers. Some people have even questioned whether it is possible to create any relationship at all through Internet trading where all that customers appear to want is a fast, efficient response and there is virtually no personal contact.

In fact, a critical dimension of the Internet is the potential emotional value that can be added to relationships with customers. There is the ability to offer value-added services that customers really like, for example obtaining information about a company's product range and purchasing these products at any time convenient to the customer. The Internet goes beyond the boundaries of traditional customer–supplier interfaces and creates a world of opportunities for establishing new relationships and enhancing existing ones.

E-VALUE: ADDED EMOTIONAL VALUE

So those companies that are consistently successful in business excel at adding emotional value to virtually everything they do. As a result, their customers like them and prefer to take their business there to gain the benefit not only of the product but of the total emotional experience.

These companies have learnt, possibly inadvertently, that the cold application of even the most sophisticated business logic and associated systems is insufficient to command customer loyalty.

With the help of inspirational leadership, these companies have evolved by adding a wide range of valuable emotions to the way they do business and interact with their customers. For example, the success of the Body Shop is a result of the incredible emotional drive (with the associated values) exhibited by Anita Roddick and her team.

Another example is Charles Dunstone who runs The Carphone Warehouse, one of the fastest-growing companies in the UK. The company was founded in 1989 and now has over 140 stores with over 1000 employees. It prides itself on its integrity and being on the side of customers. This means doing its best to meet each customer's interests and not trying to sell them mobile telephones and tariffs that are more expensive than their needs dictate. In addition to the normal mission statement, Charles Dunstone has developed an "emotional proposition" for the company to work to:

RATIONAL MISSION	EMOTIONAL PROPOSITION
Recognizable brand	Innovative
Impartiality	Young
Meaningful guarantees	Friendly
Wide range	Unconventional
Knowledge	Customers' champion

THREE INTERRELATED ATTRIBUTES OF ADDED EMOTIONAL VALUE

The added emotional value is derived from three interrelated attributes which are manifest in all these companies and their people. These are:

➤ Emotional connectivity
➤ Integrity
➤ Creativity.

ADDED EMOTIONAL VALUE AND EMOTIONAL CONNECTIVITY

Central to the theme of this book is an assertion that to deliver "most-liked" customer service a front-line person must add emotional value during each interaction with a customer, whether that is by telephone, face-to-face contact or in writing. Deprived of that emotional value, there is a high risk that a customer will defect and gravitate to any competitor that offers a warmer emotional environment for delivery of the equivalent product or service.

Adding emotional value requires a process of emotional connectivity. To create the value (what customers like) there must be emotional connectivity between the front-line person and the customer. It is not enough for a front-line person to smile, say the right things and try to be enthusiastic. The connection will only be made if they are sensitive to each customer's individual requirements for emotional value. Sometimes a smile and enthusiasm are totally inappropriate. Without emotional connectivity at a personal level there is a higher risk that a customer will defect. This applies especially if the customer has little emotional attachment to the brand.

ADDED EMOTIONAL VALUE AND INTEGRITY

This emotional connection derives from a sense of values and what each one of us as an individual feels is and is not important.

Values in turn relate to fundamental issues of principles and beliefs and thus to integrity. In fact, integrity is the cornerstone of developing an approach to business that customers like.

To achieve this it is unwise to apply the "system" slavishly and without question, no matter how good that "system" might be. Sometimes to achieve excellent relationships with customers rules have to be broken (if not challenged and changed), routines have to be departed from, authority levels exceeded and policies ignored. This requires not only a high degree of integrity and trust but also creativity on the part of the person dealing with the customer.

> To achieve excellent customer service, rules have to be broken

The trouble with the conventional approach to business is that well-intentioned organizations attempt to develop and apply bureaucratic procedures for marketing quality products and delivering excellent service, but in fact produce a set of mechanisms that effectively constrain employees from giving of their best. Thus in the most successful companies I looked at, front-line employees were authorized to give a refund to a customer if necessary, while in the less successful companies front-line employees had to refer to a supervisor or manager for permission to do so.

ADDED EMOTIONAL VALUE AND CREATIVITY

The more policies and procedures there are requiring employees to seek permission to please a customer, the less creativity there will be in the organization. The policies and procedures will drive out inspiration, will drain people of creative energy and will inhibit them from taking the all-important risks that are consistent with creativity.

Policies and procedures force employees into mind-numbing routines and an automatic mode for dealing with customers. As such, their behaviors become mechanized and devoid of the emotional energy required to generate and sustain relationships creatively.

To develop a creative approach, you have to identify and reinforce every single behavior that a customer likes as well as identifying and eradicating behaviors that a customer does not like. It should be stressed that all this needs to be within the bounds of common sense, decency, strict morality and upholding the law.

EMOTIONAL INFLUENCE AND RATIONALITY

It is well known but not well accepted that customer choice is rarely based on rational decision making alone. There is a growing body of evidence that the greater part (if not all) of customer choice is based on emotional influence. It would be totally erroneous to assume that we can eliminate emotions from our decision-making processes and that the best decisions depend solely on rationality. Rational decision making comes into play to justify and control our emotional drives. We frequently delude ourselves that we are being rational when in fact what we are doing is rationalizing our emotions.

> **The greater part of customer choice is based on emotional influence**

In business this is critically important. Customers purchase products they like from people they like rather than purchasing products they like from people they dislike. Customers like people who give them added emotional value. When there is a lack of emotional value they perceive front-line staff to be cold, indifferent, disinterested and acting in a mechanistic, impersonal way.

PRICE, VALUE AND EMOTION

The delusion of rationality extends to the issue of price. Price is no more than a function of perceived value, which itself is derived from our feelings of how important this product is to us. In other words, price is a function of emotion. It is definitely *not* a function of any logical formula. Yet business school after business school attempts to establish formulae for the determination of price.

Near where I live is one of the top restaurants in the country. A dinner for two there can set you back between £150 and £250 ($240 and $400). Not too far away is another restaurant, part of a national chain, where dinner for two will cost you between £20 and £30.

The nutritional content is arguably the same for both restaurants.

The only difference between the two lies in customers' perceptions based on status and specific sensations of taste, ambience and personal interaction, to each of which specific values are attributed in determining choice. In other words, the difference is our feelings about the two contrasting experiences.

Price is a function of how we feel about a specific product, service or experience. We rationalize our feelings and use cold logic to justify whether we spend £250 or £25 on a dinner for two. However, there is no intrinsic logic in our choice other than one based on an analysis of our feelings and emotions.

Given choice, customers will go to the company they like. It is a delusion to believe that price is the sole determinant of what customers like. The world's favorite airline is far from being the cheapest.

EMOTIONAL VALUE AND THE OBSESSION WITH MEASUREMENT

Our stress on rationality in the western world has led to the development and application of practices based on so-called scientific management. One aspect of this is our current fascination with objectivity and the requirement to measure everything.

Objectivity has reigned supreme over the last 100 years while emotions have been dismissed as of no consequence to business management. Subjectivity has been outlawed, viewed as undesirable and potentially dangerous. It is now believed that effective performance measurement helps improve performance, so everything has to be objectively measured. This is one of the biggest and most dangerous fallacies threatening organizations today.

Rationality has become the "god" of modern scientific management. Everything has to be scientifically analyzed and determined. In creating this two-dimensional world we have avoided the essential third dimension of emotion, of people's feelings. Rationality is an important force in decision making, but its potency is severely diminished if emotion is absent or ignored.

It is very evident that emotions are not admitted into the way we think about business. We have assimilated centuries of male-dominated thinking where emotions have been associated with weakness. We have been taught to suppress emotions, fearful (an emotion in itself) of the consequences of expressing them. It should become an imperative for any organization to flush out all practices that derive from the traditional "macho" approach to business thinking and decision making. This requires an acceptance of the power of emotion.

Everything we buy – a pair of shoes, a loaf of bread or a package vacation – is based on an emotional decision directed to increasing our own likeability and those of the people around us. Even when it comes to strategic corporate purchasing decisions, I would assert that the same applies. For example, I would contend that the choice of whether to purchase a fleet of Boeing jets or a fleet of Airbus jets has a substantial emotional element.

> Rationality is critically important, but without emotion it is essentially deficient

THE POWER OF EMOTION

On 31 August 1997 we learnt of the terrible death of Diana, Princess of Wales. In the UK and across the world there was a tremendous and prolonged upsurge of emotion. Weeks later journalists and pundits were still trying to trace the logic for the public's reaction to this accident and the subsequent funeral. To quote Tony Hall, chief executive of BBC News, writing in *The Times* on 10 September 1997:

> We learnt that emotion is a significant dimension, that when people give voice to their individual thoughts and feelings, we can get at some kind of truth, a truth which would otherwise elude us, no matter how many facts we assembled.

Whether we like it or not, emotion permeates every facet of our life, whether it is to do with politics, work, careers, education, families or leisure. Without emotion we just have bare facts. These are pretty useless if they are not managed with a degree of emotion. Relationships between people are not based on fact, logic or scientific analysis. They are based on emotion. And at the center of all business success are successful relationships.

When you try to reduce business to a set of logics, formulae, facts and figures you are doomed to failure. I have in front of me a college textbook on business studies. On the cover is a boring picture of a building (not of people enjoying themselves at work). The chapter headings are equally boring, with titles like "Collecting and using data", "Production", "Human resources – individuals", "Human resources – groups and organizations". There is nothing exciting or inspirational. While a knowledge of how to calculate modal salary groups and the dispersion of data on salaries might be important, much more important, in my opinion, is knowing how to initiate, develop and sustain successful business relationships. This is a subject that is not covered in the textbook. The word "emotion" is not to be found anywhere.

There's an old saying: "It's not what you know but who you know". "Who you know" extends to "what you know about people, the degree to which you understand them, empathize with them, feel for them as well as what you do for them". This is added emotional value.

A knowledge of the mechanics of marketing, of service delivery and of people management is insufficient. You have to know your customers, who they are and most importantly what they like. I would estimate that 90 percent of the organizations I give my custom to don't know that I am a customer. They don't know my name, they don't know how frequently I use them. They don't know what I like or dislike about their service.

For example, I have been traveling via the same railway station for almost 10 years. I frequently use my credit card to purchase tickets. The staff there still don't know my name. I try to smile through the glass screen, I try to strike up a conversation, but I receive little in return. There is no added emotional value.

There are many other examples. We put up with these situations because we have little choice. Give us an effective choice and someone who takes an interest in us, who really wants to find out what we like, then we might just go back to these new people time and time again, switching our custom to them on a permanent basis. These are the people who connect emotionally with us, who provide us with added emotional value.

COMMON SENSE, GUT FEEL, INSTINCT AND PERCEPTIONS

Many of us pride ourselves on our common sense. In fact, most of the successful bosses I have come across are full of common sense as opposed to theory and highfalutin ideas. They avoid jargon and speak in language most people understand. In this way they create emotional value and make an emotional connection with others.

Common sense can be seen as emotional wisdom. The word "sense" relates to perceptions, feelings, discernment and judgement. Thus we have a "sense" of what is right and wrong, or we might question the "sense" of going out in the rain and cold. In other words, people who apply common sense apply emotional intelligence. Through experience they have developed a sense of what to do in any given situation. They don't rely on textbooks, manuals or prescriptions from above, nor do they rely on logical analysis. They sense what needs to be done and they do it. Such a sensing process is fast and efficient and far more effective than processing data through the rational mind, which tends to operate rather slowly as it analyzes all the data, weighs up the options and attempts to come to a rational decision.

Common sense is emotional wisdom

There might be a logical interpretation of what is claimed to be common sense, but the emotion and the perception are there in the first place. These emotions and perceptions are based on a sensing of what is going on and are interpreted in the light of past feelings and experience. The logic follows. Invariably logic is an afterthought to explain a perception, an emotion or a feeling.

People who apply common sense rely heavily on instinct, gut feel and what they perceive to be in everyone's interests. Common sense is therefore of paramount importance, especially in business and customer service.

EMOTIONAL LABOR

One aspect of common sense relates to how we manage people to deliver excellent customer service. Common sense dictates that people don't like to be forced to do something. Yet in a traditional hierarchical organization such "force" is prevalent.

In trying to develop added emotional value for customers, there is a great risk that managers will attempt to impose specific emotional behaviors on employees. For example, they create a policy that "employees must welcome customers with a smile" and initiate training programs to indoctrinate people with this imperative.

Research by Dr Sandi Mann at the University of Salford has shown that many employees suffer from "emotional labor", in which they go through a process of hiding or faking their feelings when dealing with customers. She states that:

> many organizations have rules or regulations that ensure employees' emotional displays are in accordance with the corporate image. This can create much stress and result not only in minor ailments such as colds and flu, but also in serious stress-related conditions such as coronary heart disease, hypertension, lowered immunity and even cancers.

So attempting to add emotional value to improve service has immense implications for the way we manage people.

THE EMOTIONAL COMPUTER

Underpinning this book are some new understandings of psychology, derived from my own studies and those of other people. The key is that the brain acts as an "emotional computer". To quote Professor José Antonio Jauregui from the Universidad Complutense de Madrid:

> The brain's postal or telegraphic service is the emotional system ... This emotional system is a genetically implanted system of information by means of which the brain informs you, the subject, about what you must do ... to perform various tasks.

Dr Alan Watkins, a research fellow at Southampton University, says that the heart really does register and respond to emotions. As such, it has a vital role in helping our brains work better. The heart is the body's powerhouse, producing fifty times more electrical energy and a thousand times more electromagnetic energy than the brain.

In her brilliant book *Molecules of Emotion*, Professor Candace Pert from the Georgetown University Medical Center in Washington DC reports on decades of research into the chemical basis of emotions and asserts that it is emotions that effectively link mind and body. She even goes as far as saying that our minds are not confined to our brains but exist in other parts of our body.

Antonio Damasio, Professor of Neurology at the University of Iowa, makes a similar assertion. He states that "emotions and feelings may not be intruders in the bastion of reason at all: they may be enmeshed in its networks, for worse and for better".

The psychoneuroimmunologist Dr Paul Pearsall, in his book *The Heart's Code*, states that: "the heart stores energy and information that comprise the essence of who we are".

The overall conclusion from this research is that emotions cannot be separated from our rational thinking processes but are an inextricable part of them. In other words, emotions are neither a luxury nor a liability, they are essential for rational thinking.

WHAT IS A CUSTOMER?

It is all very well talking about adding value for "the customer" – but what do we mean by a customer? This is not as easy to answer as it appears. One of my clients is a German engineering company that manufactures and services household boilers. We had to debate at length who the company's customers are. Are they the architects who specify this type of boiler? Are they the merchants who hold them in stock? Are they the installers who collect them from the merchants and install them in homes? Or are they the householders who use the boilers? The question becomes even more complicated when you are dealing with local authorities and housing associations who have their own complicated means of specifying requirements and inviting tenders from property developers and facilities management companies.

You may define a customer as "a person who makes a purchasing decision". However, this is much too narrow. For a start, it excludes potential customers, ex-customers and people who influence customers. In many large organizations purchasing decisions are made following a process of consultation with many people, all of whom could be included under the generic description "customers".

For the purposes of this book the broadest possible definition of "customer" will be used. That is: "a customer is the person with whom you are dealing at the moment and whom you are trying to help". This help might be by the way of sales advice, marketing information or any other activity related to a customer's specific requirements within your general area of operations.

Under this wider definition we can comfortably include internal customers. We can also

A customer is the person you are trying to help

include a boss as a customer of a front-line employee where appropriate and, when circumstances require, the reverse.

Thus branch managers of a retail chain are the customers of the people in the merchandising department at head office, who send them point-of-sale material and support documentation. And shop assistants are the customers of their bosses, who will help them with the provision of expert advice in specific customer situations.

COMPANIES THAT ADD EMOTIONAL VALUE

This book is just one input to the extensive debate that is currently going on about emotional intelligence, education, customer service and business in general. The ideas and recommendations presented here are based on the following:

➤ my own direct experience of successful (and less successful) companies
➤ working with various client organizations around the world
➤ a program of informal studies that I have undertaken in 19 different countries in preparation for this book
➤ interviews with a large number of customers of many different companies around the world
➤ consultation with many other people
➤ informal studies of many people at work and interactions between front-line people and customers
➤ informal studies of many bosses and their relationships with customers and employees alike
➤ study of many books and articles connected with this subject.

Throughout the book I will use feedback from the many customers, employees and managers I have interviewed over the last few years. The key player in each company I studied was the leader of the team, not a chief executive officer in a distant ivory tower. The passion and belief demonstrated by these front-line leaders for creating emotionally valued relationships invariably showed through to the financial performance of their units. Many (but not all) of the companies I looked at were adding emotional value in the way that I advocate – at least in part of their operation. I would often discover that while one branch (or unit or department) of a company was emotionally connected, others were not.

When initiating my study of these companies I did not always start at the top. Often I would begin by talking to front-line people and then develop my investigation from there, perhaps by asking to speak to the branch manager or general manager. Thus at the J.W. Marriott hotel in Dubai, I was so impressed with the service I was continually provided with that I started chatting to the waitresses, the house-keeping staff and others. Without exception they told me that they have a great boss in Anton Najjar who encouraged them to do their very best for customers and take whatever initiative is necessary. So I asked to see Anton Najjar, who gave me a couple of hours of his valuable time explaining his approach to customer service and people management. I was truly enthralled.

During the time this book has been in preparation I have been fortunate enough to come across some really inspirational examples of highly successful and emotionally connected customer service. Appendix I provides a few examples of the companies which in my opinion are "stars" in the customer service world.

2

ADDING

EMOTIONAL VALUE

To succeed in business we need to change our own thinking and feeling patterns in order to improve the way customers think and feel about us. Part of this development and improvement process relates to how we manage our own feelings and add emotional value to what we think and communicate.

Added emotional value is based on three main attributes that create positive thinking and feeling patterns among customers. These attributes are the essence of what customers like about you and the service you provide for them. They are effectively the external manifestation of added emotional value, in that the value is passed across an external boundary from the company to its customers.

The three external attributes of added emotional value derive from three internal motivators that effectively drive each individual in the company to deliver the service that customers like.

The three external attributes and three internal motivators of added emotional value are shown in Figure 1. To add emotional value, employees need to draw on their personal reserves of motivation to create the necessary integrity and creativity for customers to connect with them emotionally. These reserves of motivation consist of energy, emotional direction and esprit.

When a company relies solely on systems and processes for delivering products and services to its customers, there will be no emo-

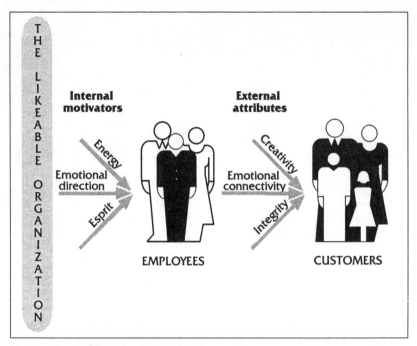

Figure 1   Adding emotional value

tional connectivity and a much higher risk of customers having negative thinking and feeling patterns. If they don't perceive integrity or creativity in their dealings with the company, customers will feel as if they are being treated as numbers and not as human beings. Furthermore, they will not see the employees as real people but rather as instruments of the system, as processors of orders and information, as robots. This is because the internal motivation latent in most employees – their energy, their emotional direction and their esprit – has been suppressed or at best directed towards efficient processing to please their bosses, not customers.

CLUSTERS

We think in patterns based on associations. These patterns are founded on deep-rooted feelings and emotions of which we are frequently unaware.

Our feelings derive from past experiences often long forgotten but still deeply embedded in our suppressed memories. Unless these patterns are brought to the surface and challenged from time to time, we are in danger of falling into routines of undesirable reactions, into unwelcome habits and into an unthinking way of behavior. Without our realizing it, our reactions become prejudicial (although we of course deny this – out of habit!).

Routines lead to automatic reactions. They are tried and trusted methods of behaving that require little effort or thought and can be exceptionally efficient. They are essentially energy-saving devices that provide us with comfort and security. However, comfort and security are no basis for competitive advantage. To succeed in an increasingly competitive world we have to challenge our routines, our standard reactions, and create new thinking and feeling patterns for ourselves and our customers.

There is a game called "clusters" which you can play with your children, your friends or by yourself. Just take any letter of the alphabet and find clusters of at least seven words which begin with that letter and which fall loosely within a broad generic classification. Here are three examples:

B IS FOR BEST	C IS FOR CEREBRAL	F IS FOR FEAR
best	cerebral	fear
better	conscious	frown
beauty	clever	fight
brilliant	conniving	fright
biggest	convincing	flee
brightest	calculating	friction
bumper	concise	flinch

Appendix III provides more examples.

The game itself is a simple method of creating new thinking patterns, based around clusters of associated ideas and feelings. It can be extended to identify all those attributes that add emotional value to customers or alternatively demotivate them (see overleaf).

e is for emotion

emotion	energy	electrify	empathy	essence
essential	efficiency	enlighten	empower	enable
esprit	enthuse	ecstasy	enjoy	enchant
emphatic	everything	ever	excite	exhilarate
excellence	exalted	ebullient	elevate	effort
entertain	enterprise	endeavor	extrovert	expert
educated	efficacy	embrace	enhance	eulogy
eureka!				

d is for demotivate

demotivate	deny	death	disconnect	deprive
draining	damaged	disaster	dented	depressed
dismissed	depraved	diseased	dictator	despot
delirious	dilapidated	disgrace	discriminate	diabolical
deprecate	delay	defecate	dejected	delusion
devil	dismal	dereliction	destruction	decay
dreadful	disgusting	despicable	despair	downcast
dreary	dirty	draconian	damnation!	doldrums

In the western world, thinking patterns tend to be based on a systematic scientific approach to the determination of facts and the establishment of reason. While the science itself is often valid, what is missing from our conventional thinking patterns about business management is the value of emotion.

When a company is able to inject some positive emotion (added emotional value) into its approach and create new clusters of thinking and feeling patterns, it is in a far better position to connect with both its employees and its customers. The end result is that employees will love working for the company and customers will love doing business with them. In the absence of these new clusters, the company and its people will go stale, relying on traditional thinking and often bad habits.

EXTERNAL ATTRIBUTE 1: EMOTIONAL CONNECTIVITY

Loyalty is based on emotional bonding between people. Customer loyalty is no different. The fashionable misuse of the terms "customer loyalty schemes" or "loyalty cards" has more to do with financial advantage than loyalty. As soon as my gas station stops giving me Air Miles I will switch my custom to one that does. Issuing freebies on a regular basis will never generate loyalty.

Human beings are social animals and as such we have a natural desire for positive relationships with others. By offering customers the opportunity of a social interaction, no matter how fleeting, a company offers something that is of value to many people.

Emotional connectivity is at the center of all relationships and is thus at the center of excellent customer service (as opposed to automated, mechanized service). It occurs when two people are able to express, share, appreciate and understand their genuine feelings about any given situation or about each other. To achieve this, each person must be tuned in emotionally to the needs of the other.

Without exception, all the companies I studied that excelled at marketing, customer service and people management had accomplished this. The majority of managers and employees were tuned in emotionally to the importance of customer service as well as to the specific needs of customers. In these companies people liked to be liked and went out of their way to do things customers (external or internal) liked. In this way they established a high degree of emotional connectivity. Furthermore, there was a great deal of emotional connectivity between senior executives, managers, employees and customers.

It would be too simplistic to equate emotional connectivity with shared passion. It is fashionable to talk about being "passionate" about service. However, passion is just one emotion, albeit a powerful one. There are many other emotions. In the companies I studied, when passion was not applicable, people drew on other emotions such as kindness, consternation and sorrow to connect with customers. Furthermore, the intensity of emotions varied widely according to circumstance. Thus customers actually liked it when front-line people showed concern (an emotion) for a harrassed mother dealing with a screaming child. Customers liked it when front-line people genuinely expressed delight (an emotion) in welcoming a new customer at the counter. Customers liked it when front-line people demonstrated genuine interest (an emotion) in the people they were serving. Customers liked it when they received signals from front-line people that they really did like them.

> Customers want to be liked by the people serving them

There were occasions when the appropriate emotional response was to add no emotion at all, for example when giving a customer "space" to think, or to relax, or to breathe. Sometimes a customer just wanted to remain silent, perhaps deep in thought, with no one approaching them. When front-line people were sufficiently sensitive to connect with the customer's feelings they exhibited no emotion (by withdrawing from the contact) and in doing so added emotional value.

To like people and to have people like you means giving a little of yourself (giving away your feelings) as well receiving and absorbing something from others (acknowledging and accrediting their feelings). It is this two-way process of emotional connectivity that helps establish mutual added emotional value.

EXTERNAL ATTRIBUTE 2: INTEGRITY

Customers will sense when a positive emotional connection has been made with them and will like it. Equally important is their sense of the degree of *integrity* exhibited by the company and its employees.

Integrity is the ability to exercise trust at every interface between the company, its employees and its customers. Customers want the company and its people to be "as good as their word". They don't like to be let down or misled, or to harbor feelings of suspicion about other people's intentions.

A cornerstone of emotional intelligence is the ability to be honest with yourself about your own feelings and to manage them accordingly. As soon as people start denying or suppressing their own feelings and emotions, they begin to behave in a way that creates suspicion. An invidious erosion of integrity takes place as they act out a role divorced from their true self.

The people and managers in less successful companies behaved like this. As a result, they were instinctively not trusted or trusting, internally or externally. They belittled emotion and resisted any expression of it, thus creating a climate of distrust and suspicion because people were unable to be themselves.

Customers don't like to feel that they are being manipulated, misled or misjudged. The majority of customers like front-line employees and organizations who both trust them and can be trusted. Every time a customer interacts with a company, they will instinctively be sizing it up to establish the degree of trust that can be exercised. Customers will measure your every word and action to see if you live up to your word and implement the actions you promise. They often equate poor service with feelings of being "let down".

Marketing campaigns, advertising and personal experience create expectations that customers trust will be fulfilled on the next occasion. They perceive an erosion of trust when such expectations are not met and promises not kept.

To achieve a high degree of integrity, executives in successful companies devoted an inordinate amount of emotional energy to creating a climate of trust throughout the organization. Openness and honesty became the foundation for all the company's transactions and interactions, internal and external, and were reflected in the everyday behaviors of managers and employees alike.

In adding emotional value, people in these companies tended to put their customers' interests before their own, for example recommending a competitor if a customer urgently required an out-of-stock item. They did not try to oversell or hide things in the small print. To prevent customers feeling bad about the company they knew they had to be scrupulously open and honest with everyone.

For example, at the Barnes & Noble bookstore near Fort Lauderdale, Florida, any customer returning a book would have it replaced without question irrespective of when it was purchased or its condition. Furthermore, customers were encouraged to enter the store, use the excellent facilities there (coffee shops, rest rooms, comfortable chairs and tables for browsing and study) without ever being put under pressure to purchase. The company genuinely wanted people to see the bookstore as a culture center for the community rather than as a retail outlet where the top 10 bestsellers were pushed at you as soon as you entered.

At HMV (UK), managing director Wilf Walsh encourages front-line people to accept customers at their word:

> We frequently have customers returning CDs which they claim are defective, stating for example that track 5 keeps on jumping. Previously we would go through the logical process of testing the CD on our own stereo system and frequently find that the CD was satisfactory and deduce that it was the customer's equipment which was at fault. This inevitably caused an argument with a customer. Now we accept the customer at his or her word. The customers like this and our front-line people like this too. If a customer perceives that a CD is defective then we replace it. Whether the CD is actually defective is irrelevant. The last thing any customer likes is to be told he or she is wrong.

All the successful companies I studied could provide similar examples. They all trusted their front-line employees to make decisions in favor of customers when there was an element of doubt.

Integrity is based on positive beliefs, values and principles. Too many companies, while accepting the importance of values, have attempted to make establishing them a policy issue. Values are written up and printed on displays in the reception area or stated in company reports and newsletters.

The establishment of values can never be an academic exercise produced by objective analysis and rational debate. Values are what people feel and are expressed in their everyday behaviors. In other words, there must be a substantial emotional element to the development and application of values. At the very core of added emotional value lie the genuine adoption and sincere application of personally held, positive values. Consider the following statements:

> As a Chief Executive Officer I really do value our people and all the hard work they put into this organization. I value them so

much that I trust each one of them implicitly to deliver the very best service to our customers. To be honest I genuinely **feel** we have a great team!

As an employee I really **feel** trusted by our bosses here. I **feel** my contribution and all my hard work is genuinely recognized and appreciated. I really do **feel** valued in this organization.

As a customer I really **feel** that the people in this company are genuinely interested in providing me with a good service. I really do **feel** they value my business.

In organizations that deliver exceptional customer service you will frequently hear these types of statements. The people making them will genuinely mean them because they genuinely feel them. Thus I often heard front-line staff at BT Mobile in Leeds, UK, say exceptionally positive things about their boss

> **Values are what people feel and are expressed in their everyday behaviors**

Richard Brimble and how they felt about him. The same applied to the customer services staff at Yellow Pages in Reading, UK, and their feelings about their boss, Debbie Hardiman. It was also the case with the staff at the Hair Advice Centre at Kings Heath in Birmingham, UK, and the way they felt about their manager, Andrew May. You will never hear this kind of statement in an organization that delivers poor service.

To add emotional value it is essential to get to grips with these genuine feelings and manage them openly and honestly.

EXTERNAL ATTRIBUTE 3: CREATIVITY

When an emotional connection has been established along with a high degree of integrity and mutual trust, there is ample opportunity to take *creative* initiatives to please customers further.

To provide such opportunities requires the abolition of fixed, rigid thinking patterns (based on the system) and the creation of clusters of new thinking and feeling patterns about ways to please customers.

When this freeing up of the heart and mind takes place, front-line employees will feel confident about deviating from routine where necessary and initiating steps that customers like. They will seize every conceivable opportunity to do something creative for their customers in their efforts to please them. Most of the time these creative initiatives will be relatively minor, for example the creative use of words in communicating with a customer. What you say to welcome one customer might be totally inappropriate for another. As soon as you have scripted welcomes you destroy the emotional connectivity and the integrity (the words are not meant), as well as suppress the opportunity for employees to be creative in the language they choose to use.

By trusting managers and front-line employees as well as encouraging them to become emotionally involved in the pursuit of exceptional service and the attainment of competitive advantage, the successful companies were able to tap a vast reservoir of creative energy (latent in most people's emotional intelligence). This could be converted into innumerable positive interactions that customers liked.

For example, at Bank Atlantic in Florida, a teller voluntarily learnt sign language so that she could communicate with two deaf customers who came into the branch every week. These customers were absolutely delighted and informed their friends in the deaf community, many of whom switched their accounts to this branch.

One British Airways customer told me that on a flight from Miami a steward serving her a glass of mineral water came up five minutes later, after the trolley service, and gave her a half-liter bottle that he had fetched for her from the galley. She had not asked for it but was delighted to receive it. Here was a steward who liked to please passengers and she liked him for it.

At the J.W. Marriott hotel in Dubai, another customer stepped out of the shower at midnight and realized he had traveled all the way from the UK without a comb. The staff there were able to deliver one to him within five minutes. The customer disliked being without a comb (it made him feel bad) and the Marriott staff welcomed the opportunity of making him feel good by providing him with a comb.

Yaya Diong, a manager with Ecobank in Côte d'Ivoire, tells of a friend of a customer who rang him in sheer desperation just as the bank was about to close. The customer had been taken seriously ill and needed to be flown that evening to the USA for specialized treatment. However, the airline concerned refused to issue a ticket until the customer's check had cleared, which would take three days. The customer had no credit card and was unable to obtain so much cash so late in the day. Yaya Diong put himself out, staying quite late to make a number of calls to the airline and then courier to it a guarantee of payment. The customer was able to fly to the USA and receive the treatment, recover successfully and now is forever indebted to Yaya Diong and the bank.

> In successful companies people used their emotional intelligence to create opportunities to please the customer

All these people were adding emotional value by creating opportunities to please customers, to do things customers liked, without fear of reprimand from their bosses, without prescription from the policy manual and without any scripted words learnt by rote on a training course.

These employees were trusted to be themselves and to create as many ways as possible to please customers. Their employers had effectively unleashed the potent forces of energy, emotional direction and esprit latent in most employees to enhance the company's prospects of competitive advantage. This is the quiet revolution that is taking place in today's most progressive companies.

INTERNAL MOTIVATOR 1: ENERGY

It is a basic law of physics and chemistry that you have to inject *energy* into the fusing of two components to create a material bond. The bond stores the energy. When the bond is broken, the stored energy is released. Unless it is controlled, the release of energy will be chaotic and potentially destructive.

The same applies to bonds between people. To create a relationship and therefore a likeable connection with another person, physical energy is required. Calories have to be generated (using a healthy dose of adrenalin) and expended to create the relationship.

Therefore physical energy is a key source of motivation. When a person is drained of energy there is little motivation.

A smile requires energy. Informing a customer of a situation requires energy. Listening to a customer requires energy. Putting yourself out for a customer requires immense energy. Virtually every interaction with a customer requires energy.

It is impossible to add emotional value to your service and get your customers to like you without investing substantial amounts of energy in each relationship.

In those companies that excelled at service, people made tremendous efforts to please their customers, while those that failed to deliver tended to take the easy way out. The choice of whether to use a standard letter or a personal letter is a reflection of the effort and energy you wish to put into a relationship with a customer. The same applies to the way you greet a customer at the front line.

In the never-ending quest for greater efficiency, companies are in danger of sacrificing the vital energies needed to sustain relationships with customers. Increasingly, customers are expected to conduct their transactions through machines – automatic telling machines for withdrawing cash, interactive voice recording for taking orders or the Internet for obtaining information. Personal contact with customers is expensive and is therefore deemed by many companies to be undesirable. As soon as you attempt to automate the relationship, you drain it of energy and the emotional connectivity is eroded.

An automated relationship is hardly a relationship at all but more a series of mechanistic interactions. Relationships require motivational energy and robots don't have such energy.

The choices you make about dealing with customers are a reflection of how you wish to direct your own internal energies – at both an individual and a corporate level.

Companies like Virgin are full of energy and there is a positive buzz about the place. In fact, the company prides itself on its "Virgin flair" – the creative use of energy in pleasing customers.

Internal motivator 2: esprit

In addition to energy, *esprit* is required to add emotional value. This motivator is effectively the proactive sparking mechanism that causes energy to be generated and released.

Esprit is the positive or negative spirit within us that defines our personality, our character, our temperament and our overall identity. It derives from deeply ingrained beliefs that we hold about ourselves, other people and the world in which we live. These beliefs reflect our values and our principles (or absence of them). Essentially, esprit is what we stand for in life and is the trigger for much of the rational and irrational thinking that leads to our behavior. If, for example, we are prejudiced against certain types of people, we will initiate certain behaviors in the vicinity of these people or when others mention them.

The outward manifestation of esprit that customers like most is integrity. Integrity is established through the motivational force of a *positive* esprit, a set of deeply held values and beliefs which spark energies and behaviors to help others. This esprit defines us in other people's eyes and give us our unique identity. It is the basis of our individual character. To quote Ben Cohen, one of the founders of ice-cream company Ben & Jerry's:

> There is a spiritual aspect to our lives – when we give we receive – when a business does something good for somebody, that somebody feels good about them!

Esprit cannot be imposed externally by words composed by senior executives. The intrinsic motivation that comes from esprit derives from people's own experience and the way they interpret it and form clusters of thinking and feeling patterns for influencing future behavior. It derives from a sense of "what is good and bad in my life" and "how I should behave to make my life and those of others better". This relates to the binary code of likeable customer service that will be dealt with in the next chapter.

INTERNAL MOTIVATOR 3:
EMOTIONAL DIRECTION

The final internal motivator relates to *emotion* itself. The energy sparked by an individual's esprit has to move in a particular direction, otherwise it would be all over the place and we would have chaos.

This directing process involves choosing from a vast number of options, some of which are obvious and many of which have to be created. Emotion is the internal motivator that directs the movement, that leads to our various expressions and behaviors.

Before giving an example of direction, it is important to differentiate between feelings, emotions, moods and temperament:

Feelings	Specific sensations ("This makes me sad")
Emotions	Short-term directed response to feelings ("I want to cry")
Moods	Longer-term collection of vague feelings ("I'm in a melancholy mood")
Temperament	Relatively permanent personal characteristics ("She always looks miserable")

Emotions are closely related to feelings. A feeling is effectively the result of a sensation. We feel hot and we move to a cooler area, we feel cold and we put on warm clothes. We feel unhappy and we move towards a situation that will make us happier. Emotion is the process of directing the behavior that results from a feeling.

In the absence of emotion we use certain automatic mechanisms (established thinking patterns and routines) to help us move. These are our habits and they will always produce the same direction of movement. For example, we follow the same routine most mornings by getting up at 6.30 am, showering, getting dressed, taking a light breakfast, watching 10 minutes of breakfast television and then driving to work, probably using the same route every day. We hardly have to think about the process.

When something different happens we sense it, or feel it, and this causes us to move out of routine, even change our habits. An emotion is created. We feel angry that there is a traffic jam on our normal route and that we have to take a detour, we feel sorry that a colleague has had an accident, we feel happy when one of the women in the office announces she has become engaged. We are filled with emotion on each occasion and take non-routine action. This action is aimed at making us and other people feel better. Thus it is "worth the effort". Creativity is the basis for generating the new direction of our behavior, away from the routine habit. Thus we can challenge the routine of a standard letter and move to a more creative approach where we choose words that more effectively connect with the customer. In doing so we sense how a customer feels and communicate in a more appropriate way than a routine, standard letter could ever achieve.

The process of feelings leading to emotions which in turn leads to directed behavior is illustrated in Figure 2.

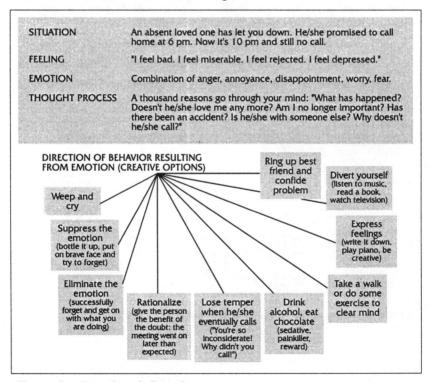

Figure 2   Emotional direction

Figure 2 relates to a personal situation. However, it is not too difficult to translate it into a customer situation. What are your customers' feelings, emotions and creative options when dealing with people in your organization? And conversely, what are your people's feelings, emotions and creative options when dealing with customers?

Figure 3 is an example of emotional direction in a customer service situation. The direction of the behavior will be determined by the emotion and its intensity. It is even possible (using one's esprit and inner reserves of energy) to change the emotion and redirect the behavior. For example, anger can be changed into sadness and compassion.

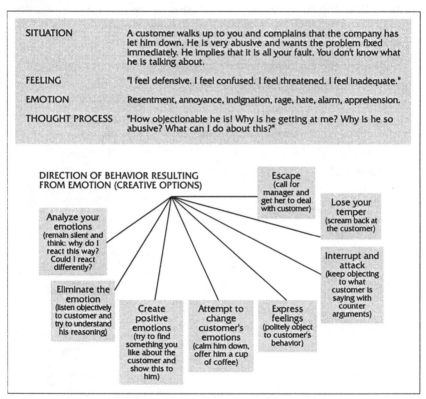

SITUATION	A customer walks up to you and complains that the company has let him down. He is very abusive and wants the problem fixed immediately. He implies that it is all your fault. You don't know what he is talking about.
FEELING	"I feel defensive. I feel confused. I feel threatened. I feel inadequate."
EMOTION	Resentment, annoyance, indignation, rage, hate, alarm, apprehension.
THOUGHT PROCESS	"How objectionable he is! Why is he getting at me? Why is he so abusive? What can I do about this?"

DIRECTION OF BEHAVIOR RESULTING FROM EMOTION (CREATIVE OPTIONS)

Escape (call for manager and get her to deal with customer)

Lose your temper (scream back at the customer)

Analyze your emotions (remain silent and think: why do I react this way? Could I react differently?)

Interrupt and attack (keep objecting to what customer is saying with counter arguments)

Eliminate the emotion (listen objectively to customer and try to understand his reasoning)

Create positive emotions (try to find something you like about the customer and show this to him)

Attempt to change customer's emotions (calm him down, offer him a cup of coffee)

Express feelings (politely object to customer's behavior)

Figure 3   Emotional direction in customer service

SUMMARY

To create added emotional value, you need to create new clusters of thinking and feeling patterns to please your customers. Added emotional value is based on three main attributes: emotional connectivity, integrity and creativity. These derive from the three motivators of energy, esprit and emotional direction.

PRACTICAL STEPS

1　Examine the clusters of thinking and feeling patterns you currently have about your customers.
2　Try to create new clusters of thinking and feeling patterns.
3　Try to assess the degree of emotional connectivity you and your people have with your customers. How can you improve it?
4　Do your customers trust you? How can you increase the level of trust?
5　What creative things can you do for your customers?
6　To what degree do you and your people possess the three key motivators of energy, esprit and emotional direction?

3

LIKEABLE CUSTOMER SERVICE

T HE ROOT OF ALL BEHAVIOR IS SURVIVAL, IN EVERY SENSE OF THE
word. When our survival is threatened we feel bad, when our
survival seems ensured we feel good. We therefore tend to move
towards what we like, towards what makes us feel good, towards
what ensures our survival. For example, we need to eat to survive,
therefore we like to eat. We need to be with others to survive, therefore we like to socialize. We need to be stimulated to survive (we
would die of boredom in a dark room with no stimuli), therefore we
like books, music, art, sport and entertainment.

Survival relates not only to avoidance of death but also to
retaining our jobs, our self-esteem, our family entities as well as
the communities and societies around us. When these are threatened we feel bad and when these are secured or enhanced we feel
good.

For many people, perhaps the more noble of us, there is also a
spiritual dimension to survival. We feel good if we make physical sac-
rifices as we move towards the attainment of higher-level spiritual
goals relating to certain eternal truths. For example, the most
ignored truth in the world is that the best way to make ourselves feel
good is to make others feel good. The evidence of war, conflict,
crime, drugs and myriad other problems indicates that many of us
have yet to discover this.

Deciding what will make us (and others) feel good requires individual choice. This applies every time we utter a word, make a decision, take an action or even think a thought. Every day we have to make "feel good" decisions such as: "Would it be better to go drinking with my friends this evening or stay home and study?" "Would it be better to stand up to my boss and tell him what I think or keep my mouth shut?"

> The best way to make ourselves feel good is to make others feel good

Our criteria each time are geared towards making us feel good and surviving. We want our relationships with others to survive, our long-term career prospects to survive and our paid employment to survive. When we lose these we believe we are on a downhill slippery slope.

Surviving and moving towards feeling good force choice on every single person, virtually every moment of the day.

THE BASIC BINARY CODE OF BEHAVIORAL CHOICE

Moving towards what makes us feel good and what we like, and moving away from what makes us feel bad and what we dislike, is the basic binary code of behavioral choice. It is also the basic binary code of business and customer service. Customers move towards products and services they like and move away from products and services they dislike. And with the people who sell the products and provide the services, customers move towards those they like and avoid those they dislike.

The likes and dislikes customers have about front-line people are not based on an objective rationale nor even necessarily on the overt behaviors, direct communication or logic adopted by these people. A customer's likes and dislikes are often based on indirect physical signals exhibited unintentionally by front-line people and the reconciliation of these signals with experiences buried deep in the customer's subconscious.

When we die we stop moving. To remain alive and to survive we have to keep moving, in every sense of the word. We move towards what we like (for example a sense of achievement) and move away what from what we dislike (for example the stigma of failure). The critical factors in all human movement are energy, emotional direction and esprit. Motivation leads to movement and if you do not move for your customers, if you give them no energy, then there is a high risk that they will move away from you. If you do not connect with them emotionally and furthermore show them no esprit, there is a similar risk.

> Moving towards what we like and away from what we dislike is the basic binary code of behavioral choice

TWO TYPES OF BEHAVIORAL TRIGGER

Our behavioral movements (towards feeling good or away from feeling bad) and thus our choices are initiated by one of two types of sparking mechanism: esprit and automatic reflex responses.

The beliefs that form our esprit derive from the vast range of experiences to which we have been subjected in life, our interpretation of them together with the influence of those people we trust.

Our customers also have esprit. They behave according to deeply ingrained beliefs about certain types of companies and the people they find in them. These beliefs are effectively clusters of thinking and feeling patterns which condition their behavior in response to the anticipated and actual service that we provide them.

When our customers have a positive esprit about us they will move towards us; conversely, when it is negative they will move away from us.

The second type of sparking mechanism is a subconscious reactive one derived from either the "hard-wired" (instinctive) part of our brain or a deeply embedded software program. For example, if we touch a hot kettle we automatically withdraw our hand. Our physical senses enable us to see, hear, smell, touch and taste and create physical sensations (feelings) which automatically initiate behavioral movement. This is necessary for our survival. When a horse charges towards us we literally do not have time to think, we jump out of the way automatically. Our "hard-wired", reflex actions are critical to avoid injury and death.

There is no conscious thought process in these reflex actions. We might rationalize after the event, but our body and mind are programmed to bypass rational thought if that is what is necessary to survive. Thus we are startled when we hear a large explosion and we blink if suddenly exposed to bright lights.

These reactive sparking mechanisms are much faster than any proactive, conscious thought process requiring rational evaluation. Rational thinking is notoriously slow and incredibly cumbersome in this context. It also requires the expenditure of vast amounts of energy. So we tend to convert our regular thought processes into subconscious routines and habits. We convert our conscious reasoning into fast-moving software programs buried deep in our subconscious.

The other evening I was having dinner with a client and I noted that she ordered the vegetarian dish. She explained that when she was 19 years old she had decided to become vegetarian. She loved animals and was horrified by what she had read about slaughterhouses. She found the whole idea of eating dismembered flesh abhorrent. Furthermore, she had learnt that vegetarians are frequently healthier and thinner than meat eaters. This rational decision-making process (to become a vegetarian) was based on emotions that moved her away from the awful feeling she had about killing animals.

Nowadays when she is presented with a menu in a restaurant she automatically chooses a vegetarian dish. What she does not do is go through the same conscious, rational evaluation that she first underwent when deciding to become a vegetarian. For her, choosing vegetarian had become an unthinking, reflex response that short-circuits the original cumbersome logic. In other words, she does not even think about dead animals when ordering vegetarian dishes. She has buried in her subconscious a sparking mechanism and a set of emotional filters that automatically direct her to the vegetarian dish when presented with a menu. This sparking mechanism is part of her esprit, in this case her values, her principles and her beliefs about vegetarianism.

If her original logic was totally rational and absolute, we would all be vegetarians. However, her rationale was based on an emotion (a move away from eating slaughtered animals). So in fact are all of our behaviors. We justify them afterwards with specific rationales. There is no such thing as an absolute rationale.

EMOTION ~ MOVEMENT ~ MOTIVATION

Our esprit sparks the release of energy from the store we have within us and enables us to move. That movement is directed by our emotions towards what makes us feel good and away from what makes us feel bad.

The word 'emotion' has the same root as the verbs "to motivate" and "to motor". They derive from the Old French word *movêre* (to move), which itself derives from Latin. Emotion is all about movement and therefore influences our motivation to make certain decisions and direct our behavior accordingly.

Emotion harnesses our feelings (external and internal sensations) and together with our esprit and our energy is the source of our motivation. The sensations and feelings which we experience and which are the spark points for our emotions have been carefully selected by our brain as a result of our esprit (our experiences, our beliefs and our values).

THE EMOTIONAL FILTER

Every second of our waking day our senses (sight, hearing, taste etc.) are bombarded with stimuli. Our brain is unable to process all the stimuli and has therefore created a large number of emotional filters that allow us to detect only those stimuli that are relevant to moving in the directions we like (or moving away from the directions we dislike).

As I write this I am sitting in an airline lounge. I have suddenly become aware that all around me are people talking, babies screaming and airline announcements being made. There are visual stimuli everywhere, indicator screens, television monitors, advertisements, the bright lights from shops and people moving about. As I return my concentration to the book I screen out all this irrelevant data, I become oblivious to it and unaware of what is happening to me. However, I have lodged in my brain one emotional filter: "Listen out for the call for my flight to Heathrow." If I miss this call I will feel bad. Returning to Heathrow will make me feel good. This emotional filter reflects my values at this point in time: the writing of my book, the importance of my family and returning home.

The emotional filters we use to select stimuli to facilitate desired movement are vitally important when it comes to dealing with customers. How we see customers depends on the filters we have selected to achieve our desired aims. And in the same way, how customers see front-line people depends on the emotional filters they have selected to achieve their aims. These filters are the clusters of thinking and feeling patterns that determine our behavioral choices.

Twenty minutes ago I approached an airline counter to check in. The agent was chatting to a colleague at the next counter. I stood with my ticket poised and waited, and waited. The agent seemed oblivious to my presence. He had not seen me. His attention was focused elsewhere and he was screening out all signals that might divert him from his focus. The result was poor customer service. He valued and liked his conversation with a colleague more than the potential interaction with me. He had not adjusted his thinking and feeling patterns to the possibility of a customer approaching at that moment. What was more important to him was the good feeling he was gaining from chatting to a colleague. The intrusion of an unexpected customer would interfere with that enjoyment and temporarily make him feel bad.

CHANGING EMOTIONAL FILTERS

To improve the way we deal with customers there is a continuing challenge to develop and heighten our awareness of customers' needs. This means challenging and if necessary changing the emotional filters we use in the vicinity of customers and also when considering any information (data, analyses, fact-files etc.) we hold about customers. It means continually developing more sensitive filters that do not screen out vital information about customers and the services we provide them. This process of challenge helps us create new clusters of thinking and feeling patterns.

> To improve customer service there is a continuing challenge to develop and heighten awareness of customers' needs

This of course begs the question of why we do actually screen out the very information needed to help us improve service.

The filters we use to select stimuli and the subsequent psychological processing of these stimuli into movement (or behavior) depend on software and hardware programs laid down in our brain. These are the two types of "sparking mechanisms" previously mentioned. One set lies in our subconscious and leads to reflex movements or reflex behaviors. It also leads to reflex screening of external stimuli.

For example, Amnesty International occasionally places advertisements showing photographs of torture victims. Personally I cannot face these grotesque sights and I automatically turn the page, screening out the images that make me feel so bad. I cannot account specifically for the subconscious program in my brain that causes me to turn away from images of torture, mutilation, severed limbs and so on. However, there can only be two possible origins of this behavior. It was either implanted as an emotional filter before I was born, or it was implanted after my birth by the conversion of some conscious experience into a subconscious reflex circuit.

Pre-birth reflexes are hard-wired into our genes. Reflex reactions are one of the first things a doctor tests for on the birth of a baby. If a newborn baby blinks when you snap your fingers close to its eyes, then in all probability the eyes are normal.

Post-birth reflexes are programmed into our subconscious by our experiences, our interpretation of them and the influence of others. For example, during the journey from the hotel to the airport this evening I put my foot down (as if there were a brake there) when the taxi approached a traffic light that suddenly turned from green to red. Yet I was in the passenger seat! Somewhere deeply embedded in my brain stem is a software program, based on binary code, that caused my foot to brake when traveling in a car that approached a red light. This experiential reflex reaction is based on binary code, as follows:

CODE 0   Drive through a red light. Put lives at risk. Threaten survival. Feel bad.

CODE 1   Stop at a red light. Secure survival. Feel good.

REFLEX RESPONSES IN CUSTOMER SERVICE SITUATIONS

The majority of our behaviors towards customers are based on reflex responses and the majority of their behaviors towards us are the same.

For example, how we look at an approaching customer, how we answer the telephone, how we reply to letters of complaint and how we process a transaction at the counter are all based on reflex responses. In fact, many companies develop training programs that encourage such reflex responses.

Furthermore, if we are afraid of a certain type of customer it is because these customers are emitting signals that elicit a "fear" response. These signals trigger a software program submerged in our subconscious that makes us automatically move away from (or avoid) these type of people. The fear is based on painful experiences in the past and, as a result, we have programmed our subconscious to provide specified reflex responses as appropriate. So we ignore certain types of customer, we become indifferent towards them, we become defensive as soon as they give us some feedback, we look the other way when they approach, we pretend to be doing something else. When we are forced to deal with people whom we subconsciously fear we act in a mechanistic way, we minimize the interaction. To protect ourselves we become cold and do not connect in any way that would make us more vulnerable to the customer we fear.

> **Most customer service routines are based on reflex responses**

By developing reflex responses we minimize pain, save energy and avoid having to think about what we are doing.

Most marketing, sales and customer service routines are based on reflex responses. These routines allow people to lay down in their subconscious sparking mechanisms that enable them to respond speedily and efficiently, without rational thinking, to specific external stimuli relating to customers.

Our esprit intervenes when we want to put one of these automatic reflex responses on hold and review the options available to us. This leads to behavioral choice. When we draw a software program from our subconscious mode into conscious mode we use our energies, our esprit and our emotions to evaluate it, modify it, replace it or even eliminate it before choosing what we consider to be the appropriate behavior.

With reflex reactions there is no choice. With conscious actions there is *always* choice. While in conscious mode we are modifying existing or creating new clusters of thinking and feeling patterns that explain our choices and justify our behaviors. They are effectively our rationales for the combination of energy, esprit and emotional direction that leads to our behaviors. When the behavior is finished we deposit these new or modified clusters of thinking and feeling patterns back into our subconscious, where they remain as latent software programs ready to respond to the next appropriate situation.

When in conscious mode these software programs, based on what we describe as logic and reason, operate incredibly slowly, are grossly inefficient and, what is worse, consume vast amounts of energy.

This conscious mode of operating is what we call "thinking". As we all know, this process can be exceptionally flawed. Yet paradoxically, it is rational thinking that has generated the human race's exceptional achievements and is the source of what we describe as civilization. It is this cumbersome, slow-working thinking process that both protects us from the law of the jungle (which is driven by reflex responses) as well as creating most of the problems in the world!

It should be stressed that the conscious process of rational thinking is inextricably linked to our emotions as well as to our esprit and levels of energy. It is a fallacy to assume that there are two parts of the brain (the left and the right) that operate independently with different roles. Recent research by Bechara, Damasio and Tranel at the University of Iowa College of Medicine indicates that an individual's previous emotional experience subconsciously influences conscious, rational decision-making processes.

The process of thinking can be, but rarely is, separated from our emotions. It is normally sparked by our esprit in response to external energy signals and used to evaluate how we feel about any situation so we can decide which is the best movement option for us. Thus when a customer walks through the door we either react instinctively towards that person (using our subconscious reflex responses) or we think about how we should behave towards them. The criteria for making the latter decision will be based on both how we feel and what we know (a combination of energy, emotional direction and esprit). Our knowledge itself is often based on what we have felt in the past. We know this is a regular customer who is always friendly and therefore we behave accordingly. We know this a difficult customer who will consume a lot of our time, ask many difficult questions and then buy very little, if anything at all; therefore we behave accordingly.

We know this because we have retained information that we feel will be useful in the future. In other words, our "memory stores" of cold data, raw information and knowledge have been created to secure our survival and help us feel good and avoid feeling bad in the future. The knowledge we acquire is thus a product of how we feel and of our emotional drives.

Our knowledge is often flawed because the thinking process we have used to record it in our memory and influence our esprit is rarely perfect. Thus we jump to conclusions, become prejudiced, are biased and make gross generalizations based on isolated incidents. We are rarely as rational as we like to think. To be completely rational would be too time consuming and drain us of too much energy. We therefore unwittingly rely on incomplete and highly imperfect clusters of thinking and feeling patterns that have been deposited from our conscious into our subconscious ready for future automatic response. The software in our emotional computer is both limited and flawed.

The biggest problem we face is that we rarely drag these software programs out of our subconscious to challenge their validity and appropriateness. We could improve ourselves immeasurably by improving the way we think and feel.

EMOTIONAL INTELLIGENCE

The application of emotional intelligence is the process of analyzing our true feelings, challenging them and then managing them more effectively to help us move in the direction that we and others like. Part of that managing process is to create new clusters of thinking and feeling patterns. It means eliminating bad old feelings and thoughts and replacing them with fresh, positive feelings and thoughts about the customers and people we come across during our everyday work.

All the time, we are absorbing life and work experiences from which we are extracting the essence to lay down in our subconscious software programs (the old thinking and feeling patterns) to facilitate an effective future response should the situation arise. It is this process that we need to challenge.

On a flight back to Heathrow one customer told me she heard a flight attendant say to one of her colleagues: "Isn't it great, this is our last sector and we only have 68 passengers."

The aeroplane could carry over 200 people. Deep down in this flight attendant's subconscious was a cluster of thinking and feeling patterns that indicated to her that full flights were hard work, exhausting and generally undesirable. In other words, the job would be great if it wasn't for the customers. This deeply ingrained attitude is passed on to the customers, who then equate it with poor service.

In this specific case the flight attendant would need to challenge herself to create new clusters of thinking and feeling patterns about customers. The following is an example:

CLUSTER OF THINKING AND FEELING PATTERNS ABOUT CUSTOMERS

Old	New
Customers are hard work	I have the best job in the world
Customers exhaust me	It is fun looking after my customers
Many are a nuisance	I love it when they ask me to help them
Quite a few are difficult	It gives me a buzz to fix difficult problems
One or two are very demanding	I always try to please them
I do not find them interesting	I meet many interesting customers
I'd prefer to be at home	I can't wait to get to work
The fewer customers the better	The more customers the better
Customers make me feel bad	Customers make me feel good

All the time customers are sending us signals, even before they open their mouths. A critical aspect of the art of dealing with customers is to become aware of these signals and then to challenge our interpretation of them. The danger is that we have deeply ingrained attitudes and reflex responses that misinterpret these signals. So we jump to the wrong conclusions and deliver poor service. For example, we only have to look at certain customers to "know" that they will be demanding and difficult. We respond accordingly, treating them defensively.

Conversely, we emit our own signals, many of which we are unaware yet which have an impact on our customers. I spend a lot of time observing people and I sense that many are unaware of the gestures they make with their hands, eyes and faces. They are unaware of how miserable they look, or how agitated they appear, or how irritable they come across as being. They definitely do not see themselves as others see them.

Recently I was dining alone in the Novotel in Accra, Ghana. Sitting at the table opposite me was a large white woman with a frail, skinny husband. Every time he opened his mouth she glared at him. Throughout the meal she looked unhappy, if not fierce and threatening. I suspect she was totally unaware of the signals she was sending out, of how she looked to any person observing her.

Let's take another, hypothetical example. A large, bald-headed man with bulging muscles walks into an exclusive department store. He weighs over 200lb, is wearing a black T-shirt with a picture of a motorcycle on it and has tattoos all over his arms. He has not shaved and has two days' growth of stubble and has a scar down his left cheek. He wears an earring and looks very serious. He is with an Alsatian dog which is straining at the leash. The man does not smile and approaches the counter.

The man is a customer. But before he says or does anything the signals he is sending out have activated our subconscious software. We have no knowledge of him except the signals he emits and we interpret these using our subconscious software as a basis for an instinctive value judgement. Our general conclusion is that we do not like this type of person and find him threatening. We react accordingly and prepare some defensive behaviors. The man dislikes our defensive, unfriendly, self-protecting, non-committing, indifferent behaviors. The service he receives is minimal and mechanistic. He interprets this as poor service and never returns. We might be happy that he never returns, but we have still provided poor service.

We should have never formed the value judgement in the first place. It was based on a subconscious prejudice and not on any current experience. This happens all the time. We rely on distorted subconscious influences to make behavioral decisions (especially relating to avoidance) rather than creating mutually beneficial experiences that enhance relationships.

A Nigerian colleague told me that she had immense difficulty opening a bank account just after marrying her husband in the UK. She worked for a reputable company, she had all the necessary documentation, all the necessary certificates, all the necessary references and the necessary financial deposits. Yet apparently because she was Nigerian her application to open an account in the UK was refused. The teller actually told her that the bank's computer threw up a refusal as soon it determined the word "Nigerian" in the nationality box.

Here is a little exercise you could undertake. What is your cluster of thinking and feeling patterns when I mention the word "gypsy"?

Now challenge yourself to read Isabel Fonseca's book *Bury Me Standing: the Gypsies and their Journey* and see if your thinking and feeling patterns alter. As a result you might choose to change your behavior towards gypsies next time you encounter some.

Emotional intelligence is all about challenging our preconceived notions about other people

Emotional intelligence is all about challenging our preconceived notions about other people – including customers. It is all about challenging how we feel about the people we come across, and it is all about acting in a more positive way that makes them feel good about us (and therefore like us) and consequently about making us feel good about them.

Emotional intelligence is also about examining the signals we send other people rather than being unduly concerned about the signals they are sending us. If we send out all the right signals, the possibility is that they will send us back the signals that they are happy to do business with us – because they like the signals we are sending them, they like us.

SUMMARY

Customers move towards people they like and avoid people they dislike. This is the binary code of behavior and customer service.

PRACTICAL STEPS

1 Question yourself frequently: "Why am I doing this? Is it a reflex response?"
2 Question yourself frequently: "Am I filtering out essential information about customers?"
3 Question yourself frequently: "Can I identify something I like about the customers I am dealing with?"
4 Eliminate from your mind all negative feelings about customers and other people.
5 Try to relate your so-called rational decisions and logic to your feelings. Can you trace the connection? If so, you will understand yourself better.
6 Avoid misinterpreting (negatively) the signals that customers send you.
7 Keep challenging your preconceived notions about other people.

4

EMOTIONAL

CONNECTIVITY

My MOTHER AND I WALKED INTO HARRY RAMSDEN'S FISH restaurant at Ocean Quay, Southampton, UK, and were greeted with smiling faces. The staff there seemed pleased to see us.

We were shown to a table towards the back of the restaurant and we indicated that we would prefer a vacant table near the window overlooking the yachts in the quay. This presented no problem and we were shown to our new table.

A smiling waitress called Gemma quickly approached and presented us with a menu, at the same time as informing us that one item was not available. She took our drinks order and disappeared.

I looked around and saw that all the staff were smiling. As they passed by each other they joked or chatted briefly. There seemed to be excellent rapport and the overall atmosphere was happy and relaxed. The staff obviously enjoyed working there. They took delight in handing out red balloons to young children or helping an old person transfer from a wheelchair to a table.

Gemma returned with our drinks. During the course of the lunch she passed by our table frequently and seemed eager to please, wanting to know whether we wanted more drinks, or bread, or anything else for that matter. She discovered that we were natives of Southampton although I no longer lived there. We also learnt a little about Gemma, that she was an out-of-work actress trying to earn some money.

There was something about this restaurant that made it tick, that made the overall dining experience so positive. It was not just the pleasant decor, the excellence of the food or the cleanliness of the toilets. What made eating at this restaurant such a pleasant event was the emotional connectivity and the value added as a result. Restaurants with "atmosphere" have emotional connectivity.

If we wanted functional dining we could visit a "waiterless" restaurant where we could poke a credit card into a vending machine to select a meal that would then automatically be microwaved. With today's technology that would be easy. If dining out was only about eating, then it would be cost effective to dispense with waiters and waitresses.

The reason we visit restaurants (and most other establishments) is because of the added value provided through an emotional connection. There is a limit to the amount of shopping we will undertake on the Internet, for example. Most of us have a basic need to connect emotionally with others and the wide range of commercial transactions with which we all become involved in our daily lives facilitates the process of meeting this need. There might be an extremely small minority of people who are recluses and who detest social interaction, but the majority of us crave it and feel bad if we are denied it. Shopping at a consumer level, and corporate purchasing at a company level, provide that essential experience.

> Those who excel at customer service have recognized the importance of establishing emotional connectivity with customers

From my studies, those organizations that excel at customer service, like Harry Ramsden's, have recognized and developed the importance of establishing emotional connectivity with their customers. They are aware that if the customer is to have an enjoyable experience, the company must have staff who enjoy their work, who inject some positive emotion into the way they connect with customers.

EMOTIONAL RANGE

However, enjoyment is just one of many different emotions that can connect with customers. Enjoyable customer service would obviously be inappropriate in the work done by undertakers, for example. Talk to most undertakers and they will tell you that they find their job rewarding. The reward is based on the emotional connectivity that they establish with their customers using compassion, sorrow, sincerity, sensitivity and understanding. The best undertakers connect with their customers using a sensitive range of emotionally considerate behaviors. It is the understanding look in their eyes, it is their soft, warm tone of voice, it is their overall demeanor and the unhurried gentle movements in everything they do. The overall impact of their behavior is to be able to provide immense emotional support (added emotional value) in times of family crisis. What undertakers do not do is provide enjoyable customer service, or customer delight. Nor do they attempt to "wow" their customers.

One of the modern myths about customer service is that it is all to do with customer delight, or customer satisfaction, or having a passion for customer service. Emotional connectivity is not about a single stream of emotions relating to passion, delight, enjoyment or satisfaction. It is the ability to draw on a wide reservoir of emotions to connect with each customer and facilitate a process of adding value to this particular relationship. Appendix IV lists over 100 different emotions, all of which could be applicable when connecting with customers.

In Table 1 on page 54 are some emotions (there are many others). Can you envisage a customer service situation in which it would be appropriate for a front-line person to display these emotions to connect with a customer?

I would assert that each of these emotions is appropriate in a specific customer service situation (Appendix V gives examples).

To understand the importance of emotional connectivity, it is important to explore the underlying reasons for any customer undertaking a transaction, whether that transaction is by way of telephone, documentation (letters, faxes, e-mail) or face-to-face encounter.

Table 1   Emotional connectivity

Would you display the follow emotions to connect with a customer and if so, when?

> Outrage
> Concern
> Anxiety
> Relief
> Amusement
> Pride
> Kindness
> Astonishment
> Revulsion
> Regret

CUSTOMER "FEEL GOOD" GOALS

For each transaction the customer will have a "feel good" goal, for example to acquire information, seek advice, place an order, enjoy an experience, complete an application, obtain help or just browse. This goal itself will be subdivided into a number of subsidiary "feel good" goals. As discussed in the previous chapter, all human behavior is directed towards the overriding survival goals of feeling good or avoiding feeling bad.

Let's take the Harry Ramsden's example from the beginning of this chapter and extract the customer "feel good" goals:

PRIMARY GOALS
Feeling good by dining out (basic survival goals of eating, socialization and the need to be stimulated with different experiences)

SECONDARY GOALS

Value for money	Easy parking
Eat excellent fish (customer likes fish)	Efficient service
Convenient location	Friendly service
Pleasant location (quayside)	

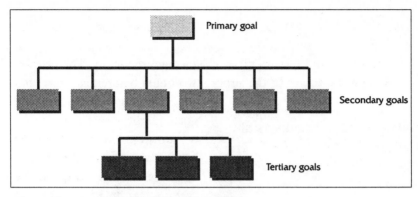

Figure 4   Cascading "feel good" goals

Failure to meet any one of these "feel good" goals creates a risk that the customer might feel better at a competitive restaurant.

Each of the secondary goals can be further divided into tertiary "feel good" goals. For example, a tertiary goal might be the allocation of a window table overlooking the quayside or to have a particularly attentive and chatty waitress (especially as, in this case, my mother likes chatting to people).

Therefore for any customer service transaction there is a cascade of primary, secondary and tertiary "feel good" goals (see Figure 4).

These cascading "feel good" goals are influenced by circumstance (external events) as well an individual's current emotional state (how they feel now). As a result, these goals are exceptionally dynamic and frequently change. It is therefore impossible to predict the total combination of cascading "feel good" goals that have to be met during any set of transactions, because the situation is evolving all the time and requirements change continually. Thus if the restaurant had been full our goal might have changed to a simple one of obtaining a table irrespective of whether it was near the window or not.

Even when customers think they have decided on their primary goals, they often change their minds. When they begin to feel differently they begin to think differently. Thus a day scheduled at the beach becomes a trip to the cinema when it rains, a wander round a shopping mall turns into an unplanned lunch at a newly discovered restaurant, the purchase of a pair of shoes becomes the acquisition of a complete outfit. I have known people who go for a drive in the countryside and end up buying a house and a new car! These people are not driven by logic but by their feelings about what they encounter.

Secondary and tertiary goals also change frequently. The primary goal might be to get to the airport two hours before departure, but an airline passenger's secondary goals might vary from journey to journey, on one occasion being happy to have the taxi driver chat away and explain the various landmarks, and on another only wanting to have some peace and quiet in the back of the taxi in order to relax after a stressful day of meetings.

> Emotional connectivity is all about sensing the dynamically changing goals of customers

Emotional connectivity is all about sensing the dynamically changing goals of customers. Some customers are much more predictable than others and it is relatively easy to sense their requirements. Others who have suffered bad experiences elsewhere have minimal expectations and it takes relatively little emotional energy to exceed their requirements. In contrast, others have exceptionally high expectations and never seem to be satisfied. There are a minority of customers with whom even an emotional genius will fail to connect.

RATIONAL INTELLIGENCE AND PROCEDURE

To apply a rational mind alone to the analysis of customer goals is to reduce a dynamic, three-dimensional, evolving process to a static, two-dimensional snapshot. The emotional connectivity is effectively removed by the statistical analysis. Anyone studying data from customer research will never be able to obtain a feel for their customers. At best, it is like comparing an old-fashioned black-and-white still photograph, developed hours or days later, with the flowing images of an instant-replay video camera.

When companies and front-line people rely solely on rational intelligence to detect customer goals, they pick up signals much too late and move much too slowly in meeting them. Customer surveys and questionnaires are examples of the application of rational intelligence to determining customer goals. Data about customer goals are pressed into patterns to create customer stereotypes, which are then used as a basis for developing transaction procedures and customer service training programs.

Such surveys can prove helpful when major changes in procedures are required, for example with respect to opening hours or the provision of additional information on a regular basis. However, they are exceptionally limited in fine-tuning how a company meets individual requirements. This necessitates an exceptionally high degree of sensitivity to myriad minor variations. The greater the sensitivity to the customer's emotional needs at the time of interaction, the greater the probability of emotional connectivity being established and value being added to the relationship.

The more a company proceduralizes its detection of customer goals and the way it meets them, the more it dehumanizes its customers. A routine sets in and this risks alienating customers.

The following are three examples of procedures developed by companies which employees are instructed to follow and in which they are frequently given training:

➤ What to do if a customer complains.
➤ What to do if the customer places a large order and requests a discount.
➤ What to do if the customer becomes abusive.

In each of the above cases employees will be expected to follow the procedure, irrespective of what they sense is the right thing to do. When the procedure has been followed innumerable times, employees lose all sense of the customers' "feel good" goals. To these employees it becomes more important to follow the procedure than to please the customer by sensing and meeting their needs.

BALANCING EMOTIONAL CONNECTIVITY, EFFICIENCY AND RELIABILITY

One customer told me that he and his family were strolling along rue Descartes, a long street in the Monge area behind the Sorbonne in Paris. The area was charming, quaint and full of restaurants. They were looking for somewhere to have dinner and were studying the menu outside one restaurant when a charming lady greeted them and persuaded them to dine there. They sat at the table, were handed menus and then waited, and waited, and waited for their orders to be taken. The three waitresses in the restaurant were incredibly charming and had excellent rapport with all the diners. However, they were totally disorganized, incredibly inefficient and the service at each stage of the dinner was exceptionally slow.

In this case the waitresses had emotionally misconnected. They thought that by charming each customer with smiles and friendly chitchat they could provide excellent service. What they were not sensitive to was the other needs of customers for a faster service, to have orders taken quickly, to have dirty plates removed from under people's noses. They were not sensitive to the secondary "feel good" goals of each party of customers.

I recently flew on a Far Eastern airline where the flight attendants were exceptionally delightful, calling me by my name at each contact and smiling sweetly at every opportunity. But they were exceptionally slow with the meal service and forgot some of the basic routines (like offering passengers on the right aisle a second cup of coffee). Emotional connectivity has to be balanced with a high degree of reliability and efficiency in the delivery of the core, "paid for" service.

Establishing emotional connectivity should never be at the expense of operating the basic systems and disciplines necessary for delivering the service. These are as essential as the emotional element. My criticism is that too many companies have concentrated solely on perfecting the basic systems and disciplines and neglected the all-important emotional side.

EMOTIONAL ENERGY

It is emotion that conveys and directs a person's energy in creating and sustaining a relationship. Cold, dry words are devoid of energy and will never create a relationship, whether they are written down or spoken. The tone of an individual's communications (verbal and non-verbal) will reflect the intensity of emotion they feel.

To create an emotional connection with a customer it is therefore necessary to transmit energy. There are two fundamentally different reactions to the emotional energy transmitted by a front-line employee when attempting to establish emotional connectivity:

➤ The energy is reflected away by the customer, dissipated and lost.
➤ The energy is absorbed by the customer, processed and retransmitted to the original sender to reinforce the emotional connection.

One of these two reactions occurs with every attempt to establish or reinforce a relation. For example, let's take the example of a front-line person giving a welcoming smile (a use of energy) to a customer to initiate the relationship.

> Injecting energy into establishing emotional connectivity is a vital factor in delivering profitable customer service

Assuming that the customer detects the smile, there can be one of two reactions:

➤ No reaction by the customer to the smile (the energy is reflected away and lost).
➤ The customer registers the smile and responds with appropriate behavior, such as a reciprocal smile, or a nod, or a word of introduction (the energy is absorbed, processed and retransmitted).

The latter reaction reinforces the process of establishing emotional connectivity.

So for emotional connectivity with a customer to be established it is imperative that a front-line person:

➤ senses customers' evolving goals for feeling good
➤ directs and transmits emotional energy towards customers to connect with each one and to facilitate the process of meeting their respective goals.

For our recent visit to Paris my family and I travelled by Eurostar. The journey was smooth, comfortable and faultless until we arrived at the

Gare du Nord. There a grim-faced taxi driver took us on a circuitous tour of Paris to reach the Royal Hotel at the Avenue Friedland near L'Etoile. I know Paris very well and I knew there was a more direct route. However, my French was not good enough for me to argue with the driver about overcharging. On stepping out of the taxi, I felt bad, I had been ripped off and I was full of negative energy.

Imagine my delight, therefore, when we entered the Royal Hotel and a radiant Anne-Sophie greeted us rapturously in English:

> Good afternoon. You must be Dr and Mrs Freemantle, we have been expecting you, how delightful to see you!

This set the whole tone for our wonderful stay in this hotel. The waitress at breakfast was no different, remembering on the second morning that my children liked hot chocolate. The concierges were equally charming, for example lending us an umbrella when it began to rain as we left the hotel one evening.

Overall the hotel had established a high degree of emotional connectivity by being consistently and genuinely warm and friendly.

Later I met the manager, Andrew Scarvelis, who agreed to be interviewed as part of my study program. The key points he made were:

➤ It is not good enough just to get the basics right (for example by setting and achieving exceptionally high standards of cleanliness). One has to generate a climate of warmth (emotional connectivity) throughout the hotel.

➤ One also has to avoid as far as possible automatic responses (e.g. "*pas de problème*") and be creative in the relationship by treating each customer as a genuine friend. (Genuine friendship is totally different from superficial friendship. The problem with "charm schools" is that the level of friendship advocated is insincere and temporary. False charm uses little energy, has no esprit, has no emotional direction and does not create genuine emotional connectivity. It is indiscriminately applied to everyone, irrespective of need and any intention to form genuine friendships.)

➤ One has to do everything conceivably possible that customers will like (to connect with them and add emotional value).

Thus on registering at the hotel Anne-Sophie informed us that there were two options for the rooms we had reserved. There were slightly smaller rooms at the top of the hotel with a view of the Arc de Triomphe, or a slightly larger room on a lower floor, but without the view.

She then took the trouble to show us the rooms. In doing so she was sensing what our goals were for feeling good. What she was not doing was attempting to impose a solution on us. She was using energy (walking upstairs with us, chatting to us) to ensure that we obtained maximum possible value from our stay.

During a spare half hour I studied the hotel's visitors' book. I found a large number of exceedingly positive comments, of which the following were typical:

> ➤ "A very lovely hotel with extremely helpful staff."
> ➤ "We enjoyed our stay and appreciated the friendly service."

A subsequent analysis of the visitors' book indicated that all the guests who had taken the trouble to comment on the hotel did so in emotional terms as opposed to making rational assessments. They did not write of the excellent cleanliness, of the high quality of the breakfast, of the fact that everything worked, that the rooms were spacious and comfortable, that the decor was graceful and refined. Perhaps they took this for granted. The words they used to describe their experience at the hotel were totally emotional. The following is an analysis of the words used:

———— EMOTIONAL ————

INTENSITY	+	TONE	=	OUTCOME
extremely		friendly		enjoyment
high order		helpful		wonder(ful)
superb		caring		delight
outstanding		warm		perfect stay
excellent		hospitable		best experience
phenomenal		welcoming		want to return
exceptional		charming		highly recommended
marvelous		courteous		very special experience

responsive	trouble-free experience
cordial	pleasurable
pleasant	lovely time
always smiling	appreciation

The emotional connectivity established between the hotel and its guests could be expressed as follows:

Emotional:

Intensity + Tone = Outcome

Level of energy + Direction > Connection > Added value

Where:

➤ **Emotional intensity** is the level of energy delivered and received by a customer.

➤ **Emotional tone** is the direction of the emotion (e.g. emotional energy directed towards a smile, a friendly welcome or some help).

➤ **Emotional outcome** is the achievement of a "feel good" goal through added emotional value.

➤ **Emotional connectivity** equals the degree of connection made in converting the employees' energy and tone into a positive outcome (added value) for the customer.

Thus the main source of the guests' perception of excellence was the wonderful staff. The other physical aspects of the hotel almost seemed incidental, if not taken for granted. When you pay for a hotel room you expect to receive the basics (a well-furnished and excellently maintained room). Most hotels can compete on these basics. What will give one hotel a leading, competitive edge in delivering profitable customer service will be the degree (or intensity) of the emotional connectivity established with each guest and the resultant added emotional value.

In the case of the Royal Hotel all the staff went out of their way to please their guests. The guests loved this and made it, in my opinion and theirs, one of the most highly rated hotels anywhere.

You can only develop a positive emotional connection with a customer if you feel good about that customer. If you feel good about a customer, there is a higher probability that the customer will feel good about you and the connection will be made.

EMOTIONAL RESONANCE AND EMOTIONAL DISSONANCE

Emotional connectivity is best established when there is a resonance between the feelings and emotions experienced by two or more people. It happens when people "feel" for one another and share the same emotional response. Effectively, people become tuned in to each other's emotions. This requires a high degree of sensitivity to various emotional states.

Emotional dissonance occurs when no emotional connectivity is established and when the feelings and emotions experienced and expressed by one person cause another to feel bad. This often occurs when one person is insensitive to the feelings of another. An extreme example would be when a very happy person cracks a few inept jokes in front of someone who has just suffered a bereavement. Another example is a miserable person pouring scorn on the achievements being joyfully celebrated by another.

A PERSONAL TECHNIQUE FOR MAXIMUM EMOTIONAL CONNECTIVITY

To achieve maximum emotional connectivity, the following technique should be used:

➤ Create a climate of warmth before customers even approach you.
➤ Send out warm and positive signals to each customer prior to the start of the transaction.
➤ Be as sensitive as possible to the customer's emotional state.
➤ Allow and possibly encourage customers to express their feelings should you feel they want to.
➤ Listen with genuine interest and feeling to what customers have to say.
➤ Try to find something you like in each customer and let it show.

➤ Never make customers feel bad for expressing their feelings, but always try to make them feel good for talking honestly about how they feel.

➤ Focus on creating and expressing your own genuine feelings if you sense customers will be receptive to and appreciative of them. (If you feel for each customer you will be able to create those feelings yourself.)

➤ Try to make these feelings positive (sometimes you can establish emotional connectivity by sharing negative feelings about a situation – but definitely not about a person).

➤ Eliminate any negative feelings you have about customers. They will show no matter whatever you say or do.

The following example shows how this technique can be applied to avoid emotional dissonance and establish emotional connectivity. It relates to an encounter that I observed between a motorcyclist and an attendant at a gas station.

ATTENDANT	"Pump number, sir?"
CUSTOMER	"Three."
ATTENDANT	"That will be $12, sir."
CUSTOMER	"But I only put $6 worth of gas in and you're charging me $12."
ATTENDANT	"That's what my screen says here. We always go by what's on the screen."
CUSTOMER	"But I only put $6 worth of gas in. Look at the pump outside, it's only showing $6."
ATTENDANT	"That's not my concern, sir. We always go by the screen here and it says right in front of me that pump number three owes $12."
CUSTOMER	(in front of a long line of other customers building up behind him) "I only put $6 worth in and I'm not going to pay any more."
ATTENDANT	"For all I know you could have put two lots of $6 in."
CUSTOMER	"Are you calling me a liar?"

During this interchange both customer and attendant remained relatively cool, neither losing his temper. However, all they did was to reiterate their own points of view.

The situation was eventually resolved when the customer demanded to see the manager who, after due consideration and inspection of the pump, decided to take the customer at his word. Meanwhile, a long line of customers had been alienated as they overheard this contretemps.

In this case the expression of two rational points of view about perceived facts did not provide an initial answer, nor was any emotional connectivity established. In fact, there was a high degree of emotional dissonance. Although he did not express his feelings directly, the customer felt bad because he was being overcharged, while the attendant felt bad because he thought the customer was trying to deceive him.

As often happens, there were different interpretations of the facts, based on feelings derived from subconscious models of how people ought to behave. The attendant felt that the customer must comply with his information on which he had been instructed to rely. On the other hand, the customer felt his own information was more reliable.

Consider an alternative scenario in which the technique described above is applied to establish emotional connectivity and avoid emotional dissonance:

ATTENDANT	"Good evening, sir. Is that a brand new Harley-Davidson you have outside?"
CUSTOMER	"Yes, I bought it a couple of weeks ago."
ATTENDANT	"They're great bikes. Anyway, that will be $12, sir."
CUSTOMER	"I think there's been a mistake. I only put $6 worth of gas in and you're charging me $12."
ATTENDANT	"Really? Let me have a look." (Attendant peers out at the pump) "You're right. I think there must be a problem with our equipment. OK, we'll make it $6 and I'll ensure our equipment is checked out."
CUSTOMER	"Thank you very much, you had me worried for a minute."
ATTENDANT	"These things happen. Anyway, I hope you enjoy riding your Harley-Davidson and I look forward to

	seeing you again soon – and hopefully we'll get it right next time. By the way, I didn't catch your name."
CUSTOMER	"Richard Wellings. I've just moved into an apartment in West Street around the corner."
ATTENDANT	"That's great, Mr Wellings, you'll like it around here. See you again soon."

In this latter case the attendant establishes emotional connectivity with the customer at the earliest opportunity and then reinforces it during the short interaction. To do so he creates a climate of warmth and sends out positive signals, taking a genuine interest in the customer. He also uses his senses to determine that the customer is new, looks honest, speaks in a sensible way and is not sending out signals that he is being duplicitous. The attendant therefore gives the customer the benefit of the doubt. Furthermore, he identifies something the customer likes (Harley-Davidson) and the customer likes him for it. The attendant has used positive emotion to resolve the problem, whereas in the earlier example the attendant relied on his narrow interpretation of the facts, a set routine and therefore limited rationality to try to solve the problem, but without success.

SUMMARY

Establishing emotional connectivity is an imperative for any relationship-based customer service interaction. The emotion itself can be drawn from a large reservoir of choices and should be managed according to your feelings about the situation. This itself relates to your perceptions of a customer's goals in approaching a transaction. These goals are dynamic and can be primary, secondary or tertiary – they are directed towards feeling good.

The key task for anyone interacting with a customer is to sense these goals and then, establishing emotional connectivity, to attempt to meet them. Emotional connectivity itself is based on transmitting and exchanging emotional energy with a customer to create added emotional value.

PRACTICAL STEPS

1 List as many emotions as you can think of.
2 Take each emotion and relate it to an example of a customer interaction.
3 Consider each customer service interaction you have today and identify the emotional energies you put into each one.
4 Try to create and transmit further positive emotional energies towards each customer.
5 In doing so, become aware of the intensity and tone you use to transmit these energies, modified as appropriate to meet the outcome required by the customer.
6 Develop your "sense" (sensitivity) of the specific outcomes a customer requires for feeling good. These are the dynamic customer goals that relate to every single transaction a customer seeks to undertake. The achievement of these goals will create added emotional value.
7 Try to search for things you like about customers.
8 Eliminate any negative feelings you have about customers.

5

THE IMPORTANCE

OF INTEGRITY

INTEGRITY IS A VITAL FACTOR IN ALL ASPECTS OF BUSINESS AND should be at the core of each company and employee's esprit. Integrity is associated with trust, openness and honesty – customers like people who demonstrate this.

Integrity can be defined as follows:

> Integrity is "wholeness". It is when the outside (the external experience) is consistent with and reflects the inside (a person's esprit), especially in relation to principles such as openness, honesty and trust. That is, words expressed and actions taken are consistent with and reflect inner thoughts and feelings.

Related to customer service, this wholeness exists when the values espoused by the company are reflected in the customer feeling valued. There needs to be total consistency between what the company and its people say and do and what customers experience.

Most customers value companies and individuals that trust them, that are open and honest with them, that care for them, that support them and take an interest in them. These are values to which most customers subscribe personally and which they value in the service provided to them. For example, customers move towards people they trust and avoid people they distrust. Trust has many facets, thus you trust someone who will not let you down, who will put your interests first, possibly at the expense of their own.

The application of a company's values (or lack of them) is experienced with every single contact a customer has with a company, whether it is an advertisement, a telephone call or an encounter in a retail establishment. In fact, everything a company says and does is a reflection of its internal value system.

When the customer's practical experience is different to the values and principles espoused by the company, there will be no "wholeness" and the integrity will be eroded.

Figure 5 shows how a company's values can be converted into a situation where customers feel good about the company. When all the connections are made there will be a high degree of integrity.

CUSTOMERS
Customers feel good about the company and its people

Customers feel valued
(Words/actions + added emotional value)
↑
Words/actions + emotion experienced by customers
↑
EMOTIONAL CONNECTIVITY
↑
Words/actions carrying emotion to reflect the value
↑
"We feel this is important in relation to our customers"
Intrinsic values (esprit)

(e.g. "Meeting our customers' needs is our top priority"
or "Our aim is to sustain our customers' faith
in the reliability and friendliness of the service we provide")

"We feel good about our customers"
COMPANY

INTEGRITY

Figure 5   Integrity comes from emotional connectivity

Integrity is a function of the way people behave in reflecting their own values, beliefs and principles.

There is a close connection between values, beliefs and principles. This is demonstrated as follows:

VALUES   What is important to me.
                   e.g. "My customers are really important to me."

BELIEFS   An act of faith that this is true (without necessary proof).
                   e.g. "The more I like my customers the more they will like me."

PRINCIPLES   My own personal rules for my own conduct.
                   e.g. "I am always completely honest with customers."

Integrity can only exist when a company's espoused values are shared and applied by its various employees and managers. You then have *esprit de corps*. It applies equally to small, one-person businesses as to large multinationals with hundreds of thousands of employees.

Below are three examples of people who demonstrated the highest degree of integrity. Each was a driver working for large taxi firms.

Taxi driver 1

Sten Larson, a store manager with a large retailer, told me the saga of a trip to Stockholm when everything went wrong. He took a taxi from Arlanda Airport to a hotel in the city center and on arrival realized he had left his hand baggage on a trolley at the airport taxi rank. The baggage he had mislaid contained his passport, his return air ticket and, most importantly, some key business documents.

The taxi driver, an Iranian who spoke five languages, took control to help Sten out of his dire predicament. Sten personally felt helpless, foolish and absent-minded. He feared that the hand baggage had been stolen and would never be found. Furthermore, he was concerned about all the hassle involved in trying to retrieve the bag. His time was precious and here he was squandering it as a result of unthinking neglect on his part.

The taxi driver spoke to the hotel receptionist and explained the situation. Then, in pursuit of the lost bag, he used the hotel's telephone to make a series of calls to different departments at Arlanda Airport before successfully locating the bag. He took Sten back to the airport where the bag was retrieved from an official (who refused a tip) and then drove him back a second time to the hotel.

This Iranian taxi driver could easily have driven away after depositing Sten at the hotel. In taking the initiative to locate the bag, he was putting his customer's interests before his own. He must have spent 20 minutes in the hotel on the telephone to the airport, with no guarantee of success or any positive outcome for himself. This is time he could have spent out on the road earning money.

Taxi driver 2
Later that day, Sten was in the picturesque Gamla Stan old-town district of Stockholm and walked down to a taxi rank by the waterfront. He asked a taxi driver to take him to his hotel a short distance away. However, what he did not know was that the road to the hotel was closed (due to a water festival) and he would have to be taken on a more circuitous route through heavy traffic. The Lebanese taxi driver, in all honesty, alerted the customer to this as they began the journey. Progress was slow and the fare on the meter began to increase at an alarming rate. Suddenly the taxi driver said "Too much!" and turned off the meter, not charging for the rest of the journey. For a second time that day a taxi driver was putting a passenger's personal interests before his own.

Taxi-driver 3
Anastasie Deboux, a senior banking executive in Côte d'Ivoire, told me about a visit to Accra, Ghana. She arrived very early for a meeting and decided to go shopping in the center of the city. Rather than drive in she parked her car at a garage on the outskirts and hired a taxi for three hours to take her shopping. The taxi driver eventually returned her to the garage, whereupon she drove to her meeting and then on to the hotel. On getting back into his cab the taxi driver counted the money she had given him and realized that she had overpaid him by a substantial amount, confused about the denominations of various notes. He looked around to find she had already driven off.

That evening he made several enquiries at different hotels, asking for a lady "who looked like this and spoke with a French accent". He eventually traced her and called up to her room from reception. When she came down to the lobby he repaid her the excess she had given him. She had not even been aware that she had overpaid him.

PUTTING THE CUSTOMER'S INTERESTS BEFORE THE COMPANY'S

In each of the above cases the taxi driver put the customer's interests before his own.

When you put your own personal or company interests before those of customers, you are in danger of being accused of being manipulative, exploitative and on a personal level selfish. When you pursue your personal interests at the expense of others, you are effectively eroding your own essential esprit. Many traditional commercial relationships are adversarial, in which one side seeks to use its power (of supply or demand) to exert its own interests at the expense of the other. The aim in such negotiations is to outmaneuver the other party to strike the most advantageous deal, irrespective of the disadvantage to your opponent.

> Integrity is putting a customer's interests before your own

In many of the successful companies I studied there was an immense amount of partnership working with customers. "Mutual benefit" was the order of the day and this was achieved by working towards shared goals. For example, Swedish company Sandvic was one of the first to develop close relationships with its customers based on partnership working. Lane Group, a UK-based transportation company, is another that has developed a similar approach where performance targets are mutually agreed, there is open-book accounting and profit margins are highly visible. Briggs Roofing, also in the UK, is developing partnership arrangements with its major customers, for example with ASDA Stores.

The end result of these partnership arrangements is an increasing amount of mutual trust, reliability and relationships based on "team spirit" or *esprit de corps*.

In contrast, where adversarial relationships persist there is a high degree of secrecy and distrust. Customers rebel against companies that exploit them, that they perceive as overcharging them, misleading them or neglecting them. The esprit is then lost and integrity eroded.

Following are some examples of a lack of integrity on the customer service front:

➤ Misleading information
➤ Exaggerated information
➤ Omitted information
➤ Selling a customer something they don't want
➤ Overselling (selling a $200 item when a $100 item would have done)
➤ Insincerity
➤ Manipulation
➤ Confusing the customer
➤ Exploiting a customer's ignorance/innocence
➤ Alarmism (creating unnecessary fears)
➤ Overplaying the positives
➤ Making promises that can't be kept

As I edited this chapter there was a headline in a British national newspaper about travel companies with a policy of charging too much. Apparently, some tour operators make people pay four times extra for insurance cover when booking a vacation. In one case a customer was forced to pay the equivalent of $200 for family insurance cover on booking a vacation when he could have obtained the same level of cover for $50 by buying direct. In no way is this putting the customer's interests before your own.

In another national newspaper there was a second instance of a lack of integrity, this time relating to a major British bank. To quote: "The bank is making up to £160 million a year by discouraging staff from directing customers to accounts paying better interest." This is also an excellent example of emotional labor, of forcing staff to go against what they feel is in the best interests of their customers.

Too many companies come up with fine words about "putting the customer first" but fail to put them into practice. The words become meaningless, they alienate customers and in the end the customers believe nothing the company says. The result is that customers perceive the company and its people as lacking in integrity.

Integrity is practicing what you preach – it is converting fine words into fine action – it is meaning what you say and saying what you mean.

Customers like front-line people who keep their promises, who ring back when they say they're going to, who actually deliver the goods on time, who follow up by fixing a problem and do not forget about it.

Customers don't like being let down, being promised superb service and then having to wait in line for long periods to be attended to. Customers don't like seeing advertisements or leaflets which emphasize excellent service and then finding that they can't get through on the telephone – and when they eventually do, finding a person at the other end who is disinterested and off-hand.

PERCEPTIONS OF FAIRNESS

Customers' feelings (and therefore likings) towards a company and its people are based on their perceptions of fairness, of the way they are treated. If customers are treated in the way they believe they should be treated, then they will perceive the company as being fair, trustworthy and demonstrating integrity. If customers feel they are treated in an unfair way, they will see the company as being exploitative, manipulative and lacking in integrity.

Yesterday I was printing a draft of the previous chapter of this book. Suddenly and unexpectedly the ink cartridge ran dry. Rather unwisely, I had not bothered to obtain a spare. I therefore drove to PC World, a computer retail store, to purchase a cartridge, only to find that the rack for this particular item was empty. I sought out an assistant and enquired if they had any more in stock. He politely explained that they had sold out of this item and that the manufacturers had been particularly slow in resupplying them. They were therefore out of stock. A little desperation (an emotion) showed through in my voice. Back in my study I had a number of important documents that urgently needed to be printed.

The assistant sensed my desperation and made a suggestion: "The only thing I can propose, sir, is that you drive a mile along the road where you will find another computer store. You could try there, they might have one." The store he recommended was a competitor. I drove there and obtained the ink cartridge I required. However, PC World has retained my business subsequently because they put my interests before theirs. It would have been so easy to say: "We are expecting a delivery of new stock next Tuesday. Why don't you come back then?"

Table 2 is some tests of integrity that you and your team might wish to consider and determine an appropriate response.

Table 2   Customer service integrity tests

1   In your opinion one of your company's products is inferior to that of a competitor. A customer asks your opinion about this product. She wants to know in what way it is better than the competitive product. What should be your response?

2   A customer returns a product complaining that it is faulty. You replace it without question. You subsequently check the product but cannot find the fault. Your manager instructs you to repackage the product as new (although it is a used product) and put it back on the shelf. What should you do?

3   A customer approaches the counter and offers to pay the full amount for a product, not having noticed that there is a substantial discount on all products purchased from that section. You are on a profit-related bonus. Do you take the full money or draw the customer's attention to the discount?

4   A newspaper article has highlighted major deficiencies in the services provided by your company to its customers. Privately you agree, as you know that the company has been cutting back on staff. However, your company has issued a PR statement refuting the allegations. What action do you take when a customer asks you directly your opinion about these deficiencies?

5 A customer contacts you and places a large and important order that he insists must be delivered within seven days. You know personally that the factory is running at full capacity and it is unlikely that the order will be met in time. You consult your boss, who tells you to take the order and promise delivery in seven days. He hints that you can fob off the customer with excuses on the seventh day. What do you do in these circumstances?

6 A customer is being abusive to one of your colleagues and is demanding to see the manager. You know that your manager is up to his eyes in work and is fed up with seeing this customer, who has been in many times before to complain. The manager has therefore told everyone that if this customer comes in she does not want to see him. Your colleague tells the customer that the manager is out, knowing full well that she's in the back office. What would you do in the circumstance?

7 It is 5.25 pm and you are about to close up. You are particularly keen to leave on time at 5.30 pm as you have planned to visit your children's school for a concert and you do not wish to disappoint your children by being late. Just as you are thinking about putting your coat on, a customer walks through the door. It is 5.27 pm. You sense that the customer is going to take a lot of time to look at the product range before making a decision. What do you do?

My own contentious answers to these tests of integrity are given in Appendix VI. I would stress that there is no one right answer and I fully expect you to disagree with my suggestions!

Maria Mercedes Rincon from Venezuela, who works for an international consultancy, told me a story about the folk dolls she collects from around the world. When she was in Turkey she began looking for a doll to take home as a souvenir. She had seen many dolls in various markets and stalls and therefore had a rough idea of the appropriate price. One afternoon she wandered along a side street in Fethiye and came across a shop selling folk dolls. She entered the shop and perused the extensive range. She found the doll she wanted and asked the price of the shopowner, who was polite, courteous and apparently spoke five languages.

"Please name your own price!" the shopowner said in perfect English.

Maria Mercedes hesitated, unsure of what to say. She was aware of the prices being asked elsewhere. She stated a price in Turkish lira equivalent to $30.

"Oh, that is much too much!" he told her. "I could never charge you that amount. I would say half that price is fairer."

She walked away with two dolls and other souvenirs. In all her life she had never had such an experience. Here was a shopowner in a back street doing very little trade, but prepared to protect a customer from inadvertently paying too much.

The amazing thing about integrity is that if you look out for it you will discover in many different corners of the world. One of the most dangerous assumptions you can make anywhere is that vendors are out to "rip you off". If you make this assumption, in all probability it will become a self-fulfilling prophecy.

THE INTEGRITY DILEMMA

However, there is a dilemma concerning integrity. Honesty, trust and truthfulness can never be absolute. If we all went around expressing exactly what we thought and how we felt, we would have anarchy. Tolerance through "biting one's tongue" is the hallmark of a civilized society.

There is always a trade-off between honesty and saving face. If being totally honest with a customer means shattering that person's self-esteem and inner dignity, then it is best *not* to be totally honest. You just cannot tell an ugly person that they look dreadful whatever they wear.

Ideally, you should try to be genuine in all your remarks to customers. However, the reality is that there are times when we have to apply the rules of diplomacy and suppress our feelings or express ourselves indirectly. In doing so, we put at risk the customer's perceptions of our own fairness and integrity. If the potential damage to our conscience through persistent diplomacy is too great, then we have no option but to seek a job with a company that expresses the values we believe in and has the integrity to apply them.

The best way to resolve this dilemma of speaking the truth without upsetting people is to focus on the positive and avoid the negative. We should go out of our way to identify and focus on the positive traits in the customers we deal with. In other words, we must go looking for things we genuinely like about our customers and screen out from our consciousness anything we find irritating or objectionable about them.

> We must go looking for things we genuinely like about our customers

As I mentioned above, integrity is closely linked to perceptions of fairness, which in turn are derived from the personal values we have developed and hold firm as a result of a lifetime's experience. These values are central to our individual esprit.

VALUES

As life progresses, we lay down in our psyche a whole series of values as a basis for influencing our future behavior. Making ourselves and others feel good is perhaps the most important goal for us in life. Thus we value things and people that make us feel good and do not value things and people that make us feel bad. Our esprit consists of these values and the principles and beliefs closely related to them.

We perceive fairness as people behaving in a way that conforms with our own personal values and unfairness as those who do not. A simple example is punctuality. Some people value it while others do not. Those who do will say: "It is unfair that this person always keeps us waiting." The unpunctual person might reply: "It is unfair that the others don't understand the pressures I am under and are therefore always complaining."

Personal values are therefore closely linked to feelings and emotions. Consider the values in Table 3 and answer "yes" or "no" according to how they apply to you and the organization you work for.

Ideally, these statements should be made by front-line employees in relation to their bosses. They should also, ideally, be made by customers in relation to the way you do business with them.

Table 3   Do you feel valued?

This is how we feel:	YES	NO
"We feel trusted"		
"We feel cared for"		
"We feel supported"		
"We feel understood"		
"We feel appreciated"		
"We feel we get a fair hearing"		
"We feel people are really interested in us"		
"We feel important"		
"We feel valued"		

You might care to establish how each individual in your team feels using the "yes/no" boxes above. If you are brave enough, you could also use this approach to consult your customers and ascertain their feelings about the service you provide.

When there is a high proportion of "yes" answers, there will be a high degree of emotional connectivity with the organization and perceived by its customers.

One of the key tasks in establishing an emotional connection to deliver profitable customer service is therefore to behave in a way that is full of integrity and makes customers feel valued. When they feel genuinely valued (through the provision of added emotional value) they will like you and give you more business as a result.

This process of valuing enhances customers' self-esteem, their feelings of self-worth and their sense of inner dignity. Furthermore, it will, in their own eyes, justify their actions and behavior in wanting to do business with you. Valuing customers (and people) reinforces them as human beings. It is essential emotional nourishment in a harsh, aggressive, competitive world where threats to our self-esteem are a frequent occurrence.

To deliver profitable customer service you have genuinely to feel not only that each person is important as a customer, but that their interests are more important (in other words, more valuable) than your own or those of the company. This is the biggest test of integrity.

The front-line people who are most likely to value customers are those who feel valued themselves, who have developed and reinforced their own esprit. The issue of leadership and motivation is critical here. If front-line people feel devalued by their bosses it is unlikely that they are going to value customers: "Why should I bother about customers when no one bothers about me?"

INDIRECT VALUE STATEMENTS

When a customer can't get through to a company on the telephone, a value statement is indirectly being made. The company is effectively saying: "Our time is more valuable than yours, therefore you can wait." The same applies to people who are forced to queue. Waiting for service effectively devalues people's time. There is a corollary statement that "the service is so valuable it is worth waiting for". This puts the company at risk, because what is important is not the company's perception of value but the customer's perception of it. There is a great deal of research evidence to show that companies lose an immense amount of business from customers who divert elsewhere because they are fed up with waiting for service.

> Forcing a customer to wait for service drains the emotion from a relationship and erodes emotional value

Successful companies develop and use emotional connectivity to communicate to customers that they value them. This is synonymous with making them feel good and doing things they like.

You might wish to examine your own company's telephone policy and practice. In most companies, if you wish to speak to a senior executive you have to go through a number of hoops. First, if you do not know the executive you have to find out their number. Then you have to ring the switchboard and wait to be connected to some executive secretary or personal assistant. This person will often ask you questions like:

➤ "Can I have your name?"
➤ "What company are you from?"
➤ "Does he (or she) know you?"
➤ "Can I ask what you are calling in connection with?"

Obstacles are frequently raised and you will find yourself diverted to a more junior person or a call-back will be promised which does not take place.

These difficulties in reaching senior people are common. It is as if they do not wish to speak to customers, especially complaining customers (the very ones who have the most important information about the company's operations).

Compare the above to the following statement which can be found (at the time of writing) on the packaging on food products in any Prêt à Manger café in the UK:

If you
would like to
speak to me or one of my
colleagues regarding anything to do
with PRET A MANGER please feel free to call on:
0171 827 6300
Thank you. Julian Metcalfe.

It just so happens that Julian Metcalfe is the company's chairman. He puts his own telephone number on the packaging of the company's food products.

Or compare the following extract from the telephone policy of the transport company TNT (UK).

A caller asking for a TNT manager must be put through directly to that person without screening, i.e. the caller must not be asked to supply his or her name or the purpose of the call before being connected.

Incoming calls to TNT managers must not be routed via secretaries or other intermediaries unless the TNT manager is out of the office.

When a TNT member of staff is not available to accept a call

always offer an alternative contact or promise a call back. Please
do not ask the caller to phone a different number.

Both of these companies value their customers so much that the top
people in the company are prepared to take calls direct from customers, without intermediaries interrogating (and sometimes intimi-
dating) these customers.

In my study of successful companies around the world, many
senior executives were prepared to allow any customer to ring them
direct, for example Arnold Ekpe, group chief executive of the West
African bank Ecobank, or Julian Stainton, chief executive of WPA
(UK), or Anton Najjar, general manager of the J.W. Marriott hotel in
Dubai.

It is also worth considering the following quotation from a senior
executive of the Body Shop:

> The difference between Body Shop and a lot of companies is that
> when you work here you don't have to leave your personal values
> at the door.

The subtitle of a book written by Ben Cohen and Jerry Greenfield,
founders of Ben & Jerry's ice-cream company, is "Lead with your values and make money, too". To quote from the book:

> Our customers don't like just our ice cream – they like what our
> company stands for. They like how doing business with us makes
> them feel.

And what about this statement from the CEO of Levi's:

> I believe that if you can create an environment your people iden-
> tify with, that is responsive to their sense of values, justice, fair-
> ness, ethics, compassion, and appreciation, they will help you be
> successful.

All the successful companies I studied recognized the importance of
values, feelings and the link between them. They were not necessarily corporately articulated values (although in some cases they were),

but they were values that every single employee felt were so important that they influenced their own personal behavior in attempting to connect with customers to make them feel valued.

Values are at the core of esprit and added emotional value.

EMOTIONAL VALUE

For a company to be driven by values and achieve the highest levels of integrity, it must also be driven by feelings and emotions. It is these feelings and emotions which reach out to customers to convince them that they are really valued and that the company is trustworthy. Words alone are inadequate for this purpose. It is the feelings and emotions (and therefore the positive energy) that are attached to these words that convey the extent of the value and the trust. Words without emotion have little value in a relationship. However, words conveying emotions that genuinely reflect feelings carry much higher value. Furthermore, when imbued with positive emotion such words will generate high degrees of trust in reflecting a company's integrity.

> For a company to be driven by values it must also be driven by feelings and emotions

This is why standardized responses to complaints and customer enquiries are so ineffective. They carry little emotional value (as well as frequently missing the point). In fact, standardized responses effectively devalue customers. They are saying indirectly: "You are not unique, you are a letter 31 stereotype."

Integrity is all about being genuine in allowing your feelings to be expressed in the process of valuing customers.

The following exercise can be undertaken in the space of five minutes and should prove productive in focusing on integrity and added emotional value.

If you work for a values-driven company, you will have no problem answering these questions. If you struggle to answer them, you (and your company) are definitely not values driven.

CUSTOMER VALUE

Be honest, what do you really value about your customers?

Be honest, what do you think your customers value about you and your company?

KEEPING PROMISES

The best way to demonstrate integrity and really convince your customers that you value them is to make them promises that you keep. The more promises you make both strategically and operationally on a day-to-day basis, the better.

Here are some examples:

➤ "I promise to call you back in half an hour."
➤ "I promise I won't keep you waiting for more than five minutes."
➤ "I promise I will mail you a written confirmation tomorrow."
➤ "I promise that we'll send an engineer within 24 hours if you experience a problem with this new equipment."
➤ "I promise that we'll refund your money if you change your mind within seven days."
➤ "I promise I will look into this and get back to you in two days."
➤ "I promise you that this product is totally reliable. I cannot recall an instance of any customer being let down by it."
➤ "I promise you that if you make a claim we will deal with it within seven days."

➤ "I promise you that should you have cause to complain we will deal with the issue and respond to you within three days."

➤ "I promise you that should you use this product for a trial period there will be no pressure on you at all to purchase it and there will be no problem if you return it."

A company that does not make promises to its customers cannot create a climate of trust, is unable to demonstrate added emotional value and therefore is severely lacking in integrity.

SUMMARY

Integrity is an essential component of added emotional value and a function of how your espoused values are reflected on to customers and received by them.

It is all about putting your customers' interests before your own and demonstrating this in everything you do. One way of doing this is to make promises to customers and then to keep them.

Integrity is vital for delivering excellent customer service and gaining competitive advantage.

PRACTICAL STEPS

1 Be honest, do you put your customers' interests before your own? If yes, how? If no, find a way to do so.

2 Go out of your way to find opportunities to make commitments and promises to customers and then honor them.

3 Keep an informal log of every time you let a customer down, then use this as a toolbox for improvement.

4 List your most deeply held values in relation to customers.

5 What do you value most about your customers?

6 What do your customers value most about you?

7 Identify ways in which you can value your customers more.

8 Go out of your way today to demonstrate to your customers that you value them.

6

CREATIVE

CUSTOMER SERVICE

CREATIVITY IS ALL ABOUT BREAKING AWAY FROM ROUTINE AND creating something new that customers value. Such creativity comes from developing new clusters of thinking and feeling patterns.

A prime example is James Dyson, who reacted emotionally to the inefficiency of the vacuum cleaner he had at home and so decided to create a new one that did not rely on old-fashioned bags that quickly became clogged up. To quote from his book *Against the Odds*:

> Our old vacuum cleaner had been annoying me for years, this poxy machine ... It just seemed to push the dirt and dust around the house ... The disposable bag had been permanently clogged. I was furious ...

A new cluster of thinking and feeling patterns emerged when he noticed how a huge cyclone was used in a sawmill to separate the dust out of the air by centrifugal force.

> It occurred to me at that moment that there was really no reason why this shouldn't work in miniature – using a cyclone about the size of, say, a Perrier bottle.

It was the emotion, the annoyance and the anger, that triggered him to invent and develop one of the bestselling vacuum cleaners in the world, the bagless dual cyclone. Had he relied on the routine of vacuuming his house and never challenged it, we would never have had this brilliant invention.

Customers will rarely value the routine, in fact they will take it for granted. Thus we take it for granted that our mail will arrive on time every morning, but treasure the moment when the person delivering the post takes the initiative to congratulate us on our birthday and even drop us a card too.

A further 40 examples of creativity in customer service are provided in the boxes in this chapter. Some of the examples result from strategic innovation, while others are of everyday initiatives in a company's operation.

When you treat your customers in a routine way, they begin to see it as a duty you must perform and as their right to benefit from it. Thus the customer assumes that there will always be a complimentary bottle of mineral water in the hotel bedroom, that there will always be a little gift at Christmas.

The routines extend to everyday behaviors too. The customer assumes that the store assistant will always approach and ask "Can I help you?" and the store assistant always assumes that the customer will respond "I am just looking."

ROUTINES AND EXPECTATIONS

By assimilating behaviors into routines we raise expectations. We expect the meal to be served on time, we expect the manager to come and chat to us, we expect the other person to behave in the way we have experienced in the past. When customers convert their expectations into assumed rights, a company is entering dangerous territory.

Rights are normally bound by law. A customer has a contract with an organization and has a right to have that contract honored. Anything over and above that contract, such as complimentary chocolates or an upgrade to first class, is not a right, although the customer frequently assumes that it is.

CREATIVITY IN CUSTOMER SERVICE

1   British Airways led the way in providing beds to its first-class passengers on long-haul flights, as well as offering meals on the ground before a night flight, thus enabling passengers to obtain maximum sleep.

2   A pilot on British Airways announced, at the end of the flight, that it was the first flight for one flight attendant. He invited the passengers to give her a round of applause. They did.

3   At the Scandic Crown Hotel in Slussen, Stockholm, there is a detailed four-color map of the city on the back of the key card for each room.

4   A customer service agent working for TNT in Amsterdam was informed that a customer had lost some critical loading documents. The authorities would not allow the shipment to be processed. If the ship sailed without the consignment, the cost to the customer would be millions. The TNT customer service agent was able to help the customer locate replacement documents and then persuade the authorities to accept them.

5   A taxi firm called Eye Africa in Johannesburg offers its customers refreshments when they get into the car.

Organizations and individuals therefore have to be incredibly careful about assimilating non-contractual actions and behaviors into routine. Unless these actions and behaviors can be sustained on the majority of occasions, it is inevitable that the customer will be disappointed. When the exception becomes routine, the expectation is raised and the action is taken for granted. Furthermore, when the exception becomes routine it is in danger of being devalued in the eyes of the customer.

We all have a natural tendency to convert our everyday behaviors into routines. Our telephone responses become routine, the way we write letters becomes routine, lunch at 12.30 pm becomes routine, the way we greet customers becomes routine. Without realizing it, our relationships with customers are put on to a routine footing. Our

CREATIVITY IN CUSTOMER SERVICE

6   Sun Microsystems, in the USA and worldwide, encourages the establishment of "Sun teams". Anyone at any level in the organization with a bright idea seeks out a sponsor for that idea and then forms a Sun team to develop and implement it.

7   An assistant at Print Dynamics in Fort Lauderdale, USA, volunteered the following information on a Friday afternoon: "If you are staying here over this weekend I'd really recommend you go down to the food and music festival at Coconut Grove."

8   As assistant in a small grocery store in Ayia Napa in Cyprus volunteered to round down the bill to £12 when the total came to £12.05.

9   A teller in the Barnett Bank of Florida offered a four-year-old child a cookie when she accompanied her parents into the branch.

10   A waitress at TGI Friday's volunteered extra napkins when she saw that a child was making a mess of her food.

interactions with them become unthinking and mechanical. Customer contact is converted into scripted welcomes, standardized letters and routine surveys.

Customers notice this and place no value on it. They see through the veneer and see that there is nothing genuine there. So they tear up your routine letters and bin them, they react indifferently to your routine calls, while your routine welcomes and sales pitches just wash over them.

The further danger with routines is that competitors will find them easy to emulate. As soon as a new creative pattern of behavior is converted into a routine, others will copy it. As soon as one British hotel put a trouser press and tea-making facilities into its bedrooms, others copied. As soon as one company started using voicemail, others followed suit.

CREATIVITY IN CUSTOMER SERVICE

11 The manager of the customer services center of Dixons at Hemel Hempstead in the UK set up the "Customer Service Olympics" in which her people could win gold, silver and bronze medals for specific aspects of their performance.

12 Here are some of the innovations introduced by the SuperQuinn chain of grocery stores in Ireland:
➤ Playhouses in all stores
➤ Candies removed from checkouts
➤ Full-time nutritionist employed to advise customers
➤ No wobbly trolleys
➤ Egg-timer on counter (you'll be served before the sand runs out)
➤ Big badges given to kids on entering the store.

13 A member of the housekeeping staff at the J.W. Marriott hotel in Dubai volunteered to obtain ice for a customer when the customer asked where the ice machine was.

14 A customer service manager at Ecobank in Abidjan, Côte d'Ivoire, concerned about a long queue that had developed, reduced the length of the queue immediately by opening another counter to deal with small transactions that could be handled quickly.

15 Kinko's in the USA opens its branches 24 hours a day and offers its customers the ability to use, on site, wordprocessors, printing and copying around the clock.

THE EASY ROUTE TO SUCCESS

We have an inclination to seek the easy route to success. Rather than be creative we prefer to copy others, deluding ourselves that we are learning. We therefore study those who have been successful and try to identify the simple short-cuts that can be taken to emulate their success, to become a millionaire, or a top salesperson or a bestselling author. Books abound with titles such as *Success Is a Choice: Ten Steps to Overachieving in Business and Life*. We look for panaceas and magic wands to transform our ailing businesses and the ruts we have got into in life. We even look for quick-fix devices to radically improve our customer service.

Having identified the simple steps, we set up procedures to secure high performance and delude ourselves that they are effective (because of the mere fact that they exist). There is a proliferation of these "procedures for success" in modern management. Total quality management, reengineering and 360° appraisal are just three examples among many. On the customer service front we routinely use customer surveys because it is standard convention to do so. The data are analyzed and reports are made. We feel good when the results show that customer satisfaction is rated above the norm and we feel bad when ratings are below average. Few people challenge the meaningfulness and efficacy of the exercise. It has become convention, it has become accepted practice, it has become routine. Why fix it if it ain't broke?

In copying other people's procedures we bypass our creative impulses to find something new and original which might just be better than what these other people are doing. A precursor to creativity is to question and challenge everything rather than accepting it and copying it.

Jack Loming, a participant on one of my seminars, told me that for years he had been filling in customer comment cards in hotels. However, he could not recall a single occasion when a comment he had made had been taken into consideration and influenced any change. For example, a number of times he had written "I would suggest that you start breakfast at 6.30 am instead of 7.00 am", only to find on his next visit that breakfast still started at 7.00 am.

For the last 14 years I have spent, on average, three nights a week in hotels running seminars for in-house clients and speaking at conferences. I can only recall one occasion when a hotel manager has come to me at the end of the session and said: "How was it? Did we serve the coffee on time?" All these hotels have customer comment cards, but it is exceptionally rare (unless you complain strongly) for a hotel manager to take sufficient interest to sit down with a customer and find out what they really felt about the experience. The whole process of obtaining feedback from customers has been converted into a routine procedure and as such has devalued the feedback and made it almost meaningless.

There are very few hotels that pride themselves on their creative approach to establishing emotional connectivity and adding emotional value to the essential task of serving their customers.

Another example of routine is customer newsletters. Most companies have got into the habit of sending their known customers periodic newsletters. Expensive as they are to produce and distribute, few people challenge the effectiveness of these glossy publications. Intuitively, we know that most customers give them five seconds' attention before tossing them into the trash.

Routines themselves are devoid of emotion. You do not need emotional energy for routine activity, in fact you can do it with your eyes shut. By following routines you shut down your emotions as well your mind. In doing so, you expend minimal energy to achieve your routine goals.

Routines are devoid of emotion

The further danger is that we begin to see the world in a routine way. We treat our customers in a routine way because we see them as conforming to stereotypes. Customers become numbers on a production line, to be processed by the system. We also drift into treating our staff in a routine way, rewarding them by routine and therefore reinforcing a mentality where the reward is taken for granted and seen as a right.

FIXED THINKING PATTERNS

Routines result in us being trapped into fixed, rigid thinking patterns. In the end we define the world by our own routine, criticizing others who have the audacity to step out of line and not conform. Customers are expected to conform to these stereotypical patterns of behavior and are readily criticized as nuisances when they expect something different.

I recall running a seminar for an in-house client in Germany. There were 30 people in the room and it was a hot day. At 11.30 am one of the participants put up his hand and requested some coffee. We had started the session at 10.00 am and no break was scheduled until lunch at 12.30 pm. I interrupted my talk, went to the phone

CREATIVITY IN CUSTOMER SERVICE

16 The bookstore Barnes & Noble, at its Plantation Branch in Florida, promotes books recommended by its staff.

17 London Underground publishes poems in the advertising space inside its trains.

18 An assistant at the ticket office at the Place Monge station on the Paris metro took the initiative to explain, in English, how to use a three-day travel pass and then filled in the necessary information on the pass which the customer should have done.

19 A teller in a Florida bank noticed that one very old customer kept on coming in to draw out cash. She was concerned that he was becoming absent-minded and losing the money. So she rang his family to alert them to the problem.

20 At the Sheraton Hotel in Jeddah, Saudi Arabia, a valet offers you complimentary pressing of your suit when you are settling into your room as well as complimentary refreshments.

and rang reception to ask for 30 coffees. Five minutes later a grumpy looking waiter appeared with some documents in his hand.

"We don't have you down for coffee at 11.30 am," he grunted, "you were supposed to have it on arrival at 9.30 am and then nothing more until 12.30 pm."

"I just want 30 coffees now please," I told him in front of the group.

"But it's not scheduled," he pleaded, "the cups are not laid out in the room."

I persisted and eventually the coffee was served, albeit reluctantly. I kept on thinking that if I was running a coffee shop I would be absolutely delighted if 30 customers came in and ordered coffee. As far as this particular waiter was concerned, I was a nuisance because I had not conformed to what he thought was the routine. He was unable to find a creative response to our request.

CREATIVITY IN CUSTOMER SERVICE

21 At Hambros Bank in Gibraltar, a teller sent flowers to a lady who notified them that her husband had just died.

22 A team at Mashreq Bank, Dubai, noticing the problems that expatriates had in opening accounts, introduced a new Quickstart account.

23 A well-known and well-established customer rang a manager of the National Bank of Abu Dhabi at midnight saying that he was leaving for the USA at 2.00 am that morning and needed $100,000 in cash. The manager obtained the cash for the customer.

24 A flight attendant on a British Airways flight, noticing a customer waiting in the aisle for a toilet to become free, pointed out that the toilet in the other aisle was vacant.

25 On Royal Brunei Airlines in business class, orders for drinks are taken before take-off.

You don't have to look far to find many other examples of how routine restricts the delivery of excellent service.

A year or so back I was undertaking a customer service assignment for a major UK bank and was scheduled to interview a number of branch managers in the Thames Valley region. My first meeting was at 9.30 am at a branch in Maidenhead. I am always punctual and arrived at 9.25 am for the meeting. However, the doors of the branch were shut and there was a plaque on the wall saying "Open 9.30 am–5.00 pm".

So I waited patiently outside in the cold rain and wind, along with a few senior citizens who were also shivering and getting wet. Precisely at 9.30 am the doors of the branch opened and by the time I found my way in and asked for the manager I was five minutes late for my meeting. I asked the manager whether he could conceivably open the doors of the branch two or three minutes early when the situation required it (for example when it was pouring with rain outside). He said he couldn't. I asked him why not. He told me it was "policy".

CREATIVITY IN CUSTOMER SERVICE

26 Kesh Morjaria of Fleet Photos in London encourages his staff to select the best photo in a film that has just been developed for a customer, put it in a small cardboard frame and say: "This photo looks great framed."

27 At BT Mobile, Steve, a customer service agent, devised "customer service bubbles" (customer quotes). Every time a customer says anything of note about the service provided, staff write it down on a specially devised "bubble form" that is then circulated for all to see.

28 A member of housekeeping at a Ritz Carlton Hotel, noticing a guest waiting for the gift shop to open (at 8.55 am), volunteered to obtain the gift for the guest, to save her waiting, and deliver it at the conference coffee break.

29 At Winn Dixie's supermarket in Lauderdale-by-the-Sea, Florida, customers can have their blood pressure and pulse measured free of charge using an automatic machine.

30 At Lloyds Bank in Windsor, UK, the manager dresses up as Father Christmas and serves champagne, orange juice and mince pies to all customers on Christmas Eve.

The amazing thing was that during the day I met five further branch managers, one of whom actually did confess to opening the doors of his branch two or three minutes early when the situation required it. A few weeks later I asked the bank's senior retail operations director whether he had any problem with his branch managers opening the doors a few minutes early. His reply was significant.

"No," he said. "But most of these branch managers have got it stuck in their heads that they can't do it. If I begin to rewrite the operations manuals to state all the detailed things branch managers can or cannot do then we would have 20 volumes requiring three feet of shelf space. Also we would defeat the object of this exercise – which is to encourage people to think for themselves."

And that is the problem with routine. People stop being creative in trying to please their customers. They stop thinking for themselves, especially if the routines are laid down by the organization or the "system". Front-line people subjected to routine start subjecting customers to unthinking, automatic responses. The front-line employees effectively become automatons who treat their customers as items to be processed rather than as human beings with unique needs that require a creative response.

It is the creative response which adds emotional value, while the routine, deprived as it is of emotion, is very rarely valued.

Compare the above experience with that at Bank Atlantic in Florida. There, a teller at a drive-through counter noticed that senior citizens regularly drove to the bank with their pet dogs in the back seat. This teller dipped into her own pocket and bought some dog biscuits, so that each time a senior citizen came to the drive-through counter with a dog in the back seat she could pop a dog biscuit into the dog's mouth. Needless to say, both the senior citizens and the dogs loved this and thereafter were emotionally attached to the bank.

CREATIVE OPPORTUNITIES

If you remove routine from relationships, every single interaction becomes an opportunity to do something creative and positive for a customer. How you welcome a customer becomes a creative opportunity, as do the words you choose to address a customer. Your whole body language can be used creatively to express the way you value each customer. By developing your senses about what the customer's specific goals are, you can seek creative opportunities to please the customer and make them feel good.

Customers really do like front-line people who take initiatives, who go out of their way to do something different, who are able to fix apparently intractable problems. Such creative initiatives add emotional value not only for the customers but also for the employees, most of whom abhor the boredom of routine and get a real buzz from doing something unusual to please customers.

A study published in the USA shows that the most admired companies in America are those that are the most innovative. The innovation permeates every facet of the organization. Creativity and innovation are not just a matter of strategic conceptualization and implementation, but also everyday behavior.

None of the creative initiatives mentioned above represents the industry norm. They were all taken by people who wanted to do something different and special for customers. The exciting thing about striving for service excellence and competitive advantage is that most days present opportunities for taking such creative initiatives. As soon as you open your mouth you have a choice about the words you use, the gestures you make and the emotions you display. One of the keys of emotional intelligence is to become aware of these words, gestures and emotions and in doing so to become more creative in their use.

Take this opportunity to list some creative initiatives that you are aware of in your company. Also list the creative initiatives that you have taken recently.

Creative initiatives for customers by my company	Creative initiatives for customers by myself and members of our team

CREATIVITY IN CUSTOMER SERVICE

31 A Volkswagen dealer in Sweden invites customers who have recently purchased a car to come and have a meal with him at the dealership.

32 Taxis in Sweden take credit cards.

33 At the Novotel in Accra, Ghana, guests are presented with a little gift on checking out.

34 Jean Aka, Managing Director of Ecobank, Ghana, sends flowers to customers who are in hospital.

35 Greg McGarry, General Manager of the Royal York Hotel in York (UK), occasionally books rooms in his competitors' hotels for his team sessions.

CREATIVITY, GIVING AND VALUE

Creativity is synonymous with giving that extra value to customers to differentiate a company from its competitors and thus provide competitive advantage. A significant part of this extra value can be added emotional value. It is all about giving more than is expected, surprising the customers with things they did not expect. Creativity is a way of demonstrating that you really want to please your customers, that you really value them and want to do as much as possible for them. You can never demonstrate this by routine.

So creativity is closely associated with integrity, with giving more than you take, with creating trust. It is also associated with adding emotional value through emotional connectivity, because by taking these creative initiatives you make your customers feel really good. Simply put, it is what your customers like about you.

This can be expressed as follows:

CREATIVITY ———▶ GIVING ———▶ VALUE

CREATIVE STRATEGIES FOR SERVICE EXCELLENCE

While every transaction with a customer presents a creative opportunity, there is also need to be creative in developing your longer-term strategy for service excellence and competitive advantage.

Many people become too immersed in the pressures of their everyday routines and lose sight of the creative opportunities all around them, both short term and long term.

To maximize your own creativity and that of your team, it is important to find "space" away from your normal environment, together with some stimuli for sparking new concepts and developing exciting fresh strategies for developing your company's approach to customers. This will enable a free flow of ideas.

The more creative managers take their teams away for a "retreat" to brainstorm ideas for improving service. In doing so they will agree conditions for such creativity. Below is a typical set of conditions:

➤ Be free of constraints (the words "this is not allowed" are not allowed).
➤ Be free of fixed, rigid thinking patterns (routines and habits are out).
➤ Be free of entrenched attitudes (prejudices and stereotypes).
➤ Be free of negativity (eliminate "it can't be done" statements).
➤ Be free of tradition (do not refer to the way we did it before).
➤ Be free of history (do not refer to incidents from the past).
➤ Be relaxed (you can never be creative if you are tense and under stress).
➤ Be positive (it can be done).
➤ Be open to all conceivable ideas (even the most outrageous ideas will be considered).
➤ Challenge yourself and each other in a constructive way.
➤ Seek stimuli by looking at other people's exciting ideas outside your own specific domain – look at case studies, videos, books, draw on your own experiences, listen to outside lecturers etc.
➤ Allow one crazy idea to spark another and another so that you eventually arrive at one that is both exciting and feasible.

➤ Be prepared to give the idea a go – if it doesn't work out after the pilot, drop it.
➤ Believe in the idea.
➤ Be prepared to evaluate the idea and pilot its implementation with a carefully prepared plan (in other words, give it a whirl!).
➤ If you really believe that your idea will bear fruit, work hard to implement it. Discipline and energy are essential in the creativity process.

Here are some important criteria that should apply to the strategic implementation of any creative new idea:

➤ Is it unique?
➤ How do I/we feel about the idea?
➤ Does it make sense?
➤ Is it worth developing?
➤ What do I/we aim to achieve by implementing this idea?

While routine devalues a relationship, creativity adds value to it. Creativity enables you to offer more than your contractual commitment, more than the competition, and thus to be ahead of everything else on offer in the marketplace.

Creativity is effectively an attitude of mind driven by the emotional desire to do even more for your customers. As mentioned above, creativity is synonymous with giving customers added value while routines are synonymous with minimizing value. You just have to review your own recent experiences as a customer to come to the conclusion that only a small percentage of people working at the front line seem really keen to please you, to do things that will make you feel good and that you will like.

A smile in the right place can be incredibly creative, a kind word to a tense customer can be incredibly creative, a nod to the effect of "I'll be with you in a moment" can be incredibly creative when you see an impatient-looking customer waiting.

Cast your mind back to the last time you experienced really superb customer service and identify to what extent this resulted from a creative initiative as opposed to some routine endeavor.

CREATIVITY IN CUSTOMER SERVICE

36 An officer in charge of a day center for people with learning difficulties in Maidenhead (UK) trained up some of its "clients" to work on reception and answer telephones.

37 Alan Levan, President of Bank Atlantic, Florida, runs an annual convention for all his staff at the Fort Lauderdale Convention Center. One year he approved a major systems conversion which, during implementation, went drastically wrong. His staff suffered as the system frequently collapsed, screens were slow to come up and transactions were not processed. At the annual convention each employee received a red polystyrene ball, bought from Toys 'R' Us. Alan stood up in front of everyone, admitted his mistake with the systems conversion and asked his employees to imagine that the red balls were tomatoes and to throw them at him. They did. They love him!

38 A waitress at the Marriott Hotel in Portsmouth, UK, came up and had a chat to explain what was happening with all the refurbishment that was taking place.

39 A barman at SHL's residential training center at Long Ditton, UK, was put through the company's training programs for customers (on occupational testing and various other psychometric tests) so that he could sense which customer trainees were struggling with the course and thus help them.

40 A customer came into the Hair Advice Centre in Kings Heath, Birmingham, UK, and started crying while her hair was being cut. Manager Andrew May comforted her and gently enquired what was wrong. Apparently the customer's pet dog had run across the road the previous Saturday and had been killed. After the customer left, Andrew went to a card shop, selected a card with a picture of dog on it and sent it to the customer with a message of condolence.

SUMMARY

Customers like companies and employees who are creative in responding to their needs. Routines tend to dehumanize relationships and lead to an unthinking approach to customer service. Creativity adds value to a relationship and is a key factor in helping companies establish a leading competitive edge through customer service. Creativity applies at a strategic level and also at an operational level in people's everyday behaviors.

PRACTICAL STEPS

1 Identify and list all the routines you apply to your relationships with customers (e.g. scripted welcomes, standardized letters etc.).
2 Try to reduce the routines and replace them with creative actions and behaviors that demonstrate how much you value your customers.
3 Review all the initiatives you and your team have taken on behalf of your customers over the last four weeks. Then assess the impact of these initiatives on your customers' perceptions.
4 Schedule some time off site, in a relaxed environment, and brainstorm as many ideas as possible to be included in a long-term customer service development strategy.
5 Examine your own behaviors (the way you answer the telephone, the way you reply to letters, the way you greet and talk with customers) and identify creative ways in which you can develop these behaviors.

7

EVERYDAY LIKEABLE

BEHAVIORS

CUSTOMERS MOST LIKE YOU WHEN:

➤ You connect emotionally with them to deliver added emotional value.
➤ You demonstrate integrity in all your dealings with them.
➤ You are creative in responding to their needs.

The challenge for each of us as individuals is to develop and exhibit a range of likeable behaviors that will reinforce and confirm these attributes.

Likeable behaviors can be grouped according to the following seven attributes:

1　The emotional eye
2　The emotional ear
3　The emotional voice
4　Behaving with integrity
5　The challenge of creativity
6　The feeling mind
7　Emotional energy

The emotional eye

The most powerful emotional connection is made through the eyes. This is a much neglected aspect of customer service. We tend to become unaware of what is happening between our eyes and those of the customer, yet without realizing it the impression the customer gains of us often stems from what they see (or do not see) in our eyes. Whatever words you use, it is often your eyes that will give you away, that speak the truth and determine the reaction you will get from customers.

There are five key likeable behaviors relating to the emotional eye.

Keep an eye open for customers

It is critical that any front-line person is continually alert for new customers entering their sphere of influence and activity. One of the biggest complaints customers make is that they are ignored, that nobody pays any attention to them. Even before any transaction begins, the customer is already feeling bad. By keeping an eye open for customers coming into your domain you can take the initiative to greet, welcome, acknowledge or put them at ease as appropriate. Even if you are dealing with another customer, it is not difficult to gesture to a new customer that you will come to them in a moment or two. Such small gestures add a high degree of emotional value.

Keep an eye on customers

As soon as a customer has entered your domain (your sphere of influence and activity) you must be aware of what that customer is doing. This means being sensitive to the requirements (the goals and expectations) of each customer. It means being sensitive to what they are thinking and feeling and then responding appropriately. It means being aware that a customer has taken a sudden interest in a different product to the one you are showing, or is only concerned about the price, or is getting impatient, or wants to learn more about the features of comparative products. By being aware, by being sensitive, you add emotional value and the customer will like you for it.

ALLOW YOUR EYES TO LIGHT UP FOR CUSTOMERS

Customers love front-line people with a sparkle in their eyes. Delight at seeing an approaching customer is best expressed through the eyes. To achieve this means delving deep inside yourself to discover the genuine good feeling you have when a person who pays your salary, a customer, walks through the door. This good feeling, this rapture, must show through your eyes. When this connection is made you add immense emotional value.

LET YOUR FEELINGS SHOW THROUGH YOUR EYES

After the initial sparkle at seeing a customer approach, you will need to become sensitized to each customer's particular situation and their evolving needs. If, for example, a customer has a major problem and is seeking help, you will need to let your sympathy show through your eyes. If a customer is excited about the prospect of a potential purchase, you will need to let your enthusiasm for that product show through your eyes. If a customer tells you that she has been badly treated elsewhere, then you will need to let your anger show too. This is all to do with empathy and being sensitive to and understanding each customer's feelings. The eyes are a major instrument of empathy. By letting your feelings show, you connect with the customer's feelings and therefore enhance the value they receive.

MAINTAIN FREQUENT EYE CONTACT WITH CUSTOMERS

Since your thoughts show through your eyes, by avoiding eye contact you are attempting to hide your thoughts and you are probably indicating to a customer that your interests are elsewhere. To achieve excellent customer service you must focus all your energies on each customer you come across. This energy shows through the eyes and through frequent eye contact with customers. There are limitations, because many customers have their own thoughts to hide and will avoid eye contact with you. However, the more you can sustain eye contact the more likely it is that you will deliver excellent service.

THE EMOTIONAL EAR

The ear is a much misused instrument. We frequently allow it to screen out vital information while selfishly letting in only those sounds that are of interest to us. Properly used, the ear can detect the emotional tone in a customer's voice and pick up the fine but important nuances of a customer's requirements. Thus the voice of a customer who is nervous about buying a major item might tremble slightly. If you detect this, you can reassure the customer and put them at their ease. There are a range of behaviors relating to the emotional ear.

LISTEN CAREFULLY TO WHAT THE CUSTOMER SAYS

Try not to think *for* the customer, or about what you are going to say in response. Ignore your own value judgements about any contentious issue the customer raises and refrain from expressing your own opinions until such time as the customer is ready to receive them. Genuinely try to get inside the customer's mind by concentrating on what they have to say. You must avoid the syndrome commonly described as "in one ear and out the other".

LEARN FROM WHAT THE CUSTOMER HAS TO SAY

Avoid jumping to conclusions and making assumptions about the customer's requirements. Don't put words into their mouth. Try to learn in depth about the customer's specific goals for feeling good. In doing so, go beyond the immediate transaction and seek out a little more about the customer and the context within which they are making the purchase. Discover the customer's motives, their reasons for making a particular purchase. You can do this by asking indirect questions. For example, rather than asking "What type of white shirt do you require?", ask "Will you be requiring this white shirt for everyday work, for an important business occasion, or for a casual dinner one evening?"

The more you can understand "where customers are coming from" (the context), the better position you will be in to connect emotionally with them and help achieve their evolving goals.

TUNE IN TO THE CUSTOMER'S EMOTIONAL TONE

Try to detect the fine nuances of the customer's emotional tone to determine and understand each point they are making. Train your ears to detect the various emotional modulations in the voice of each customer. You will need to weigh the words customers use with the emotion attached to them. If there is coldness in the customer's voice, you will need to identify whether they are suspicious about you, the company and its products, or whether they are really not interested. You will then need to reassure them subtly that you will be acting in their best interest.

Other examples of emotional tones used by customers are as follows:

➤ A worried tone (the customer is unsure about the purchase).
➤ An excited tone (the customer has special plans following this purchase).
➤ A sad tone (this is a distress purchase).
➤ A hurried tone (the customer has little time to make the purchase).
➤ A confident tone (the customer knows exactly what he or she wants).
➤ A happy tone (the customer is delighted to have found, at last, the product he or she has been looking for).
➤ A challenging tone (the customer wants evidence that the product is all it is made out to be).
➤ A friendly tone (the customer is as much interested in having a chat with you as in purchasing the product).
➤ A shocked tone (the customer is appalled at the price).
➤ A disinterested tone (the customer is not interested in you or the product he or she is purchasing).
➤ A pleading tone (the customer is desperate for help).
➤ An angry tone (the customer has been waiting a long time).
➤ An inquiring tone (the customer requires information and advice).
➤ An authoritarian tone (the customer demands action of you).
➤ An obsequious tone (the customer craves a favor of you).
➤ A sympathetic tone (the customer understands the pressures you are under).

Having trained your ear to recognize the wide range of emotional tones customers use, it is equally important to become aware of your own emotional tone. This leads on to the importance of the emotional voice.

THE EMOTIONAL VOICE

When you deprive your voice of emotion you are left with cold, dry words that at best convey information but in fact communicate little about your real self. No matter how good your logic and the words used to express it, you will fail to convince people unless your beliefs and feelings show through in the way you use the words. This is vital in dealing with customers. There are therefore two critical behaviors you need to adopt to develop an emotional voice that will enable you to connect with customers.

DEVELOP AWARENESS OF YOUR TONE OF VOICE

In talking with customers, it is absolutely critical that you become aware of the sound of your own voice and the emotions this conveys. Every individual's voice varies in pitch, pace and range and has a unique "voice print". The best way to learn about these voice prints is to tune in to the sounds of other people's voices and the emotional tones they use (as discussed in the previous section).

Listen carefully to your customers. What emotions do they convey? Discipline yourself to listen carefully to other people and identify those voices you feel comfortable with and those that alienate you. Identify the emotional qualities of those voices you like and those you do not like. Then try to compare your own voice with those you like. Every time you speak, try to put yourself into your customer's shoes and determine how they might react to your voice. What emotion are you conveying with your voice, if any?

At Yellow Pages' customer call center in Reading, UK, a computer selects random examples of each agent's calls for recording, playback and review. In this way agents can assess their own emotional tone and the impact on each customer.

Modulate your voice to establish an emotional connection

Having become tuned in to the emotional tone of your own and other people's voices, you will need to modulate your voice to reflect genuine feelings for each customer and to develop their feelings for you. For example:

➤ If a customer comes across as cold and diffident, convince yourself that beneath the surface is a warm, caring, loving human being. Try to reach that suppressed warmth by injecting emotional warmth into your own words.

➤ If a customer comes across as being overpowering and effusive, convince yourself that beneath the surface is someone who is desperate for recognition and admiration. Therefore in responding to the customer, try to underline your words with a tone of emotional approval.

➤ If a customer comes across as being kind and caring, then respond in the same way, ensuring that your voice is soft, rounded and undulates smoothly to reflect your own feelings of compassion.

By drawing on your feelings and emotions to fine-tune the way you use your voice, you will be much better able to connect emotionally with customers and become someone they really like.

Using the examples from the previous section, here are some emotional tones that you can develop and use in response to customers:

Customer's emotional tone	Your emotional tone in response
➤ Worried	➤ Reassuring
➤ Excited	➤ Happy
➤ Sad	➤ Compassionate
➤ Hurried	➤ Understanding
➤ Confident	➤ Approving
➤ Happy	➤ Happy
➤ Challenging	➤ Reassuring
➤ Friendly	➤ Friendly

- ➤ Shocked
- ➤ Disinterested
- ➤ Pleading
- ➤ Angry
- ➤ Inquiring
- ➤ Authoritarian
- ➤ Obsequious
- ➤ Sympathetic

- ➤ Understanding
- ➤ Polite
- ➤ Helpful
- ➤ Soothing
- ➤ Helpful
- ➤ Pleasing
- ➤ "Firm and fair"
- ➤ Appreciative

If possible, tape record your own voice in everyday conversation and listen to it carefully. How do you think other people react to the various tones you use in your voice? If you are brave enough, ask them!

BEHAVING WITH INTEGRITY

All the emotional behaviors listed above ideally reflect your own genuine feelings for customers and your desire to connect emotionally with them. Integrity is the cornerstone of all these behaviors. By acting with integrity you allow your own values, beliefs and feelings to show through. You will be acting as a "whole person" whose words and actions are perfectly aligned with your real thoughts and deep feelings. Unfortunately, some people who have the highest integrity inadvertently behave in a way that convinces otherwise, and this makes customers suspicious. These people are cumbersome in the way they express themselves and quite unwittingly send out the wrong signals.

While traveling on trains or the metro, I frequently observe other people's behavior. Many are oblivious to their own mannerisms, to the signals they are sending out. They seem to be unaware that their eye movements, facial expressions and hand gestures are giving their thoughts away. You can sense the stress they are under, or their irritation, puzzlement, delight, boredom or annoyance. All the time we are sending out such signals.

To behave with integrity therefore requires a high degree of consciousness of every movement of your body, every word you use and the way you use it. This level of consciousness requires a lot of energy and is too much for many, who prefer to revert to routine, unthinking, subconscious behaviors that consume little energy. Assuming that you really value your customers as well as like them, there are four key behaviors you can adopt to help you behave with integrity.

Be demonstrative

Use every possible opportunity to demonstrate behaviorally that you genuinely value each customer, no matter how insignificant the transaction. This means demonstrating with your eyes, your arms, your hands, your voice and the words you use that the customer in front of you is the most important person in the world. If you genuinely feel this, you will find it relatively easy to develop gestures and voice tones to demonstrate it.

This does mean getting in touch with your values. Those people who do not think about their values will need to search for them. Normally they exist but are suppressed and hidden away. Your values need to be brought to the surface, examined, developed and applied. If trust is an important value for you, then you need to reflect on it and be totally aware how it can be demonstrated in every facet of your dealings with a customer. If accountability is an important value for you, then you need to seize every opportunity to show customers that you are taking accountability for satisfying their needs for excellent service.

The most impressive front-line people and managers I have met are those who have brought their values into focus and applied them consistently, day in and day out. For example, Charlotte Horne of BT Mobile in the UK goes out of her way every single day to create opportunities to please people. It has become a driving force in her life. Every evening she goes home, she asks herself: "In what way have I made a customer feel better today?"

Treat customers as equals

There is an old adage: "treat customers as you would want to be treated yourself". This holds true. However, it does mean you have to become aware of how you want to be treated yourself. This could well mean enhancing your own expectations and self-esteem. For a start, if you believe that you are genuinely open, honest and trustworthy, then it is essential that you treat each approaching customer as genuinely open, honest and trustworthy.

TAKE AN INTEREST IN EACH CUSTOMER

Treating people well often means giving them time and listening carefully to their viewpoint, without making value judgements. Try treating customers in the same way.

Most people like to talk about themselves and like people who will listen to them and find out about them. One of the most neglected behaviors in establishing an emotional connection is to ask a few simple questions: "Where are you from?" "Do you live locally?" "Are you going to the carnival this afternoon?" "What do you think of this new shopping mall?" "Did you hear the news about our local mayor?"

There can be no set pattern for taking an interest in customers, except that the more you do it the more emotional connections you will make and the more emotional value you will add. Your interest must be genuine and you must be prepared to learn from what each customer has to say. Your overall goal is to determine what each customer stands for and what their goals are, so that you can help them reinforce their values and meet their goals. Such interest and reinforcement contribute to added emotional value.

When you are experienced, you will intuitively know the type of things that interest various customers and you will be able to develop a conversation around these topics, thus initiating and reinforcing relationships with them. To develop these relationships it is important to acquire a wide range of interests yourself, whether it be sport, music, travel, politics, the state of the housing market or whatever. This will give you an excellent reservoir of conversational opportunities to connect emotionally with each customer through their own area of specific interest.

Too many front-line people have too narrow a focus of interest in their life and therefore are unable to connect with the majority of customers and their broad range of interests.

BE SCRUPULOUSLY HONEST AND TRUSTWORTHY

Never, ever try to mislead customers or hide vital information from them. It is essential that in every interaction with a customer you come across as being honest and trustworthy. This means that you must be, as a person, completely honest and trustworthy. You cannot pretend, instead you have to *be* so. This means getting in touch with your own conscience, with your own values and beliefs, and allowing these to show through to the customer. If you try to act out a role that is inconsistent with your values and beliefs, then the customer will instinctively sense this and become suspicious.

THE CHALLENGE OF CREATIVITY

Every day, every week, you need to find new, different and possibly better ways of interacting with customers. As already discussed, this will require an immense amount of energy. You must resist, with all your might, the temptation to fall into a rut, to get into set ways, to yield to an unthinking, mechanical approach.

There are three main behaviors you can adopt to help you. They are all high-energy behaviors.

CHALLENGE YOURSELF CONTINUALLY

Never merely accept that your behaviors and actions reflect best practice. You have to be convinced that you are continually capable of change and improvement. Repeated practice in a relationship is not always best practice. Predictability (as opposed to reliability) can lead to stagnation. It is varied, spontaneous, creative practice that effectively becomes best practice along with reliability and trust. You therefore frequently need to:

➤ Challenge the way you welcome customers to your building.
➤ Challenge the telephone greetings you use.
➤ Challenge the initiatives you take to create a relationship with a customer.
➤ Challenge the way you write letters to customers.

➤ Challenge the way you talk with customers.
➤ Challenge the way you listen to customers.
➤ Challenge the way you learn from customers.
➤ Challenge the way you say "goodbye" to customers.
➤ Challenge the way you establish eye contact with customers.
➤ Challenge your own facial expressions and other gestures.
➤ Challenge the way you do things for customers.
➤ Challenge the systems and tools you use for delivering service excellence.

If you undertake this challenge, you will be surprised to find that creative new ways of doing these things will spring to mind.

For example, don't send your secretary down from the third floor to main reception to welcome a visiting customer – instead, go down yourself and greet the person and then show them around.

Or give all your customers your home telephone number (as well as your private line number) and invite them to call you at any time if they need to.

SEIZE THE INITIATIVE

As soon as a problem is identified, either by yourself or a customer, seize the opportunity to get it fixed. Take full accountability for the resolution of this problem, even if it means harassing your boss for a decision.

Furthermore, if a customer alludes to something, then seize the opportunity to pick up on this idea and get something done about it. For example, a customer might allude to the difficulties he had with car parking. Take the matter up with the appropriate people and pester them until the car-parking situation is eased.

Too often a problem gets shunted off to some other person in the hierarchy and is lost. Whoever encounters the problem first should be accountable for its creative resolution, from start to finish.

In all the companies I studied that were emotionally connected and delivered excellent service, the trust was sufficient to allow front-line people to resolve most customer problems, rather than shunting the problem up the hierarchy which results in a high risk of delays and problems being forgotten about (see Figure 6 opposite).

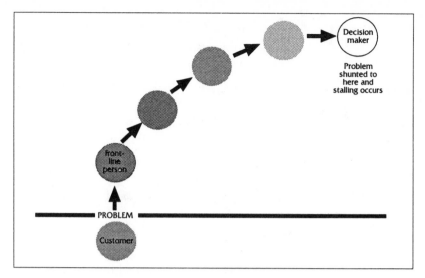

Figure 6   The "shunt and disown" syndrome

Allowing front-line people to fix customer problems adds immense emotional value – denying them the opportunity devalues both the front-line person and the customer.

If, on rare occasions, a decision has to be made by a senior executive, then the front-line person should still "own" the problem and progress the resolution of the issue, if necessary by chasing the senior executive for a decision. In other words, on certain issues it is quite possible for ownership (of the resolution of the problem) and decision making (deciding on the resolution) to be separate.

DO THINGS DIFFERENTLY

Get into the habit of getting out of the habit. Before you practice on customers, practice on yourself. For example, most people park their cars in the same space every day (normally as near to the entrance as possible). Why not park in the most remote part of the car park? The extra exercise will do you good and give you extra thinking time.

Vary the clothes you wear to the office, arrive at work at different times and use different routes to get there. Why try to save two minutes by using the same route every day? Invest the extra two minutes in seeing a different part of the locality.

Having practiced doing things differently on yourself, then practice on customers. Vary the way you sit customers in your office, vary how you show them around, vary the presentations you give them.

> **Get into the habit of getting out of the habit**

At the front line, encourage your people to vary the way they deal with customers, for example where they stand in the showroom, the things they put on the counter or on the desk. Encourage them to vary the way they speak to customers, for example by changing their words of welcome from one customer to another.

The more variations you adopt in your service approach, the fresher and more spontaneous you will be personally, thus enabling you to become more effective in connecting emotionally with customers.

THE FEELING MIND

Feargal Quinn, chairman of the Irish retail chain SuperQuinn, said:

> Getting customers to come back again and again depends critically on your ability to develop a *feel* for the customer. It's a feel that can never be achieved through indirect means such as market research.

Developing a feel for customers means developing a heightened sensitivity to their broad spectrum of needs. There is no one specific behavior for this. To develop a "feeling mind" requires a high degree of alertness, awareness, empathy, finely tuned observation and extreme sensitivity, together with a reluctance to overreact or rush to value judgements.

Next time you are in a public place, a café, a train, a bus or a shop, practice using your feeling mind. Try to develop a feel for what is going on around you – for example with that family over there, or with this old gentleman here, or with that assistant behind the counter. By developing a feeling mind, you will learn a great deal about what is going on around you and therefore be in a much better position to connect with your customers.

PAY COMPLETE ATTENTION TO YOUR CUSTOMERS

The one key behavior for developing a feeling mind is to pay complete attention to your customers.

The more you take your mind off your customers, the greater the probability that they will take their minds off you and defect to competitors who give them their due attention.

Customers want to do business with people who pay attention to them. Paying attention means training your mind to focus only on customers when they are in the vicinity. Paying attention to customers is another form of added emotional value.

Sara Lee from Singapore told me that while she was working in central London she went to a branch of her bank to pay in a couple of checks. It was just after 9.30 am and not the busiest time for the bank. Only one counter was open and the teller there was processing a long and complicated transaction for the customer in front of her. She looked around. There was a foreign exchange counter nearby where a bank employee was shuffling paper, eyes down behind the screen. Another person was sitting at a customer service desk idling time away. Other bank staff milled around. She counted six bank staff in total. Three of them were talking to each other on various bank matters. Not a single member of staff seemed to be aware of her existence, no one paid any attention to her despite her long wait.

Eventually, out of frustration, she approached the foreign exchange counter and managed to attract the attention of the cashier there. He begrudgingly pushed aside his paperwork and processed Sara's check deposits. There was no emotional interaction at all. Her overall reaction was: "Why the hell do I deal with this bank?" Perhaps one day she won't.

The hardest task of all in customer service is to keep your mind on customers, as opposed to processing papers, undertaking administration and doing something more tangible. The hardest task for any manager is to persuade their staff to keep their minds on customers all the time.

Amazingly, front-line people frequently forget about customers. They think about their next coffee break, or having a chat with that friendly colleague over there. They think about the row they had with their spouse this morning, or about what to get the kids to eat this evening. They think about whether they'll have time to get to the grocery store during the lunch break. One minute they are thinking about their next vacation and the next minute they are thinking about what mood the boss will be in today and whether they can ask for an extra day off.

What they forget to think about is the very people who pay their salaries, their customers. As their minds wriggle down nefarious personal routes and into futuristic fantasies ("Tonight I'm going to win the lottery, now how am I going to spend ten million?") they screen out anything to do with customers. Minimal attention is deployed to the specific transactions they have to undertake, they count the money, check the checks, tick the boxes, fill in the odd form and stamp the pay-in slips. They are hardly aware of the customer standing across the counter. It is just another blank face, another number.

Thinking about customers and paying attention to them requires immense powers of concentration and a lot of energy. It helps if you like them because this will lower the energy barriers and allow you to relax a little more and enjoy the interaction. I

The hardest task of all in customer service is to keep your mind on customers

would estimate that this happens on 10 percent of occasions. When it comes to retail customer service and routine transactions (buying a newspaper, a bottle of mineral water, a railway ticket, a theater ticket) I frequently do not exist as far as the other person is concerned. I am a transaction but not a human being. I am one of a hundred items being processed on the manufacturing line during the day.

The joy when someone genuinely pays me attention and thinks about me is immeasurable, yet it happens only on a minority of occasions.

Rupert Johnston, a senior executive with a building company, told me that there are over 20 different coffee shops in his town center, yet he only goes to one. That is because the coffee shop manager always recognizes him and goes out of his way to have a chat with him, occasionally offering him a complimentary coffee. Rupert told me that when he goes elsewhere nobody ever bothers, the order is taken and that is it. For him it was a joy to have someone acknowledge him as a human being and chat to him for a minute or two.

There are five main tests for developing a feeling mind and paying attention to customers:

1 Are you really pleased to see each customer?
2 Do you show that you are genuinely pleased to see each customer?
3 Are you thinking about your customers all the time?
4 Have you developed a fine sense of what customers are thinking and feeling?
5 Do you really pay attention to the customers in your vicinity?

Be scrupulously honest in answering these questions. Then sit down with your team and invite them to answer the questions too. Afterwards, try putting into practice the behaviors implicit in each question.

Keep these questions in mind with every single customer you deal with. For example, ask yourself:

➤ How can I show I am pleased to see this approaching customer?
➤ How can I show I am thinking about each customer?
➤ How can I pay better attention to the customers around me?

You will be amazed at how customers respond, how delighted they are because you have tried to please them. Don't be deterred by their grim, blank faces as they approach. This is because they expect the worst and have set up defense mechanisms. Break down their defenses by showing that you are pleased to see them, by showing that you are thinking about them, by simply paying attention to them. It is the surest way to connect.

Expressed another way, thinking about customers and paying attention to them increase the possibility that they will feel they are being treated like human beings. Your behavior towards other people, including customers, either humanizes them or dehumanizes them. Ignore a customer and you dehumanize that customer.

EMOTIONAL ENERGY

To humanize another person you must focus and apply your positive energies to them. As previously explained, the source of all behavioral movement is energy, emotional direction and esprit. When you attempt to minimize your emotional energies, you minimize the probability of connecting with another person. Dry words that carry no emotional weight (such as can be found in legal documents) are very unlikely to connect with most people.

Generating and applying emotional energy is perhaps the most important aspect of creating everyday likeable behaviors for dealing with customers.

INJECT POSITIVE ENERGY INTO EVERY INTERACTION

If you genuinely value your customers, then you will wish to add value to the relationship (to establish and reinforce the emotional connection) by injecting positive energy into every interaction with every customer.

This requires a degree of adrenalin as well as esprit to create and draw on your own personal reservoir of positive emotional energies. Such a reservoir might comprise the deep-rooted feelings of goodwill you have towards your customers. To deposit these feelings you have to create them. You have to look for the good in your customers and when you find it, draw it into your reservoir. You also have to look to your own set of values (your esprit) which has become the driving force in your life. If necessary, you need to eliminate the negative values (which drain energy) and develop positive values which create energy. Examples are given opposite.

You must avoid taking the easy way out, the low-energy route of doing the bare minimum or passing the buck back to the customer or to someone else. Injecting positive energy into every interaction means seizing opportunities to do something extra special for each customer. It means drawing on your deepest reserves of energy to demonstrate warmth and care, it means making the effort to find ways of pleasing each customer, it means taking the time to go out of your way to fix a problem that has been plaguing a customer.

Adding emotional value to your interactions with customers is hard work. It saps your energy, but it can be exceptionally rewarding.

The following are some examples of valued (positive-energy) behaviors and non-valued (low- or negative-energy) behaviors. There are many more.

Valued behaviors (Positive energy and added emotional value)	Non-valued behaviors (Low or negative energy and customer feels devalued)
A genuine smile	An intimidating stare
Using a person's name	Ignoring a person
A warm welcome	Keeping someone waiting
An enthusiastic response	Not returning telephone calls
Taking a real interest	Indifference
Eye-to-eye contact	Looking out of the window
Nodding in agreement	Sighing in disagreement
Listening carefully	Fidgeting
Keeping promises	Breaking promises
Making commitments	Avoiding commitments
Looking out for customers	Avoiding customers
Putting yourself out for people	Avoiding extra work
Asking questions	Making assumptions
Asking opinions	Jumping to conclusions

AWARENESS OF YOUR OWN BEHAVIORS

In developing your approach to customers you need to become aware of the minutiae of your own behavior. The behaviors discussed in this chapter are relatively high level. Each of them can be broken down into minute behaviors such as facial expressions, movements of your hands and arms, the way you stand, the precise intonation applied to your words and many other signals. You will need to develop a range of minute behaviors that are valued by customers while eliminating those behaviors that devalue customers.

Most importantly, however, these behaviors must reflect your own deepest held values about customers and people.

SUMMARY

There is a range of likeable behaviors that anyone dealing with customers can develop, the most important of which are to pay attention to customers, to think about them all the time and to inject positive energy in the relationship with them.

The following practical steps recap the 19 behaviors discussed in this chapter.

PRACTICAL STEPS

1   Keep an eye open for customers.
2   Keep an eye on customers.
3   Allow your eyes to light up for customers.
4   Maintain frequent eye contact with customers.
5   Let your feelings show through your eyes.
6   Listen carefully to what the customer has to say.
7   Learn from what the customer has to say.
8   Tune in to the customer's emotional tone.
9   Develop awareness of the tone of your own voice.
10 Modulate your voice to establish an emotional connection with the customer.
11 Be demonstrative.
12 Treat customers as equals.
13 Take an interest in each customer.
14 Be scrupulously honest and trustworthy.
15 Challenge yourself continually.
16 Seize the initiative.
17 Do things differently.
18 Pay attention to customers.
19 Inject positive energy into every interaction.

8

INFLUENCING HOW
CUSTOMERS FEEL
ABOUT YOU

B RAINWASHING IS UNACCEPTABLE. ANY ATTEMPT TO IMPOSE A thought pattern on another person is unethical and it is to be hoped that such practices will be consigned to the annals of history and to the biographies of dictators.

But we all do it. We attempt to condition our children to think and behave in certain ways (for example, to be polite and courteous towards our aunt). We also attempt to condition our employees to think and behave in certain ways. We often force people who speak for the company to parrot the "company line". They end up by believing this company line no matter how indefensible it is (think of tobacco companies or of companies that pollute the environment). If they do not believe it, they will not be able to communicate the message effectively to the public. These people have been brainwashed.

PERSUASION AND INFLUENCE

Persuasion and influence are lesser attempts to change people's thinking. Every day we are bombarded with communications that attempt to influence us, to persuade us to purchase a certain product or vote for a particular political party. Furthermore, every day we seek to use our influence to persuade others to think our way, to agree with us that our football team is the greatest or that we are the best person for the job.

In the western world competition is synonymous with persuasion and influence. Without it there would be no competition, just diktat. The key difference between persuasion and brainwashing is choice. When you are being brainwashed, you are being forced to think in a particular way, there is no choice. When you are being persuaded, you are being given a choice to think (and therefore to behave) in a different way. People will freely accept this choice provided that they are not penalized for making what you consider to be the wrong choice. Peer-group pressure, intimidation, blackmail and threats attempt to force people into choices they might not otherwise make if the pressure was not there.

By definition, to get customers to like you so they want to buy your products and services, you have to encourage them to think and feel about you in a positive way. This will depend not only on their total past experiences of using your products and dealing with you and your company, but also on their subconscious thinking and feeling patterns.

EMOTIONAL BLACKMAIL AND INFLUENCE

Emotional blackmail is one of the least overt forms of brainwashing.

➤ "Unless you agree with my request I will scream and shout, lose my temper and make your life a misery."
➤ "Unless you agree with my request I will not talk to you, I will totally ignore you and make your life a misery."
➤ "Unless you agree with my request I will take the thing you want most away from you and I will make your life a misery."

➤ "Unless you buy this product now there is a high probability that we will sell it to another customer and you will lose out."
➤ "Unless you buy this product today you will not benefit from a special discount."
➤ "Unless you buy now we will make you feel bad."
➤ "If you complain I will make things even worse for you."
➤ "If you speak up I will make you look silly."
➤ "If you cancel the account there will be a penalty charge."
➤ "If you transfer your account to a competitor we will make life very difficult for you."

These statements are usually implied and are rarely stated directly by the emotional blackmailer to the victim.

Emotional blackmail when dealing with customers is a form of attempted influence that plays on people's fears and aims to make them feel bad if they do not go along with you. In the short term such blackmail might work, but in the long term it will always backfire.

BRAND IMAGES

It is only right that people with precious information, up-to-date knowledge, professional expertise and acquired wisdom attempt to influence people whom they feel might benefit from all this. However, failure to benefit implies a disbenefit that will make customers feel bad. As a consequence, emotional blackmail is invidious and creeps into many forms of advertising, publicity and the ways companies present their products. Basically they are saying: "You will lose out and feel bad if you do not buy this."

It is natural to want customers to think of us in the best possible way. Most advertising and public relations is aimed at achieving the simple goal of "think well of our company, its products and services". The concept of developing "brand images" is all to do with establishing thinking and feeling patterns (brand associations) in customers' minds and hearts.

In the media and politics we have "spin doctors" whose prime job is to ensure that the correct message is put across to reinforce the appropriate image in the public's mind. When it comes to customer service, we want customers to view our service in an exceptional light. We want them to develop an image that our service is the very best available, that its high reputation is justifiably deserved. In other words, we want to be a good influence on our customers.

THINKING AND FEELING

Thinking and feeling are interrelated. Our emotions have a significant impact on the way we think and the way we think has a significant impact on our emotions. As continually stressed in this book, we frequently delude ourselves that we have gone through a rational thought process to arrive at a conclusion and decision, while failing to acknowledge the vital role that emotions have played in influencing this decision.

> Feelings have a critical role in the way customers are influenced

Feelings therefore have a critical role in the way customers are influenced. Each time we arrive at a decision (to behave in a certain way, for example to purchase a product) we do not and cannot rely solely on an empirical, analytical, conscious thought process. We cannot decide "from scratch" each time to buy Kellogg's cornflakes or Sony hi-fi equipment. We cannot decide "from scratch" each time whether to do our grocery shopping at Tesco's as opposed to Sainsbury's. Such decisions are substantially influenced by the way we feel about these companies, their products and their people.

The quality of our decisions will improve if we bring to the surface and acknowledge our preprogrammed subconscious thinking and feeling patterns. This means challenging our habits as well as examining and understanding our deep-rooted emotions about how we feel about Kellogg's, Sony, Tesco's and Sainsbury's (and many others).

To influence a customer's behavior in favor of dealing with you and making a purchase requires changing their thinking and feeling patterns. The two cannot be separated.

Five critical criteria must be applied in any attempt at influence:

1   The attempt must be genuine and sincere.
2   The attempt must be aimed at helping the other person.
3   The attempt must be based on the highest standards of integrity (total openness, honesty and trustworthiness).
4   The attempt must result in the customer having a genuine choice of how to think and behave, without fear of being penalized for appearing to make the wrong choice.
5   The attempt cannot be based on words alone but must be supported by genuine, emotionally valued actions.

ACHIEVING INFLUENCE BY MAKING REAL IMPROVEMENTS

Integrity demands that if a customer's perceptions are based on real deficiencies in the company's approach (say in service), then the company should make the necessary improvements. Such improvements will have a positive influence on customers, who will change their thinking and feeling patterns accordingly.

Skilled communication and explicit action on the part of every employee will be required to convince customers that the company's approach is improving and that they should return to experience it and benefit accordingly. Emotional connectivity is vital to this process. A front-line employee who genuinely believes that the service has improved will be better able to influence a customer of this than one who is cynical about it.

A few years back British Airways mounted a campaign stating that it was "the world's favorite airline". This was after various polls had voted the airline the best. It also coincided with increasingly healthier revenues and profits. The campaign effectively encouraged frequent customers to go down a thinking route that ended in a choice about "their favorite airline". The training given to British Airways staff also effectively took them down a thinking route that ended in a choice about "what I can do in my job to reinforce this perception of British Airways being the world's favorite airline".

The perception of being the favorite and the articulation of this in a focused campaign forced everyone, customers and employees alike, to think of ways in which the company could remain the favorite. As a result, innumerable innovative improvements have been made to the service (for example, the provision of beds in first class, meals on the ground to first- and business-class passengers before long overnight flights, electronic ticketing to facilitate a customer's passage through an airport).

The focus on the word "favorite" influenced both staff and customers. British Airways was effectively adding emotional value in influencing people.

POTENTIAL PERCEPTION POINTS (PPPS)

Each contact a customer has with a company is a "potential perception point" that influences a customer's judgement (or a series of judgements) about the company. These judgements can be positive, neutral or negative and add up to a final choice on the part of the customer of whether or not to make a purchase from you, the salesperson (and your colleagues, the sales team).

Companies and their people are sending out signals all the time that customers pick up to determine their perceptions and thus influence them. These signals not only come through the personal behavior of company employees but also in its advertisements, its signage, its car parks, the state of its reception areas and its rest rooms. In fact, there are myriad potential perception points in every sales situation.

Table 4 opposite is a hypothetical example of a series of 30 potential perception points that may influence a customer in a typical sales and customer service situation.

Each customer is different and it is impossible to predict which potential perception points will influence their decision. There is no option but to ensure that the company operates to a standard of excellence at each point.

INFLUENCE AND TOLERANCE

Tolerance is an important factor here. Most people (and therefore most customers) are quite tolerant and will readily forgive a company and its people if something goes wrong. We all accept that

Table 4 Customers will potentially be influenced by their perceptions at the following contact points

1   Initial advertisement inviting telephone call for information.
2   Standard of response to customer's initial telephone enquiry and request for information.
3   Dispatch of leaflets, related documentation and personalized cover letter.
4   Telephone follow-up after provision of documentation and suggestion of appointment to see a demonstration of the product.
5   Confirmation of appointment together with directions to get to company's premises.
6   Ease of car parking.
7   Signs to building.
8   Initial reception at company's premises.
9   Impression of reception area.
10 Secondary enquiry at reception ("Can you tell me where the rest rooms are, please?").
11 State of rest rooms.
12 Initial welcome by salesperson.
13 Conduct of salesperson during meeting with customer (comprising a whole range of behavioral opportunities).
14 Introduction to other members of the company's team.
15 Provision of refreshments.
16 Demonstration of product.
17 Handling customer's queries.
18 Discussion with customer.
19 Closing of sale (as appropriate).
20 The way the meeting is concluded.
21 The way the customer is escorted from the meeting room to the reception area/car park.
22 Keeping a promise to send out a contract within two days.
23 How any subsequent enquiries by the customer are handled.
24 Follow-up call to customer after receipt of contract.
25 Confirmation of receipt of contract.
26 Invoicing and payment procedures.
27 Delivery of product.
28 Installation and set-up of product.
29 Provision of technical support.
30 Follow-up calls.

occasionally a machine breaks down, that a traffic jam causes a delay, that from time to time a product proves faulty, that there is an error in the paperwork, that the wrong order is dispatched or that a front-line person might forget to do something. What we find much less acceptable is perceived indifference when handling the resulting problem. We develop perceptions based on the emotional conclusion that no one is bothered, that no one cares, that no one is taking an interest in fixing a problem created by the company but identified by the customer.

When something goes wrong, what influences the customer is not necessarily the problem itself but the way it is handled.

INFLUENCE AND COMMUNICATION

Failure to handle customers' problems is often exacerbated by a lack of communication. More negative perceptions are created by a failure to keep a customer informed than by anything else. Often it is not the lack of action that creates the negative perception, but the lack of communication.

The simplest rule in the world is to keep customers informed

The simplest customer service rule in the world is to keep customers informed. Customers warm to front-line people who let them know what is going on and are influenced by them. This does mean that a front-line person has to know as much as possible about what is happening up and down the line and all around. This is an important management issue that will be dealt with in Chapter 11.

A participant at one of my seminars in South Africa told me that two weeks previously she had sent off a completed claim form to an insurance company. She had not received an acknowledgement and had no indication as to what was happening to the claim. She did not even know if the claim (to which valuable documents were attached) had been received. On the explanatory guideline sent to her with the blank claim form was a statement: "Should you have any enquiries regarding your claim, once submitted, please write to us, do not phone."

This is an insurance company whose parent company prides itself on excellent service and frequently boasts of quick responses to customers. The participant told me that her perception of the company was one of disinterest. The lack of response made her feel helpless and frustrated. She kept asking herself: "Does this insurance company have something against me because I've made a claim? Doesn't the company like me? Does it think I'm trying to defraud it with this claim?" She told me that these thoughts kept racing through her mind, driven by a strong set of emotions based on perceived rejection. All of this was because of a lack of response, a lack of communication from an insurance company. The overall result was that she was influenced to change to a competitive company when her policy was next renewed.

Sensitive, effective and timely communication is thus vital in creating positive perceptions and influencing customers. In the absence of communication from the company, a vacuum is created and the customer tends to fill it with negative, suspicious and distrusting thoughts. The vacuum becomes a bad influence.

FOUR ZONES OF CUSTOMER INFLUENCE

There are four zones of customer influence, as shown in Figure 7.

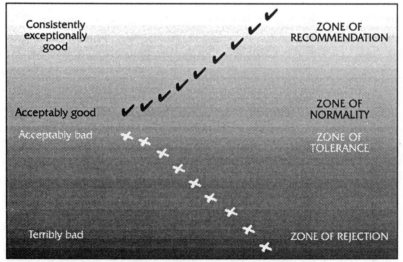

Figure 7   The four zones of customer influence

Each of the ticks and crosses in the diagram represents a potential perception point of contact between a customer and the company. Each contact generates an experience that customers perceive as excellent, acceptable, acceptably bad or terribly bad and will influence them accordingly. Because all customers think and feel differently, what is acceptable to one customer might be unacceptable to another. The degree of influence will therefore vary widely.

Some customers are influenced to reject a company (defect to a competitor) after one bad contact, while others reject a company only after a series of bad experiences.

The four zones of customer influence can be explained as follows.

ZONE OF RECOMMENDATION

In this zone the service is, in the eyes of the customer, consistently excellent. In fact, it is so good that the customer is prepared to recommend it to family, friends, neighbors and colleagues at work.

The influence level is consistently high and consistently positive.

In the zone of recommendation there is an immense amount of added emotional value. Front-line employees are always going out of their way to do more to please their customers.

ZONE OF NORMALITY

In this zone the service is taken for granted, hardly noticed. The impression created is minimal, although not bad. The service is OK but not exceptional. In most countries the majority of customer service experiences falls into this zone.

The influence level here is minimal but marginally positive.

In the zone of normality there is relatively little added emotional value to influence the customer. The customer experiences a "matter-of-fact" service that is efficient but lacks emotional warmth.

ZONE OF TOLERANCE

This is the danger zone. Here the customer tolerates the service although it is bad. They accept the fact that they cannot get through on the telephone, that they don't receive a reply to a letter and have to chase the company. In this zone the customer "puts up" with the company either because there is little choice or because they want the product badly enough to suffer the poor service.

The influence level here is also minimal but marginally negative.

The risk for the company, if it allows its service to fall into the zone of tolerance, is that it will never know when a customer will "flip" and suddenly say: "I've had enough, I'm going to take my money and custom elsewhere."

In this zone the customer feels devalued and negative emotions begin to arise. This can generate a negative influence in the face of intensifying competition.

ZONE OF REJECTION

In this zone the customer perceives the service to be so bad that the company, its products and people are rejected in favor of the competition.

The suppressed negative emotions eventually surface and are directed to a rejection of the company.

The influence level here is exceptionally high and exceptionally negative.

As stressed above, different customers' perceptions of the same contact experience vary widely. The experience of one customer may fall into the zone of normality, while the same experience for another customer is in the zone of tolerance.

The challenge therefore is to strive to make each single contact experience as positive as possible so that the customer has a perception of excellence and is influenced to purchase as well as to recommend the company to others. Creating these positive experiences and influences is the essence of added emotional value. It is what customers like, it makes them feel good.

Meeting this challenge is a major task for every manager and employee. It requires creating an awareness of how everyone's decisions, actions, behaviors and communications can influence the perceptions of customers and therefore their decisions.

INFLUENCING CUSTOMERS WITH NEGATIVE ATTITUDES

When a person with a negative attitude, a previous bad experience, an emotional problem or an unreasonable demand approaches the front line, the employees there have an exceptionally complex challenge in influencing them.

The easiest thing is to turn your head the other way and avoid the problem. Alternatively, it is relatively easy to confront the difficult customer head on and "get back" at them. In many countries the culture of pride is such that if a customer shouts at you, you shout back.

Your task is to help customers change their thinking and feeling about you and therefore your company and the service it provides. This means facing up to the reality that the customer's thinking about you and the company is bad and establishing a simple goal of converting this from bad to good, so that the customer begins to like you.

You do not have to be a psychologist to accomplish this. Many front-line people have a natural aptitude for influencing customers who have negative perceptions.

First of all, you have accept that you cannot tell a customer what to think and feel. However, two things can be done to help:

➤ You and your organization can behave in such a way that every potential perception point is positive and adds emotional value. This will have a gradual positive influence on any negative customer.
➤ You can try to understand customers' thoughts and feelings. In doing so, you will probably help customers understand themselves a little better. This in turn will help influence customers' own thinking and feeling patterns.

To accomplish the latter, some simple steps are recommended:

➤ Take a genuine interest in customers.
➤ Show that you are genuinely interested in them.
➤ Give customers as much time as they require.
➤ Allow customers to tell you "war stories" from the past.

➤ Sympathize with their bad experiences.
➤ Ask questions to determine precisely why the experience was so bad.
➤ Declare your intention to make sure that the experience will not be repeated.
➤ Offer a hand of friendship, inviting customers to turn to you should they encounter future problems elsewhere in the organization.
➤ Do not attempt to persuade customers that their perception was wrong, that they did not understand, jumped to the wrong conclusion or were partly at fault for the bad experience that occurred.

The more you allow customers to talk and vent their problems, the more they will like you and be influenced accordingly. There is no way you can solve problems that occurred a long time ago, but you can declare that you will take responsibility for any problems that occur from now on. You might need to demonstrate this by giving special attention to this specific transaction.

THE INFLUENCE OF DESIRES AND FEARS

In attempting to influence a customer in favor of your company, it is important to recognize that at an emotional level most customers have deep-rooted desires and fears. These relate to the goals of feeling good and avoiding feeling bad.

Desires and fears are in effect powerful emotions existing as software programs in our subconscious that initiate behavioral responses to specific external stimuli, in the case of desire attracting us to what makes us feel good and in the case of fear protecting us from harm.

To add emotional value and to get a customer to like you requires you to develop a sensitivity towards each customer's specific desires and fears. By getting a better understanding of these you will be in a much better position to influence the customer, responding to their desires and countering their fears. Such a response adds emotional value to the transaction process.

Accomplishing this requires no more than taking a genuine interest in each customer and attempting to identify these desires and fears.

DESIRES

The desire to feel good can be manifested in many different ways. Some lonely people, for example, go shopping just for the social contact. They merely want someone to talk to, to listen to them. Busy people, by comparison, desire fast, efficient service and no social contact. Some people simply want clear advice on which product to buy, while others seek compliments by asking a store assistant their opinion on how a particular item of clothing looks. Some people are solely interested in value for money, while others wish to make a purchase to impress their friends. Certain individuals are forever curious about new products, while others are forever seeking new ideas to help their business. Many people will be desiring reliability, quality and peace of mind in whatever they purchase, while others will want to be assured that they are up to date with the latest equipment.

FEARS

While many people are reluctant to express their true desires, there are many more who resist expressing their fears. Yet fears can have an incredibly negative influence on the way customers think about you, your company, its products and services.

Here are some examples of fears that customers feel when it comes to dealing with a company (and there are many more):

➤ Fear of being made to look silly by a front-line assistant (e.g. when purchasing a product of which the customer has little knowledge).
➤ Fear of rejection (e.g. when making an unusual request such as a variation from the set menu).
➤ Fear of embarrassment (e.g. of saying the wrong thing).
➤ Fear of speaking up (e.g. when there is a delay in service).
➤ Fear of being branded a troublemaker (e.g. when complaining).
➤ Fear of making a bad decision (e.g. when choosing between two different products).

➤ Fear of making a nuisance of oneself (e.g. when demanding additional time and help from an employee).

➤ Fear of being let down (e.g. of being promised delivery of an important item by a specific date and then not receiving it).

➤ Fear of not being trusted (e.g. when claiming that a product is defective).

➤ Fear of not being liked (e.g. when complaining).

➤ Fear of repeating a previously bad experience (e.g. of experiencing a real hassle in getting to talk the right person).

➤ Fear of losing one's self-esteem and inner dignity (e.g. by being proved wrong).

An employee with a high degree of emotional intelligence will be able to sense any overt fears that customers are exhibiting. By getting to know a customer they will be able to identify and understand even more deep-rooted fears. Such understanding enables a front-line person to put customers at their ease, to reassure them that everything will work out satisfactorily, that they will not experience anything untoward. As soon as you remove or reduce fear in a person their thinking and feeling patterns change, they become more relaxed, more open, more accessible and more appreciative of the service you are providing. When this happens they are more susceptible to influence.

Fear is often founded on suspicion and distrust. Again, emotionally intelligent employees will sense this and go out of their way to allay these suspicions. For example, many customers are suspicious of the "small print" or "hidden clauses in the offer". An experienced front-line person will be sensitive to this and take the trouble to reassure the customer that there is no "catch".

There are other customers who have experience of being fobbed off when things go wrong, for example with excuses for non-delivery, for failure to call back or for not keeping a promise. Understandably, these customers begin to develop a distrust of the system and the people who operate it. This shows through when approaching a new supplier. With emotional intelligence the employee whom the customer approaches will be able to sense this and feel able to make a personal commitment to deliver on the promises that others failed to keep. The customer's feelings will change accordingly.

The extent to which you influence customers will therefore depend on the degree to which you meet their desires and allay their fears. The desires and fears themselves are expressed through a range of emotions that can be paired with other (genuine) emotions for response purposes.

THE INFLUENCE OF PAIRED EMOTIONS

What customers like is front-line people who quickly get to understand their requirements, their desires, their wants and their fears and so are able to do their best to meet them. Once again, words alone are insufficient to express these desires or fears. The skilled front-line person will use emotional connectivity to determine the emotional content. As soon as a connection has been established (by taking and showing a genuine interest in a customer), it is possible to respond to the emotion a customer displays with the appropriate counter-balancing "paired" emotion. The following are examples:

EMOTION UNDERPINNING THE DESIRE (CUSTOMER) *The customer feels...*	EMOTION UNDERPINNING THE RESPONSE (EMPLOYEE) *The employee provides/expresses...*
Anxiety (desire for reassurance)	Reassurance
Joy (desire to share delight)	Delight
Kindness (desire to give)	Appreciation
Depression (desire for help)	Understanding
Indignation (desire for redress)	Sorrow
Grief (desire for understanding)	Sympathy
Astonishment (desire to tell someone)	Surprise
Embarrassment (desire to save face)	Reassurance
Relief (desire to express gratitude)	Relief

There are many more of these emotional pairings. They are based on empathy. The greater the degree of empathy, the higher the probability that the customer will like an employee and will be influenced accordingly. Using these emotional pairings to establish emotional connectivity results in the customer feeling (and therefore thinking) less bad than they did before entering the transaction.

Simply put, if you make a customer feel better they will think better of you. That can only be a good influence.

INFLUENCE AND FRIENDSHIP

By helping customers address their desires and reduce their levels of fear, employees enable them to build up their levels of confidence and self-esteem. What these employees are effectively doing is enabling customers to achieve more (the added emotional value) than they would if they had to suffer the inadequacies of the system. This is tantamount to offering a hand of friendship.

Friends are people you can trust, to whom you can take your problems, whose company you enjoy, with whom you can share experiences. Friends are also people who influence you.

> Friendship is not about smiling nicely at a customer but about integrity and trust

When you have friends you "feel for them", you sympathize with their problems and help them out where possible. You give them time and are prepared to put yourself out for them. Having friends makes people feel valued and wanted. It makes them feel special and gives them confidence. Friendly customer service accomplishes the same at a business level. It gives customers confidence, it makes them feel valued and wanted. It enables customers to feel that they have "friends" in the organization who can fix their problems, alleviate their fears and deliver what they want (their desires).

As soon as you discover that you have a "friend" in a company, your thinking about that company changes and you are influenced in a positive way. If that person subsequently lets you down, then there is an erosion of trust and the friendship is put at risk. The influence is then negative.

The friendship must be genuine as opposed to false. Too many salespeople pretend to be friends with customers and then forget about them as soon as the sale has been closed.

Friendship and friendly customer service relate to the basic definition of integrity given in Chapter 5 – putting a customer's interests before your own. As soon as you do this, you remove fears of exploitation and manipulation and provide reassurance that every effort will be made to please.

Simply put, the friends you have tend to be drawn from the people you like. It is difficult to have a friend you do not like. Of course, as soon as you get to know people well you will discover facets of their personality and behavior that you don't like. However, on balance you will like them and the aspects you do not like will be addressed with a combination of tolerance, acceptance and honesty. In the absence of friendship, people (and customers) are less tolerant, less accepting and tend to be less honest, because they suppress the truth.

Nando's, a chain of chicken restaurants in South Africa, dares its employees to make the customer a friend. Friendship becomes a vital factor in the customer service equation. Friendship is not about smiling nicely at a customer, it is all about integrity and trust, the alleviation of fear and the pursuit of joint "feel good" goals. It is about energy, it is about giving, it is about doing things for people you like and who like you. Friendship is about added emotional value and is a key influence.

THE INFLUENCE OF HABITS

Habits are behavioral and thinking routines. As we saw in Chapter 6, we all develop habits and routines for dealing with customers, to save energy and to ensure that we don't have to think about everything we do. They can be useful, but we need to ensure that we review and question them continually to prevent them from becoming mechanistic and automated.

Frequently, our habits drift into becoming bad habits. These are the ones we need to eliminate. We need to bring our bad habits to the surface and make a conscious effort to eradicate them. Our bad habits can have a bad influence on customers who might resent the fact that we never smile at them, never chat to them or never take an interest in them.

Here are some good habits we can develop to influence customers:

➤ The habit of greeting a person warmly.
➤ The habit of using a customer's name frequently.
➤ The habit of smiling.
➤ The habit of showing appreciation.
➤ The habit of positive thinking.
➤ The habit of creating opportunities to please others.

Many front-line people also have annoying habits that irritate customers. For example:

➤ Talking to a colleague when dealing with a customer.
➤ Not paying attention to what a customer says.
➤ Keeping customers waiting, without acknowledgment, while completing a previous task.
➤ Smiling insincerely at a customer.
➤ Not calling a customer by name.
➤ Not thanking a customer when the transaction has been completed.

When front-line people develop a fresh set of positive habits, these can be an incredibly positive influence on customers.

THE BAD INFLUENCE OF INCOMPLETE THINKING PATTERNS

One of the bad habits we get into is *not* challenging our interpretation of the external information and data we receive through our senses and allow to be filtered into our conscious brain. In other words, we jump to conclusions. This can have a negative influence on customers.

When a picture is incomplete we tend to draw on previously instilled subconscious thinking patterns and complete the gaps with what we think is the missing information. This process is instinctive.

For example, in my seminars I often ask people to complete the following words:

bright -ellow
fancy -ink
pure --ite
natural gr--n

About 95 percent of people give me the following answers:

bright yellow
fancy pink
pure white
natural green

They see a pattern of colors and fill in the gaps accordingly. But there are other options that they fail to see. For example:

bright fellow
fancy mink
pure spite
natural groan

The danger is that we jump to conclusions by interpreting incomplete information in a different way from others. Such different interpretations cause misunderstandings, conflict and many problems. They also do not allow us to influence others. If we are seeing incomplete pictures in different ways, then there is no merging of minds and no mutual influence.

Lack of customer influence often arises from this process of prematurely jumping to conclusions, missing vital information or misinterpreting it. To avoid such misunderstandings, we need to challenge the way we think and feel about our customers. We need to develop a habit in which we always question ourselves as to whether there might be a more effective interpretation of the information we have at hand about our customers.

We need to look at how our feelings influence our interpretation of the facts and the conclusions we draw. The most obvious example of this relates to the handling of complaints, where many companies draw the wrong conclusions about those complaining, often branding them as troublemakers and unreasonable. Such an interpretation, based on unacknowledged deep fears and vulnerabilities, results in the company becoming defensive in the face of complaints. Furthermore, it misses out on the opportunity of obtaining valuable information that could help it learn and improve as well as influence customers more effectively. A defensive response will never influence customers.

The interpretation of information we have about our customers is not only influenced by

> To influence others we have to look at what influences us

immediate events, but also by our deep-rooted subconscious esprit and the emotions that flow from it. If our desire is to have an easy time at work, then there is a risk that we see customers as nuisances, as people who ask difficult questions, who are demanding and who distract us from the pleasure of chatting to our colleagues.

In other words, when we wish to influence others we have to look at what influences us. This means looking at and challenging our own habits, our own thinking and feeling patterns and our own subconscious esprit.

SUMMARY

It is not possible to influence customers by imposing thinking patterns on them. However, it is possible to influence customers by improving the basic service you provide them. Their thinking then becomes a product of the positive emotional experience you provide.

Words and logics alone are insufficient to persuade people to think, feel and behave differently. These words and logics need to be carefully weighed with emotion, behavior and action to convince a customer to move in your direction. Customers' desires and fears need to be taken into account in order to help them develop more positive thoughts about you and your organization.

Establishing emotional connectivity will help employees identify these fears and desires and address them. In doing so, employees effectively befriend the customer and create a relationship of mutual influence based on integrity and trust.

Finally, we have to be cognizant of our habits, constantly challenging ourselves to eliminate bad habits and improve on the good ones. To influence others we have to look at what influences us.

PRACTICAL STEPS

1 Examine your own recent experiences as a customer. Dig deep into your subconscious and identify your main desires and fears when dealing with different companies.

2 Are you clear about the desires and fears of your customers when dealing with your organization? If so, state them. If not, go out of your way to spend some time with your customers and listen to them.

3 Now apply the lessons from the above two questions to identify the changes you and your team need to make in terms of basic service as well as in the way your relate to customers, in order to improve and change the way your customers think about you.

4 Avoid telling your customers what to think.

5 Always listen carefully to your customers.

6 Demonstrate that you take a genuine interest in your customers and are always prepared to help them.

7 Try to identify your own habits (especially your thinking and feeling habits). Challenge them and try to eliminate the bad habits and improve on the good ones.

9

WHY IT ISN'T

FASHIONABLE

TO BE LIKED

R EGRETTABLY, THE WORDS "EMOTION" AND "LIKE" HAVE NOT been readily evident in the vocabulary of managers over the last 50 years or so. In fact, in many quarters it has been fashionable for managers not to be liked. This chapter examines why modern-day managers have been so resistant to the view that emotions, feelings, likes and dislikes play an important role in business.

One reason is that managers are often afraid to declare what they like or dislike and tend to confine such admissions to the safe territories of their homes, clubs and quiet corners at work where they can confide in the few people they trust. Expressing a like or dislike often invites a rebuttal and an accusation of being subjective and not fair.

> "Reason is itself a matter of faith. It is an act of faith to assert that our thoughts have any relation to reality at all."
> (G.K. Chesterton)

Another reason is that many businesspeople believe that the issue of likes and dislikes has little place in running a business. They pride themselves on their analytical skills and decision-making prowess. Figure work and data are the order of the day as a perceived essential foundation for extrapolations and projections for future success. Measurement has become an obsession. We measure customer satisfaction, employee performance and a thousand other parameters correlated with success, or what we think is success. Business schools echo this rationality with their focus on analysis, process and measurable results.

At best we are allowed to like inanimate objects. We are allowed to prefer "model A" as opposed to "model B", provided, of course, that we have measurable reasons for doing so.

However, we must definitely not allow our likes and dislikes for other people to influence our decision making. This is perceived as favoritism or bias or partiality, leading to inequity in the treatment of people. The greatest sin in modern management today is alleged to be subjectivity.

THE OBSESSION WITH OBJECTIVITY

In our fear of likes and dislikes and our subsequent quest to eliminate them, we have become obsessed with objectivity at the expense of subjectivity.

To ensure objectivity we have systems, policies, procedures, processes and an ever-increasing amount of bureaucracy as we attempt to measure and control everything within defined boundaries.

Measurement has become an obsession

What a load of bunkum! To quote James Dyson:

> There are five billion people out there thinking in train tracks, and thinking what they have been taught to think … Go in and be illogical … I can never be bothered to think anything through logically.

Modern management has created a monolith of unworkable ideas, based on supposed rationalities that bear little relation to reality, let alone success. The truth, if you are prepared to accept it, is as follows:

THE TRUTH ABOUT MODERN MANAGEMENT – PART ONE

➤ Performance appraisal systems fail to improve performance in the majority of cases.
➤ Objective setting is no more than a tribal ritual.
➤ Most measures of customer satisfaction are meaningless.
➤ When customers tell you they are satisfied, they are not telling you how they feel or what they really think, they are just using the word to satisfy you.
➤ Modern management has become a word game that bears little relation to actual practice.
➤ We are driven by our likes and dislikes, but do not like to admit it.
➤ Most managers waste too much of their time "feeding the elephant" (their head office) with meaningless data.
➤ Customer service has become lip service.

Other examples of unworkable ideas will be given throughout the chapter.

LOVING AND LIKING IN BUSINESS

The reason it is not fashionable to talk about loving and liking in the world of business is not only that we fear such talk, but that we feel safer with routines and systems. Loving and liking are areas of high risk where we face the prospect of emotional rebuttal. We protect ourselves against this by deluding ourselves with carefully constructed rationales and reasoning processes, which at best convince us of the correctness of our decisions but do not always convince others. Thus we resist liking and loving our customers and instead subject them to routines and systems which make us feel safe but in fact can alienate the very people we want to please.

Relating to customers by way of routine and systems makes the rational assumption that customers will accept and conform to the imposed routine. When the system delivers what the customer likes, this is fine. However, this does not often happen. Every customer is unique and it is difficult to force everyone into the stereotype and routine demanded by the system.

CUSTOMER CHOICE AND FREEDOM

Fifty years ago customers expected to shop between 9 am and 5.30 pm and only up to 1 pm on Wednesdays and Saturdays. Today there are shops, even supermarkets, that open 24 hours a day, seven days a week. The previous routine limited the choice of when to shop. Now I have a choice and I like it. Excellent customer service is giving me a freedom I like. It allows me to move away from the routine drudgery of Saturday morning shopping.

What I like and dislike as a customer are therefore critical. Success can never be achieved if business managers have no sensitivity to people's likes and dislikes and discard them in favor of presumed rationality and traditional routine.

I value choice and I like it, I value freedom and I like it. Giving people choice and freedom – on both sides of the customer/ employee interface – enhances the prospects of service excellence and competitive advantage. So employees are free to do things they like to please customers, and customers are free to choose to shop when and where they like and to give their custom to the people they like. Emotional connectivity, integrity and creativity contribute to these freedoms, while rules and regulations are relatively useless.

THE LAW OF UNINTENDED CONSEQUENCES

The emphasis on rationality and the lack of emphasis on subjectivity, emotion, feelings, values and personal likes and dislikes are products of the "law of unintended consequences" (itself a much neglected law of life).

The law of unintended consequences states that every decision we make has an intended consequence as well as an unintended consequence.

THE TRUTH ABOUT MODERN MANAGEMENT – PART TWO

➤ What we know about customer service is a mere 0.0001 percent of what we don't know. Yet most people think it is the reverse.

➤ Rational intelligence, however measured, bears little correlation to success. Yet we think it is the answer to all our problems.

➤ Emotionally intelligent people are more likely to be successful than people who are merely rationally intelligent.

➤ Customers are not always right, but most of them know more about the service you provide than you do.

➤ Financial performance incentives are performance disincentives.

➤ The best managers love their people.

➤ The best people love their managers.

➤ The best customers love the companies they deal with.

➤ The best companies love their customers.

➤ Customer service is a new label for an old idea.

➤ Success in customer service is founded on spirit, belief, vision, energy, commitment, hard work, risk, innovation, flair and an overwhelming obsession to please people.

➤ In practice this means adding emotional value to relationships with customers with the application of integrity and constant creativity.

➤ Combine all this and it is about giving something for nothing (a smile, an extra piece of information, genuine care, little extras etc.) so the customer genuinely feels valued.

➤ Adding emotional value requires discipline and hard work.

➤ How many of our top business leaders went to business school and gained an MBA? (If it was a high percentage the business schools would be shouting this all over the front page.)

➤ Most schools and universities teach people how to pass exams.

An intended consequence is one that we plan for, that we have thought about and that we want to achieve. An intended consequence is the accomplishment of our personal goals.

An unintended consequence is an outcome resulting from our decision that we did not want, possibly did not forecast let alone think about. An unintended consequence is an unexpected outcome and can be either desirable or undesirable.

Here are two examples of unintended consequences:

➤ When Gottlieb Daimler and Carl Benz pioneered the manufacture of automobiles in the 1880s, their intended consequence was to help people travel more quickly. The unintended consequence of this (as Henry Ford capitalized on the process with mass production in the early 1900s) was the decay of city centers many decades later, the rise of suburbia, people traveling greater distances to work, the demise of railways in the USA, pollution and global warming. I am convinced that Daimler, Benz and Ford never foresaw and never intended global pollution as a consequence of their decisions.

➤ When the US Government's Advanced Research Projects Agency developed a long-distance computer network in 1969, the intended consequence was to connect 200 computers in military and research establishments throughout the USA, with a few overseas links. No one ever foresaw or intended in 1969 (or even 20 years later) that this network would develop into the Internet, with its all-pervasive applications around the world.

Virtually every decision we make has an unintended consequence. When we marry, the intended consequence is to live in harmony with our spouse, to bring up a family and to be secure and prosperous in sharing our lives together. The unintended consequence, since one in three marriages ends in divorce, is often that our dreams are shattered.

When we overindulge in the wrong foods, fail to take exercise, smoke, drink alcohol and so on, the unintended consequence is that we become ill, sometimes with a life-threatening disease.

As a result of the law of unintended consequences, the actions we take can often lead to other actions we did not intend. This is of particular relevance to the way we behave with customers in our pursuit of competitive advantage.

THE TRUTH ABOUT MODERN MANAGEMENT – PART THREE

➤ Little learning about life (home, work, customers, people) takes place in the average classroom.
➤ Most learning derives from how we feel about our experiences.
➤ What companies tell their customers is not what they tell themselves.
➤ What customers tell companies is not what they tell themselves.
➤ What people tell themselves is based on how they feel.
➤ However, in most places it is not permitted to express how you feel.

SCIENTIFIC MANAGEMENT

Scientific management (with its consequent systems, processes, procedures, controls and measures) has had an unintended consequence for business and specific aspects of it, such as marketing, customer service and people management. This is a denial of the importance of emotions, feelings, values, likes and dislikes in the business arena.

Who is to blame for this obsession with a scientific approach to management and its all-pervasive systems? Socrates? Descartes? Max Weber? Frank Winslow Taylor? Well, actually all of them!

Greek philosopher Socrates was executed in 399 BC because his quest for reason led others to accuse him of atheism. He believed that there had to be a reason behind every statement and sought that reason through the relentless questioning of others. For him, reason was the certainty of knowledge. Without that certainty there was no knowledge and therefore no reason. This was the birth of rational thinking.

Twenty centuries later in 1644 the great French intellectual Descartes extended the thinking of Socrates in his seminal work *Principia Philosophiae*. He asserted that all of nature could be accounted for by scientific and mathematical principles based on perfect (objective) knowledge. Subjectivity implied doubt.

With the Industrial Revolution in the nineteenth century the rationalism of Descartes was applied to the way organizations were managed. Max Weber (a German social scientist who died in 1920) asserted that an organization could be defined precisely by the way its labor was divided, by its authority structure and by the rules that regulate the relations between organizational members. His was a bureaucratic organization characterized by a "rational" and impersonal regulation of inferior–superior relationships using well-defined administrative procedures.

Influenced by Max Weber, an American mechanical engineer called Frederick Winslow Taylor developed his *Principles of Scientific Management*, published in 1911. Much modern management practice can be traced back to Taylor's assertion that the task of factory management is to determine the best way for a worker to perform a job, to provide the appropriate tools and training, and to offer incentives for good performance. Taylor asserted that every job could be broken down into its constituent motions, analyzed and timed. From this analysis factory managers could develop a machine-like routine that a worker could follow. This analysis would allow non-essential activities (unnecessary motions) to be eliminated and enable efficient routines to be developed based only on essential activities (necessary motions). In other words, every single activity undertaken by a worker could be measured with a view to obtaining higher efficiency.

Taylor's approach led to the introduction of work-study departments in factories, together with piecework schemes (by which workers were paid for each individual piece they produced).

All of this was, of course, highly rational and highly logical. Except that history shows that it did not work! The unintended consequence of Taylor's approach and the introduction of piecework schemes led to rampant wage drift and a vast array of industrial relations problems in engineering and manufacturing companies.

You will no longer find work-study departments and piecework schemes in most manufacturing companies.

THE TRUTH ABOUT MODERN MANAGEMENT – PART FOUR

➤ What people **feel** is the basis for all trading, service and business success.

➤ Words are limited as a basis for describing reality, yet we use words as the medium for all rational argument and creating a reality we can hardly see.

➤ Most customers are the equal of the people they deal with. It's just that many employees and many companies do not see it this way. They delude themselves about their own superiority, their own value and that they know better than the customer.

➤ Defensiveness and lack of learning are the biggest problems in customer service.

➤ What customers like about you is what you like about them.

THE MYTH OF PERFORMANCE MANAGEMENT AND PRP

Somewhat irrationally, companies have tried to extend these principles of scientific management to non-factory workers through the adoption of performance appraisal schemes and various versions of performance-related pay (PRP). All the evidence points to the conclusion that, rather than enhancing performance, PRP is divisive, demotivational and counter-productive. In other words, it fails to achieve the very thing it sets out to do – improve performance!

An article by A. Kohn in the September/October 1993 issue of *Harvard Business Review* produced a wealth of research evidence to show that performance-related pay had no significant effect on performance.

Similarly, a research report by Bevan and Thompson in the November 1991 issue of *Personnel Management* stated:

We found no evidence to suggest that improved organizational performance in the private sector is associated with the operation of a formal performance management system (including PRP).

In a study of 122 companies carried out by my own company, only 10 percent reported that they had PRP systems that were effective in improving performance.

To quote John Tusa from the BBC in his James Cameron Memorial Lecture in 1994:

> Is the tidy driving out the inspirational? You cannot after all set a quota for inspiration, a performance indicator for genius. But if all the time is spent on measuring the routine, where is the intellectual space for fostering the remarkable?

When piecework incentive schemes for factory workers have failed on the shopfloor (and therefore been abolished), it is totally irrational to attempt to apply the same performance incentive rationale to office workers and professionals. If you cannot effectively measure the output of an individual factory worker, how can you expect to measure that of a secretary, accountant, personnel officer, systems expert or any other office-based employee? Yet performance appraisal and PRP are based on the premise that the performance of professional and administrative people can be measured objectively!

The above is yet another example of an unintended consequence, a scientific approach to improving performance that in practice often leads to reduced performance.

Most companies are desperate to establish a scientific basis for delivering excellent customer service. In doing so, they invent systems, procedures, measures, rules and regulations – in compliance with all the rational thinking of the last two thousand years and in denial of all the evidence that scientific management alone will have a minimal impact on customer service and business success.

Systems are necessary in the same way that tools are necessary. Both have to be used effectively. The tool will not work by itself. The effective use of any tool requires a high degree of skill as well as a positive attitude and an emotional involvement. Owning a paintbrush, a canvas and some oils does not make you a great painter. The use of a wordprocessor does not make you any more creative as a writer than if you used an old-fashioned pen and paper. It is similar with performance management systems. In fact, a blank notepad and a pencil are perhaps the most effective tools for measuring the performance of an office-based worker or a professional. Tickbox and ratings systems for performance measurement are limited and dangerously misleading.

FOUR FLAWS IN SCIENTIFIC MANAGEMENT

The first flaw in the thinking of "scientific managers" is that the introduction of systems (such as performance appraisal, total quality management, business planning) into the organization will convert poor performers into high performers. What they won't accept is that the high performers never needed these bureaucratic systems in the first place, they were already applying the underlying principles – but without the use of a bureaucratic procedure imposed by senior management.

It is just that these high performers had never relabelled what is ostensibly good, common-sense management practice with such jargon as performance appraisal, 360° appraisal, total quality management or customer focus. Nor had they bothered to proceduralize it. They were just doing it, without a fashionable name and without a formal procedure. The so-called head-office experts then came along and deluded themselves that they were inventing good management by developing formal procedures that had not previously existed. Therefore, by a process of totally irrational deduction, these head-office experts concluded that good management did not exist, because the procedures did not exist. They became organizational missionaries whose aim was to convert the "heathens" who resisted the new procedures. Of course, the underlying principles were totally lost sight of in the quest to fill in forms and produce compelling measurable evidence that this was an organization with progressive management.

The second flaw in scientific management is that it forces employees to "serve the system" rather than allowing the system to serve them. The system becomes an end in itself as opposed to a tool that serves managers and employees. For example, the order of the day becomes: "You must comply with the rule that you must performance appraise your people every November. Furthermore, you must ensure that you use the correct form, complete every box on it, obtain the necessary signatures and return it to the personnel

THE TRUTH ABOUT MODERN MANAGEMENT – PART FIVE

➤ Achieving customer service excellence is very simple. All you have to do is give your front-line people total freedom to do what they feel is in the best interests of their customers and then train them, encourage them and support them in exercising this freedom.

➤ Delivering dreadful service is a result of managerial interference and a tendency to restrict front-line people from applying common sense.

➤ Customer relations are no different from human relations.

➤ Front-line people who value themselves and who are valued by their bosses will value their customers. The reverse is also true.

➤ If there was a system for delivering business success, we would all follow it and we would be in paradise.

➤ Those who purport to have all the answers about business and customer service are those who haven't asked enough questions.

➤ It is more important to question yourself than to question your customers.

department by 15 December." It would be far better to say: "Here is a useful tool that you might wish to use in achieving your goals."

The former is based on the scientific principle of "command and control" and is prevalent in traditional, hierarchical organizations, whereas the latter is based on the exercise of freedom and common sense and is prevalent in emotionally intelligent and empowered organizations.

The third flaw of scientific management is that it tends to focus on the means rather than the end. There is a dangerous tendency to measure what people *do* rather than what they *achieve*. The task becomes more important than the end result. It is relatively easy to measure the task – we see it being undertaken every day and can gauge whether the person was working quickly, slowly, with or without a smile, was tidy or untidy, communicated well or poorly and generally had a positive or negative attitude. What is often neglected are the key "output" measures by which the ultimate success of the business is judged. This is because these measures are very difficult to establish for any one individual or team of people.

The final flaw of scientific management is that it creates a delusion that we are managing in a totally objective way, that subjectivity has been eliminated. Scientific management thus becomes a rationalization in which we deny that our emotions, our feelings, have influenced us. We produce artificial rationales for justifying that this person should be promoted (because they had higher ratings) or this other person should be paid more money. The existence of the rating convinces us that we are being objective and therefore scientific.

What we fail to acknowledge is that the rating was based on a subjective assessment in the first place. In other words, all scientific management does, when it comes to performance management for example, is to quantify our feelings about other people. We feel good that Jane has taken this initiative, is putting in a lot of hours, has a positive attitude – so we rate Jane highly and in doing so delude ourselves that we are being objective. The unintended consequence is that we lose sight of the end result – the value Jane adds to the business – because we are not even aware of it.

NEGLECTING THE POWER OF EMOTION

So the unintended consequences of the obsession with rational thinking, scientific management, objectivity, command and control and measurement have been the repression, denial and therefore total neglect of the most dominant force in customer service and business life – the force of emotion.

In reality, the emotion has been there all the time. It is just that nobody likes to admit it. We look the other way and pretend that it does not exist or is unimportant. This attitude was prevalent in the less successful companies I studied. Scientific management was rampant and emotion was suppressed and deemed to be undesirable.

As a result of scientific management, an all-pervasive and prejudicial view has crept into our thinking and that is that emotion should be banned in the mainstream of our work. In our pursuit of total objectivity we are asked to purge ourselves of this alien thing called

---

THE TRUTH ABOUT MODERN MANAGEMENT – PART SIX

➤ Customers see you for what you are. You are the only person who is not aware of this.
➤ There is no end to the improvements you can make in customer service and your business.
➤ Forgetting to say "thank you", forgetting to call customers by their names and forgetting to smile are improvement opportunities.
➤ Customer service is all about choice – the choices customers make about you and the way you choose to behave towards them and communicate with them.

---

emotion, thus allowing ourselves to be clinically efficient in reaching "businesslike" decisions.

The unintended consequence of this is that we become wary of declaring our likes, dislikes and feelings and prefer to delude ourselves and others with pseudo-scientific analyses, meaningless theories and false projections. We refuse to recognize, let alone acknowledge, that often our figure work (in budgets, in surveys, in performance data) is but a fiction of our own making to support our personal preferences – which our gut instinct tells us are right.

In other words, we create rational arguments to support what we want to do – and what we want to do is feel good! Here is an example:

> We as senior executives do not feel good about trusting our front-line people. Of course we cannot trust them because they do not have the skills and the experience that we, as senior executives, have gained over many years. Furthermore, we have much anecdotal evidence from the past that front-line people, when allowed to make decisions, have totally screwed up and this has cost the company dearly. Therefore to prevent our front-line people making mistakes and ruining the company we must have a system of controls in place. We will therefore issue an edict that no front-line person can make a refund to a customer or make any other type of payment without the express written permission of a supervisor. Furthermore, when a refund or payment over $200 is

required, the supervisor must obtain further authorization from a senior manager. When this edict is in place and being applied we will feel good (because we will have control of the business).

This is all very logical and various versions of this "command and control" logic are still evident in a large number of companies.

However, what is denied in the above statement is the following:

We do not feel good about our people, we do not trust them, we do not like it when they make mistakes. We like to have power over our people so that they do the things we like.

This type of thinking can be extended to the following rationale:

The mere fact that we have been appointed as senior executives must mean that we know more than our front-line people. This means we are invariably right in everything we say and do. We trust ourselves and we rarely make mistakes (because if we did make mistakes we would not have been appointed as senior executives in the first place). We therefore don't like it when our front-line people criticize us because we know they are wrong.

Denial thinking

Many disasters occur as a result of this type of "denial" thinking. For example, after the *Herald of Free Enterprise* disaster in the English Channel in 1987, when 188 people died as a result of the ferry's bow doors being left open, Mr Justice Sheen, who headed the inquiry, rebuked the senior management of ferry company Townsend Thoresen for rejecting proposals from the captain to improve the safety of the ferry. The senior managers thought they knew all the answers and ridiculed the captain for his ideas. To quote Mr Justice Sheen: "The shore management took very little notice of its captains."

The same applied to the captain of an aircraft that crashed at Kegworth in the UK in 1989. He would not listen to cabin staff who informed him which engine was on fire. His instruments said otherwise. He therefore shut down the engine that was working.

The same applied to the collapse of Baring's Bank in 1995. Internal audits had warned senior executives of potential "control" problems, but these had been ignored.

In his book *On the Psychology of Military Incompetence*, Norman Dixon recounts a similar story relating to the fall of Singapore to the Japanese in the Second World War. To quote: "Why did General Officer Commanding Singapore, Lieutenant-General Percival, ignore the urgent advice of his subordinate, Brigadier Simpson, and of his superior, General Wavell, to implement these defenses?"

There are many other examples and you will not have to look too far to come across this "denial syndrome" in many organizations.

Peter Senge comments in *The Fifth Discipline*:

> In most companies that fail, there is abundant evidence in advance that the firm is in trouble. This evidence goes unheeded, however, even when individual managers are aware of it. The organization as a whole cannot recognize impending threats, understand the implications of those threats, or come up with alternatives.

By emphasizing the logic behind our decisions (to reject ideas put forward by our people) we deny a greater truth (that we do not feel good about our people).

When you feel good about your people, you trust them, you like them, you love them, you support them, you tolerate their mistakes, you help them, you encourage them. What is more, you love to give them leeway, you love them to make decisions on behalf of customers (whether they be refunds, ex-gratia payments, gifts or whatever).

Judith, a customer service agent at BT Mobile Call Centre, Leeds, UK, said the following about her manager Richard Brimble:

> When I first joined BT Mobile five years ago I really wanted to do my best for our customers. Yet I used to go home and cry because of the constraints our managers put us under. They just wouldn't allow us to do anything – it was so frustrating and I was really unhappy. It was often obvious what we had to do to please our customers, but we were never allowed to do it without first taking it to a higher level. Now it's all changed, it's a joy to work here. Richard, our new manager, gives us total freedom. He never

interferes. We can please our customers by doing whatever we feel necessary. I can make any decision I want. Richard is very supportive and very encouraging.

Compare the above with a statement made to me by a manager from a well-known international bank:

The problem in our bank is that as middle managers we cannot make decisions. Frequently we recommend to senior management that a customer's application for a loan should be granted, only to have the application turned down. We are not told why and we find it incredibly embarrassing to have to go back to the customer with a rejection – especially knowing that he (or she) is credit worthy and having encouraged him to apply for the loan in the first instance.

We don't like these decisions, yet they are frequently imposed on us for no apparent reason at all. It demoralizes us and it doesn't help us in our relationships with customers. We can't tell them lies, so we can't tell them anything.

INTOLERANCE OF EMOTIONAL JUDGEMENT

The scientific approach to marketing, customer service, selling and people management leads to an intolerance of emotional judgement that mitigates against employees and customers. Managers who pride themselves on their total rationality define and measure everything they can think of in their attempt to impose the "rules of logic".

Here are some of the rules you frequently find in these organizations:

➤ A rule for "who can do what" based on measures of skill and experience.
➤ A rule about "who can spend what" based on measures of hierarchical position.
➤ A rule about personal expenses (so much for a lunch, so much for a 10-mile journey, which hotels you can stay in etc.).
➤ A rule for "what you can and cannot say to a customer" (for example, the scripted welcome).

➤ Rules for when you can go to the toilet, taking lunch, what you can wear, who you can talk to (definitely not the person at the top), when you can have a break.
➤ A rule for what you must do if a customer complains.
➤ A rule for what you must not do if a customer wants something extra special, and so on.

Nordstrom, a chain of retail stores in the USA, only has one rule for its employees and that is "Use your good judgement in all situations." Anton Najjar at the J.W. Marriott hotel in Dubai gives his people the same freedom. To quote him: "I tell all of our staff here, if it is necessary to break the rules to please a customer then you must do so."

Andrew May, who runs the Hair Advice Centre in Birmingham, UK, similarly trusts his staff. Recently he did something most managers would find unthinkable. He closed his salon for the morning and invited his staff to work together to review the prices they charge their customers and to set the new price list for the coming year. He gave them no criteria, no guidelines. He just left it to them. They set the prices that they felt were fair. Those prices are now in place.

As indicated in Figure 8 opposite, the traditional and scientific way of reaching a decision is to review the available data in the light of prior knowledge and then decide on the best future option. Frequently this decision-making process is influenced by how people feel and their values and leads to decisions being made (through the emotionally connected route) based on perception, interpretation and opinion.

Scientific managers are reluctant to acknowledge the left and right sides of this process and thus are reluctant to accept that feelings and added emotional value are critical for delivering the service that customers like. They believe that the central, rational route is one that can be applied in all situations and that feelings and values have little influence on this rational decision-making process.

The emotional connection is created when people are emotionally intelligent. In examining these two disparate approaches (scientific and emotionally connected), it is necessary to define what is meant by emotional intelligence and rational intelligence.

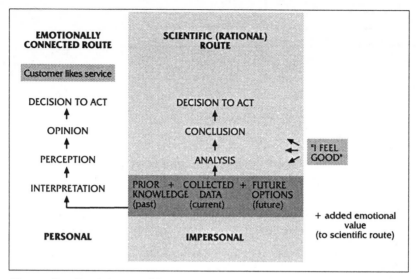

Figure 8   Decision making

The definition of emotional intelligence in Figure 9 overleaf distinguishes between the positive and negative aspects of emotional intelligence and the way emotions are managed.

It would be wrong to deduce from this discussion that emotional intelligence is all important and that there is no place for rational intelligence, defined in Figure 10. Rational intelligence is critical in most walks of life. However, it can only be successfully applied if it is supported by a high degree of emotional intelligence. Rational intelligence alone is insufficient.

Scientific Managers and Emotionally Connected Managers

Rules are a product of rational thinking. Managers who pride themselves on scientific thinking often discard or suppress their emotions and therefore do not allow their feelings and personal likes and dislikes to enter into the argument. The rules they invent are therefore rarely based on any sense of feeling for the real situation on which customers and front-line employees form their perceptions. Scientific managers tend to be devoid of emotion and are therefore in danger of dismissing the one factor that has a prime influence on customer choice.

Emotional but not intelligent	Emotions out of control (e.g. hysterical) Non-awareness of emotions (e.g. insensitive)	
POSITIVE EMOTIONAL INTELLIGENCE	Awareness and understanding of emotions Creating positive emotions Emotions under positive control Emotions expressed in sensitive/acceptable way Eliminating negative emotions	Intuitive Creative
Lacking emotional intelligence	Emotions under negative control (e.g. vindictiveness) Emotions expressed in insensitive/unacceptable way (e.g. ridicule) Habitual suppression of emotions (e.g. coldness) No emotions (e.g inhuman)	

Figure 9   Emotional intelligence

Lacking in rational intelligence	Unable to reason Illogical	
RATIONAL INTELLIGENCE	Logical Analytical Systematic Measurable Rational	Able to: (a) think clearly (b) give good reasons (c) solve problems (d) perform efficiently (e) achieve results
Lacking in rational intelligence	Confused Irrational Unreasonable Emotional (uncontrolled, hysterical)	

Figure 10   Rational intelligence

Such scientific managers will say that they do not care whether they are liked or disliked by their customers or front-line staff, asserting that their obligation is to make decisions in the best interests of the company, irrespective of whether people like or dislike these decisions. As such, they will come across as uncaring of people and customers. It will be perceived as if the only thing they do care for is bottom-line profitability. Profitability and financial performance become the underlying rationale for all their decisions.

Emotionally connected managers will harness and combine their own rational intelligence and emotional energies to come to a totally different set of conclusions. While not denying the importance of financial performance, they will say that non-financial performance is equally important. They believe that if you care for people, these people will care for customers and the bottom-line profit will take care of itself.

At the annual conference of the Institute of Directors in London in 1993, the keynote speaker, Richard Branson, head of the Virgin Group, said:

> We have three priorities in our company. The first is people, the second is customers and the third is shareholders. If we get the first right the second follows. And if we get the second right the third follows. Sadly the majority of western companies have the inverse of these priorities.

Emotionally connected managers will say that it is in the best interests of everyone (the company, the customers and employees) to give people the freedom to do the things they like. The whole concept of adding emotional value and thus excellent customer service is based on this freedom of harnessing emotional energies to deliver the very best. Rules solely based on simple rationales will suppress if not try to eliminate these emotional energies, thus constraining people in their freedom to do their best.

Managers who pride themselves on their rationality will focus solely on an analysis of all the facts before identifying the various options and then presenting their reasons (their logics, their rationales, their theories) for taking action.

Emotionally connected managers realize that this analytical process alone is insufficient to deliver a sensible decision. They will supplement it with a "feel" for what needs to be done. It is almost as if they use a common-sense check and balance against the rational argument to ensure that the decision "feels right". When the decision does feel right, emotionally intelligent managers will communicate this decision (with feeling) to the appropriate people.

Furthermore, emotionally connected managers discover (by listening with genuine interest) what others feel needs to be done on a specific issue. They will discuss with interested parties their feelings on the various options, agree on the action and then do it. These discussions will of course be supplemented by any scientific analysis of hard data and any review of options that is available. But such scientific analysis is always considered in the context of the total emotional situation, in other words in the context of how people feel and what they value in the circumstances.

You can observe the difference between a scientific manager and an emotionally connected manager any time. The former tends to be dry, two-dimensional, dour, cerebral and very serious. The latter tends to be passionate, enthusiastic and a positive believer. The former tends to be a matter-of-fact, keep-to-the-point, no-chit-chat, no-small-talk, give-me-the-facts type of person. The latter tends to be a human being who actually likes being with people, who enjoys their company.

RATIONAL COMMUNICATION AND EMOTIONAL COMMUNICATION

The key differentiator is communication. Facts, logics and conclusions are relatively easy to express. One comes up with a rational thought process and expresses it in a rational sequence of words. However, in themselves these rational thoughts carry no emotional weight. When you add emotional weight (for example passion, enthusiasm and excitement) to your thoughts they carry much more conviction and are much more persuasive.

Nevertheless, it is not as simple as identifying your emotions and applying them to the words you use in expressing your thoughts. It is not as if your rational thoughts come first and then, after the event, you apply your emotions to add weight. The reverse tends to apply.

Most of us have a complex set of emotions, feelings and values that we struggle to understand (through rational thinking) let alone express. If we can apply rational thinking to our emotions then we are better able to express them using words. Even so, words are very limited in communicating our emotions and feelings. As a result, these are frequently expressed in other ways, for example through our eyes, our gestures, our attitude and our tone of voice.

In Figure 11 the central vertical arrows represent the approach of the scientific manager. When combined, the three sets of arrows represent the approach of the emotionally connected manager who adds emotional value to his rational approach. The single central (rational) route of vertical arrows produces only a third of the power in achieving personal goals compared with the three routes when combined.

The figure also demonstrates that a person's rational thoughts, communications and actions are driven by emotions, feelings, values, likes, dislikes as well as by hidden, subconscious factors.

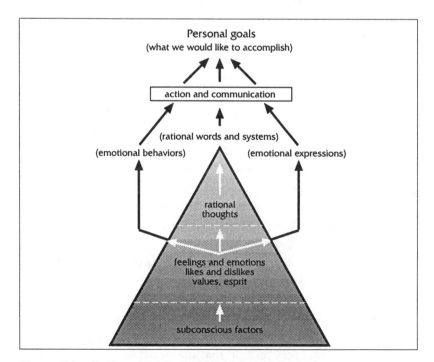

Figure 11   Rational and emotional communication

LIMITS OF SCIENTIFIC THINKING AND COMMUNICATION

Because many people struggle in their use of rational language to communicate their innermost thoughts and feelings, they often resort to art as a way of expressing themselves. Thus they paint, write poetry or play music.

The reason most of us love music, for example, is that it often expresses certain feelings which we are unable to express but with which we are able to identify. Through the medium of music we are able to get in touch with our innermost feelings and are thus moved emotionally. The same applies to other forms of art. This morning I was driving back from the leisure center where I regularly go for an early morning swim and I heard on the car radio the song *The winner takes it all* by Abba. I had not heard this song for many years. For some reason the piano introduction, the soulful voice and then the song itself moved me beyond words.

We live with a thin surface of rationality that frequently cracks to allow our emotions to seep through. The mistake is to believe that below the surface there is nothing and that emotions do not exist (because they can be suppressed or eliminated). We cannot avoid these emotions. If we try to avoid them they will appear at the most unexpected time, when the surface cracks. The wise approach is to accept and become aware of these emotions and manage them in a positive way. This will make the surface (for example the interface between customers and employees, or between bosses and employees, or between husbands and wives) much stronger. This is the emotionally intelligent approach.

Trying to limit relationships with customers to a set of rational words, a set of procedures, a set of systems and a set of rational thoughts eliminates the very dimension of emotion that ensures excellence. Such emotion is based on what customers and front-line people like and dislike about their everyday interactions.

In Dubai, I chatted to a Filipino waitress, Melba, in a café in the Hamarain shopping mall. She told me that she works over 11 hours a day (10.30 am to 3 pm and then 5 pm to midnight), that she is given two days off every month, that she sleeps in a room with five other waitresses, that she gets back to the Philippines for one month every year to see her children (who are looked after by her mother) and her husband. For 11 months a year she does not see her family. Melba was happy, she loved her husband and she was not complaining. She told me that she was saving up a thousand kisses for him. She was paid 1000 dirhams ($220) per month plus food and lodging.

Melba had never been on a training course in her life and she was only vaguely aware of the term "customer service". Yet she loved to please customers, to chat to them, to put herself out for them. I was moved. There was an emotional connection. She was adding emotional value to the simple process of serving a coffee. Next time I am in Dubai I will return to see her.

Whether my brief encounter with Melba was a textbook customer service interaction is irrelevant. It was just an experience I liked.

Such an experience can never be the product of a policy or a set of procedures or a prescriptive training course. Melba was giving me the benefit of her experience and felt good in doing so, and that made me feel good too. She liked to talk and I liked to listen, it was as simple as that. Sometimes it is the reverse. Essentially, a positive customer service interaction is a positive human interaction.

SUMMARY

For the last two thousand years the dominant fashion in thinking has been to be rational, to be logical and to devise systems and rules for exercising these logics.

Conversely, it has not been fashionable to allow one's personal feelings, likes and dislikes to enter into the process of making business decisions.

The reality is that at the front line it is these emotional aspects that are the key driving force in customer decision making and the provision of service by employees.

The key to success in customer service is to express your own feelings and thoughts, to be yourself as opposed to being a product of a company policy. Words are limited as method of expressing such feelings.

PRACTICAL STEPS

1 Make a list of all the rules, regulations, policies, procedures, processes and systems that apply to your front-line customer service.
2 Sit down with your people and agree with them which of the procedures, processes and systems it would be sensible to retain to help them serve their customers more effectively. Abolish the rest.
3 Now tell your people that you love them all, that they are wonderful and that you trust them completely.
4 Encourage them to do whatever is necessary to please customers (within, of course, the boundaries of the law, common decency and common sense).
5 Explain that your role is to provide whatever support they deem necessary to deliver excellent service.
6 If they don't believe you, it is because you do not believe it yourself.
7 In which case, challenge your own beliefs and learn to love your people and your customers. They will like it.

10

THE LIKEABLE

ORGANIZATION

CUSTOMERS WILL LIKE YOU WHEN YOU LIKE THE ORGANIZATION you are working for. Should you dislike it for any reason, this will be reflected on to the customer and they will dislike you.

In other words, motivated employees will motivate customers and demotivated employees will demotivate customers. Customer care is a reflection of staff care. Those front-line employees who care best for their customers are those who feel cared for by their employers.

Most people are influenced by the society around them and the people they work with. In fact, many people become conditioned by their social environment. A process of osmosis takes place in which the customs and mores of the people we come across permeate the surface of our psyche and seep into our subconscious. Unless we have truly discovered ourselves for what we are and become "our own person", we tend to be influenced by our families, neighbors, friends and colleagues. By imbibing their values and behaving accordingly, we earn their accreditation and become accepted into the group. This gives us self-esteem and diminishes the fear of rejection latent in everyone.

The lubricants for this process are our personal likes and dislikes together with those of the people with whom we are in regular contact. We tend to like people who exhibit at least some of the values we hold dear and dislike people who affront us personally with behaviors that go against our own values.

EFFECTIVE ORGANIZATIONS ARE
LIKEABLE ORGANIZATIONS

Effective organizations are likeable organizations. These are those where there are teams of managers and employees who tend to share the same values and "feel good" goals. People enjoy working with one another because of the sharing that takes place on a daily basis.

In contrast, in an organization where there are disparate values and goals there tends to be a high degree of internal politics, morale is low and there is emotional dissonance. In these organizations people gravitate towards small groups with similar vested interests and battle indirectly with other groups with different values. Thus you frequently see friction between the line and head-office departments. Operations and sales managers rebel against edicts emanating from head-office personnel, while those at head office rail against the uncontrol-

> In effective organizations managers and employees tend to share the same values and "feel good" goals

lable mavericks on the front line. Senior executives are often seen as remote, out of touch and living in an ivory tower, while they see the "troops" as intransigent and reluctant to go along with the changes they deem necessary.

An organization can be extremely dislikeable where morale is low and where there is a great deal of in-fighting. Employees dislike the lack of trust, the insecurity, the perceived unfairness and injustices that seem to occur. They dislike the edicts that are imposed from on high and the fact that they are unable to express their true feelings, despite proclamations from the chief executive to the contrary. In these organizations there is a surfeit of propaganda and a simmering cauldron of unrest beneath the surface.

Customers suffer the repercussions of all this. When employees feel bad about the organization they work for, they feel bad about themselves. This in turn shows through to the customer. In these dislikeable organizations you will frequently hear the following types of statements:

➤ "Why should I bother about customers if my bosses don't bother about me?"

➤ "Why should I care if no one cares about me?"

➤ "Why should I put myself out when I get no appreciation for anything I do?"

➤ "It's best to keep your head below the parapet because if you speak up you get shot at."

➤ "I've heard it all before, it's fine words but they don't really mean it."

➤ "It's pointless saying what you think here, nobody ever listens. They just go through the motions."

➤ "I've raised that issue with the boss three times in the last six months and he just ignores me. He does nothing about it."

➤ "They tell you nothing here. You only find out through the back door."

➤ "You never know where you stand in this organization, they are forever moving the goalposts. It's one thing one day and a totally different thing the next day."

➤ "We just go from one fashion to another, from one quick fix to the next. It's 'flavor of the month' management."

➤ "If you speak up here you get shot down in flames."

➤ "The last person who disagreed with the boss got fired."

These statements of festering discontent infect newcomers to the organization and disillusion those who are keen to contribute ("You're a fool to put yourself out for the company, you'll get no appreciation" or "Are you trying to curry favor with the bosses with all that extra work?").

The infection spreads quickly and comes across as indifference and disinterest at the front line. Customers become inconsequential because the employees at the front line feel inconsequential themselves. If the front-line people do not feel valued they are definitely not going to value the company's customers.

The type of malaise is prevalent in many of the organizations I studied around the world. I have seen it in South Africa, in the Middle East, in Sweden, in the USA, in the UK and in many other countries. The following are characteristic of executives who create dislikeable organizations:

➤ Very autocratic.
➤ Obsessed with financial results and short-term gain.
➤ Dismissive of ideas that go against their own thoughts.
➤ Insensitive to the feelings of both employees and most customers (with the exception of the most important ones).
➤ Status driven (big cars, big offices, first-class travel etc.).
➤ Pay lip service to customer service (they say all the right words but fail to put them into practice).
➤ Have a belief that there is a systems solution to every problem (including people problems, for example performance problems are addressed with bureaucratic performance management systems).
➤ Defensive, irritable, bad-tempered.
➤ Difficult to get hold of (you have to book time with them three months in advance).
➤ Exceptionally nice to VIPs as well as to chauffeurs, car park attendants, security staff, gardeners and other employees who "salute".
➤ Very little attention to teamwork.
➤ Allow grapevine communication, rumor-mills and gossip.

These executives tend to drain the organization of all positive emotions. Negative emotions prevail and when they are suppressed the place becomes cold and impersonal. There is a harsh, aggressive atmosphere where people are indifferent to each other's feelings and survival of the fittest rules. Praise is a rare commodity and "bawling out" is the order of the day.

EROSION OF GOODWILL

When executives like these take over there is a gradual erosion of goodwill. First it is the goodwill of the employees that begins to diminish and then, in due course, it is the customers who suffer and then defect.

Coincidentally, as I write this there is a report in the newspaper of an outcry from a group of highly professional people about some action taken by their chief executive. This is a high-profile public service organization in the UK. To quote: "The chief executive has been labelled 'the most feared man in the industry', he is seen as a 'corporate monster'." Another report states: "They [these professionals] include some of the most calm, sensible and level-headed individuals, but today they are distressed and deeply passionate." These highly experienced people have written to the chief executive expressing their "dismay, verging on despair" at the changes he is trying to impose on them, very quickly and without prior consultation.

It does not follow that to make a profit you have to be disliked. It does not follow that in order to make tough business decisions you have to be disliked. If you are open and honest with people and treat them with respect, they will often accept the harshest decisions.

THE LIKEABLE ORGANIZATION

From my studies of a large number of organizations around the world, those that tended to provide the most impressive (and therefore the most likeable) customer service tended to have teams of likeable people. These were people who liked (if not loved) working together and liked the work they did.

Appendix I gives over 30 examples of teams that provide likeable customer service.

In the likeable organizations senior executives tended to be likeable. They were less imperfect than they made out, although they made occasional mistakes and were happy to declare these to the world.

In these likeable companies there is a positive flow of emotional energy across the organization. For example, walk into the reception of the health insurance company WPA at Taunton in the UK and you will feel the positive atmosphere immediately. It is the way the receptionist greets you, it is the way a senior executive comes down to meet you at reception, it is the way people smile and talk to each other.

All this is reflected on to customers. Independent surveys show that WPA is rated as the best by customers in its particular marketplace.

At the Mount Alvernia Hospital in Guildford, UK, the ethos of the organization is built around "care". The hospital's philosophy is based on care, the style of Paul Nicholson, the administrator, and his team is based on care. There is a conscious program of communication and training to keep this core philosophy in front of staff. It has repercussions for the patients, the majority of whom report very positively about the total caring approach of the hospital. It is a hospital that is well liked by its patients.

Or, to quote Charlotte Horne, a customer service agent at BT Mobile, Leeds, UK:

> We love it here. It is not to do with the money. It's just that we love what we are doing and the support we get from each other. For myself personally I want to help other people and I do. I am learning all the time, I am improving. We are one big family here.

Such spirit flows through to customers and the overall satisfaction ratings at BT Mobile have improved dramatically since Richard Brimble began developing this positive, trusting, loving approach with his people.

It is a rare and precious spirit that I do not come across very often. However, all the evidence is that when this spirit exists, customer service is exceptionally good.

Another incredibly likeable company that achieves phenomenal levels of customer service is TNT. This UK company has won award after award for quality and much of this can be attributed to the pioneering, inspirational spirit of Alan Jones, the chief executive. He is totally obsessed with ensuring that TNT's employees are highly motivated and that the company's customers receive the highest levels of service. Thus when Alan visits a depot he has one aim, to leave the depot with the staff there "on a high". In other words, he wants them to feel more motivated than when he arrived.

> **In these likeable companies there is a positive flow of emotional energy across the organization**

One customer I interviewed told me he had to make some travel arrangements for a visit to Spain. First of all he rang Marriott, the hotel group. The lady he spoke to there was incredibly charming. She chatted away to him while dealing with his complicated arrangements and processing his reservation. Nor did she complain when he asked for additional information about car hire and various facilities at the hotel. He rang a travel agent next to arrange the flights and received a totally different response. First of all it took him 10 attempts and 10 minutes before he got through to a recorded message on the phone. The woman who eventually dealt with him was pleasant but totally devoid of personality.

Later, when he arrived at the Marriott Beach Resort at Marbella, Spain, he knew instantly that here was a team of people who liked working together and liked to go out of their way to please customers. For a start, the security man at the entrance was smiling and charming, while each of the receptionists provided a warm welcome. All these people seemed to like working there and to like pleasing customers. In fact, they saw their job as pleasing customers and everyone liked that.

EMOTIONAL CONNECTIVITY IN LIKEABLE COMPANIES

In likeable companies there is a high degree of emotional connectivity between the bosses and their people, while in dislikeable companies this is never the case, in fact there is emotional dissonance. People distance themselves from the company and its bosses.

To maximize performance, to achieve incredible customer service, one of the prime tasks of any manager is to generate a feeling of goodwill in addition to developing the requisite skills and ensuring that people have the right tools to do the job and the appropriate reward structures. This feeling of goodwill, which reflects on to customers, will exist when employees are able to express their feelings, take initiatives and do their genuine best for customers.

Expressed another way, the prime role of any boss is to add emotional value to the work their people do. This added emotional value can then be passed on to the company's customers.

The following are some examples of the goodwill (added emotional value) that managers need to generate:

➤ "We feel valued in this organization."

➤ "We feel trusted."

➤ "We feel supported."

➤ "We feel cared for."

➤ "We feel appreciated."

➤ "We feel that our bosses respect us (and we respect them)."

➤ "We feel understood."

➤ "We feel that we are fairly rewarded."

➤ "We feel that our bosses are interested in developing our skills and talents."

➤ "We feel that all decisions are fairly made."

➤ "We feel that we can be open with our bosses and they with us."

➤ "We feel accountable for what we do."

➤ "We feel that we can take a few risks without getting into trouble if they backfire."

➤ "We enjoy working here, it's fun."

➤ "There's always a good spirit about the place."

The likeable organization is driven by feelings, emotions and values, not by facts and bureacratic performance measures.

THE LIKEABLE ORGANIZATION AND INTEGRITY

To create a likeable organization that benefits customers as much as employees and that delivers consistently high profits, there must be total integrity in the way the company goes about its business.

Customers value companies that act with integrity and like their people for it. This external perception of integrity can only be accomplished if there is genuine integrity within the company. In fact, there must be a "wholeness" in everything the company and its people do. This means that there must be total consistency between all the words uttered and actions taken by managers and employees.

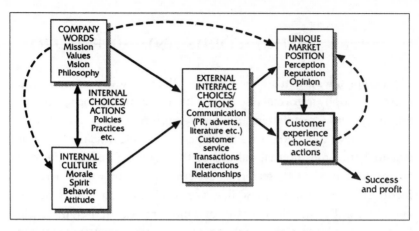

Figure 12   Total integrity in the likeable organization

INTEGRITY IMPERATIVES

To become a likeable organization there are five "integrity imperatives" that must be created and maintained to ensure its totality. Virtually all these integrity imperatives will be influenced by people's
emotions and the way they feel about the relationships between the
company's actions and words.

The five integrity imperatives are:

1 The internal culture of a company must reflect its formally stated
   core philosophy.
2 A company's policies and procedures must reflect its formally
   stated core philosophy.
3 The company's external communications must reflect its internal
   culture.
4 The company's external communications must reflect its formally
   stated core philosophy.
5 The company's position in the marketplace must reflect its external communications.

These five integrity imperatives rely on achieving a high degree of
consistency in everything that the company says and does.

FINE WORDS AND FINE ACTION

Most companies articulate their mission, their values, their vision and their philosophy in formal documents such as annual reports, sales literature, internal newsletters and display posters.

To achieve total integrity and become a likeable organization, it is essential that the internal culture of the company reflects the fine words contained in these formal statements. If employees perceive inconsistencies between these fine words (on mission, values, vision and philosophy) and the behavior of senior executives, then there will be a negative impact on morale, spirit, behavior and attitude. When this happens, positive emotions will slowly decay into negative emotions with a consequential impact on front-line customer service performance.

Here is an example from one multinational's vision statement, taken from a newsletter:

The seven key elements of our visionary strategy are:

1   Focusing on service excellence.
2   Innovating to remain ahead of the competition.
3   Optimizing the value of sales and maximizing profitability.
4   Improving operations performance.
5   Recruiting, training and motivating first-class people.
6   Developing effective measures of success.
7   Creating a culture based on our key values.

Our key values are:

A   Personal challenge.
B   Empowerment.
C   Action.
D   Trust.

These are exceptionally fine words and nobody I know in this particular organization disputes them. However, the real challenge has been to convert these fine words into fine practice in the eyes of all its employees and customers. There is a danger that such words wash over people without any direct impact on the culture of the organization, let alone on customers.

EMOTIONAL DISSONANCE

Emotional dissonance occurs when the policies and practices of senior executives bear little relationship to the mission and values that the company espouses.

For example, one company I studied espoused the importance of trust in its values statement. Yet the company, a financial institution, was hideously bureaucratic and middle managers were unable even to order a working lunch with a visitor in a conference room without first obtaining permission from a director. The culture was one of distrust. The official policies and practices were constraining and totally out of line with the company's values statement that stressed the importance of trust. Cynicism, low morale and a high degree of emotional dissonance occurred as a result.

Another example of emotional dissonance relates to a building services company for which I was running a series of two-day customer service seminars. I invited the chief executive to "top and tail" each seminar. He dutifully came along at the beginning and gave a 20-minute talk stressing how important customer service was to the future of the company. This was the only way, he said, that it would differentiate itself from its competitors. At the end of each seminar he came along to hear presentations from branch managers on the actions they planned for improving service. He listened carefully and was generally very supportive.

Yet despite this, his branch managers had consistently told me that the chief executive was not interested in customer service, despite hiring me and investing heavily in this program of seminars and despite committing a great deal of his own time to attending each seminar. The reputation of the chief executive was that he was only interested in one thing and that was financial results.

Three months later I ran a series of follow-up sessions to learn about progress and to help the branch managers develop further. Regrettably, there was an even higher degree of cynicism about the chief executive's intention. In the intervening three months he had visited a number of branches across the country. During each visit his sole focus had been the financial results. Not once had he sat down with a branch manager to review progress in implementing the action plan for improving customer service.

The end result was a high degree of emotional dissonance in the organization. While the chief executive espoused the importance of customer service, his actual behavior was at variance with this. People saw him driving hard for financial results and sensed that this was much more important to him than all the fine things he said (but did little about) in relation to customer service.

LIKEABLE ORGANIZATIONS AND EMPOWERMENT

Likeable organizations are empowered organizations.

Here is a simple test of empowerment: do you permit your front-line people to spend money on a customer without reference to a supervisor? And if so, how much? $20, $200 or $2000?

The Ritz Carlton hotel group, a company that has pioneered a very progressive approach to customer service, permits its front-line employees to spend up to $2000 to redress a guest's grievance. Lloyds Bank in the UK also allows its front-line people to spend up to £250 ($400) to resolve a customer problem.

In all the successful companies I studied, front-line people were given immense discretion to go out of their way to provide the service their customers wanted. At WPA, front-line people working on claims had final accountability for making a decision on whether or not to meet a claim. At TNT, front-line people were given total responsibility for making decisions to ensure that a consignment was delivered to a customer on time and in perfect condition. On one occasion this involved a front-line supervisor chartering a Boeing 727 aircraft to avoid a considerable delay due to a ferry strike and deliver a consignment on time.

Empowerment exists when people feel trusted to make decisions in favor of a customer without reference to their boss. Customers like it because they can obtain instant decisions and employees like it because the trust they enjoy enhances their self-esteem. This is the real power, the power of personal value. When empowerment exists there is a high degree of trust and integrity.

This does mean that front-line people have to take personal accountability for the initiatives they seize and the action they take. It also means that their bosses have to be incredibly supportive, especially when mistakes are made. A culture of intimidation and fear can quickly be created when so-called empowered people make mistakes and are reprimanded or punished for this. Too frequently I go into organizations and hear about the "blame culture" that exists. The top bosses talk glibly of empowerment but within the organization the talk is of "witch-hunts" when things go wrong, or people being held up as scapegoats when there has been a screw-up.

In an empowered organization people do not become defensive if they make a mistake and are prepared to learn from it. In these organizations everyone sees their job as contributing to the delivery of excellent customer service. Pleasing the customer is the ultimate goal. In a

> In an empowered organization people don't become defensive if they make mistakes

traditional, hierarchical organization, everyone sees their job as doing what their boss requires and therefore pleasing the boss. The first is a customer-serving organization and the second a boss-serving one. The mindsets and emotions associated with each are fundamentally different. An empowered organization is one where there is a high degree of emotional connectivity, whereas in a traditional, hierarchical organization there is a high degree of emotional deficiency.

This is demonstrated in Figure 13 overleaf.

SEMCO

A vivid example of an empowered, supportive organization is Ricardo Semler's Brazilian company Semco. In his book, *Maverick*, he portrays a company that has become emotionally connected. To quote:

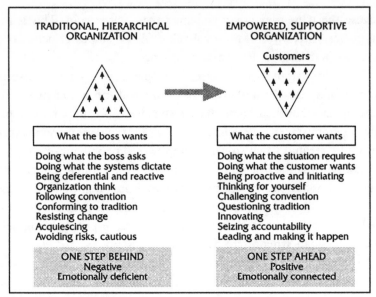

Figure 13   Emotionally deficient and emotionally connected organizations

We have absolute trust in our employees. In fact, we are partners with them ... We're thrilled that our workers are self-managing. It means they care about their jobs and about their company, and that's good for all of us.

The keys here are trust, care, a consensus about what is good and of course the emotion of being thrilled. What Ricardo Semler has created is an incredibly likeable organization.

NORDSTROM

Rich Gallitelli is the epitome of an empowered employee working in a likeable organization. He is one of the most likeable store assistants I have ever come across and demonstrates all that is best in customer service. To achieve this, he exercises an exceptionally high degree of emotional intelligence – not that he would necessarily call it this. He is the type of store assistant that gives Nordstrom, a US retail chain, such a high reputation for outstanding service.

I came across Rich in the menswear section of the Short Hills store in New Jersey. He went to great lengths to ensure that my specific requirements for a white shirt were met, if not exceeded. For a start, he was exceptionally pleasant and personable, as well as quietly enthusiastic about the products on offer and his company as a whole. He gave me as much time as I needed, never rushing me or pressurizing me to purchasing anything. Furthermore, he revealed an in-depth knowledge of the qualities of the wide range of products available. Impressed by this, I enquired how he came to acquire such a degree of expertise about men's clothing. He told me that he seizes every opportunity of a visit from a sales representative to discover as much as possible about the product being sold. For example, he'll find out about the pros and cons of the various weaves and stitchings for different types of shirt, he'll discover why Egyptian cotton is so special and he'll get to know how to distinguish a sturdy button from one that will break with constant washing. He goes out of his way to develop his expertise and knowledge about the product to enable him to give his customers the best possible advice.

In addition to learning about the product, Rich also went out of his way to learn about his customers. He took a genuine interest in my reasons for visiting Nordstrom and in my specific requirements, establishing that I was in the USA to give a seminar and needed a white shirt for that purpose. He offered me a coffee at the Starbucks café annexed to the store and explained that he'll even buy a customer a meal if the situation demands it. It would be unthinkable for him to ask permission from his boss to spend money on a customer. If Rich deems it necessary, he'll do it.

Even so, I decided to ask his then boss, store manager Barbara Kirk, about this. She was full of praise for Rich Gallitelli. To quote her:

> Rich enjoys providing the best possible service to his customers.
> He truly is the epitome of Nordstrom service.

The key word here is "enjoys". Rich does what he enjoys. In other words, he does what he likes to please customers and as a result the customers like him. What Barbara Kirk revealed was a high degree of trust in Rich's abilities to exercise emotionally intelligent judgments and add emotional value in dealing with customers and so getting them to like him and the service he provides.

Nordstrom is not a company that suppresses its employees with an overbearing and constraining set of rules and policy procedures. In fact, its employee handbook consists of one page only and reads:

WELCOME TO NORDSTROM

We're glad to have you with our Company.
Our number one goal is to provide outstanding customer service.
Set both your personal and professional goals high.
We have great confidence in your ability to achieve them.

Nordstrom Rules:
Rule # 1: Use your good judgement in all situations.
There will be no additional rules.
Please feel free to ask your department manager, store manager, or division general manager any question at any time.

This is one of the reasons for Nordstrom's success. The company relies on allowing its front-line employees to add emotional value in providing the best possible service. This involves a high degree of mutual trust and the exercise of total freedom to be creative in providing exceptional service to customers. The end result is an incredibly likeable organization. The employees love the company and so do its customers. To quote Rich Gallitelli: "I am not here to take money off customers but to help them, to please them, to serve them."

THREE MORE EXAMPLES OF LIKEABLE ORGANIZATIONS

Marks and Spencer's is one of the most liked and most respected companies in the UK. The reason is simple. It has a clear set of values based on trust and quality and these form the basis of its day-by-day operations. These values are well understood within the company as well as by its customers, who experience the application of them all the time. Go into the food section of any Marks and Spencer store and you won't find a rotten tomato. Return an ill-fitting pullover and it will be replaced without question. The customer is trusted.

The Swedish automobile company Volvo has built up a reputation for safety and reliability. The company values safety more than anything else and its customers know that.

The US company 3M values innovation and has a worldwide reputation for bringing exciting new products to the market. The Post-it note™ is the most famous example of this.

These companies (and there are many more) succeed because their whole operation is reflected in their values. It is reflected in the behaviour of individual employees and managers as well as at strategic level. At Marks and Spencer you would expect a front-line store assistant to remove any item from the shelves if they perceive it to be of substandard quality. At a Volvo dealership you would expect a front-line service engineer to be meticulous in maintaining your car to the highest standards. At 3M you would expect any employee to put forward and pursue any bright new idea that they had.

LIKEABLE ORGANIZATIONS AND ADDED EMOTIONAL VALUE

There is only one way of achieving the necessary integrity to become a likeable organization – to add emotional value to everything the company does and says, internally and externally.

This integrity will exist when employees feel that the company's values are a reflection of their own personal values. For this to occur employees must understand what the company's values are, like what they find, and want to behave in a way that is consistent with them. This will then be translated into everything that happens at the external interfaces with their customers.

It means living and breathing the values espoused by the company and its people. It is a cliché to say that "actions speak louder than words", but in likeable organizations this is always the case. Employees and customers alike tend to judge a company on what is done rather than what is said. If the words are to have any significance, then it must be to support the actions. In less successful companies the words (the values, the principles, the beliefs) come first and it is hoped that the actions (the application) will follow, but they rarely do.

For an organization to be likeable, employees must therefore experience a high degree of consistency between the following:

➤ The words stated by senior executives.
➤ The actions expected of them by these senior executives.
➤ The actions they themselves want to take.

Furthermore, employees must be able to relate emotionally to the words and actions of their senior executives.

When people feel that their company stands for the right sorts of things, that it is going in the right direction, that their senior executives are both competent and trustworthy, then their performance will reflect these feelings and is likely to be compatible with the expectations of both customers and senior managers.

In other words, a company can be energized by the positive feelings of its people. When customers like these feelings they are more likely to do business with the company than when the people are drained of energy.

> A company can be energized by its people's positive feelings

The key task for every senior executive and manager is therefore to generate these positive feelings. To accomplish this, they must live and breathe the very values they espouse through the company's formal words.

When employees feel emotionally valued by their bosses, they will be able to add emotional value to their interactions with customers.

When this happens you will have a likeable organization, excellent customer service and an exceptional advantage over your competitors.

LIKEABLE ORGANIZATIONS AND CREATIVITY

Another facet of likeable organizations is their creativity. People like to work in companies where there is a high degree of creativity and flair. It gives them a buzz and enables them to give vent to their own creative impulses.

In dislikeable companies creativity is suppressed and there is a high degree of autocratic management. Virtually every decision, however minor, has to go to the boss. As a result, initiative, innovation and creativity are stifled.

Creativity can only exist when there is a high degree of trust and integrity. When there is a lack of trust and integrity, people will be fearful of the backlash that might occur if they take risks to do something new and out of line with accepted policies and practices.

A creative organization is a vibrant organization that both customers and employees like. Marks and Spencer has already been given as an example of an organization that has a strong set of values and exercises trust in its dealings with customers. It is also incredibly creative, not only in the exciting new products it puts on its shelves but also in the way it works with employees. For example, it employs a resident poet who gives regular poetry workshops for employees. The ultimate beneficiary will be the customer.

Customer service is an art as well as a science. The creative and artistic side has been much neglected by many companies – yet it is this aspect of customer service that both customers and employees most like. When given the freedom and the opportunity, people love to express their creative impulses through work and will do everything to please their customers.

SUMMARY

Likeable organizations are more likely to achieve service excellence and competitive advantage than organizations that employees and customers dislike. Likeable organizations are those where employees feel good about the way they are treated – this in turn enables them to treat customers well. To accomplish this, there must be total integrity in the way a company's formal words are reflected in its internal culture, in the way senior executives behave and in the decisions and actions taken in relation to its customers.

When employees' personal values are reflected in their company's values you will have a likeable organization. When these values include trust, employees will be able to be incredibly creative in the way they please customers.

PRACTICAL STEPS

1 Do you honestly know how the people in your team feel about your company's values and the way you as a boss apply them?
2 Sit down with your people and review how their behaviors and yours relate to their values and the company's values.
3 Now agree a plan of action to ensure total reconciliation between your stated values and everything you say and do for your customers.
4 Ask your team whether they feel that they work for a likeable organization.
5 Then find a way of asking your customers the same question.
6 Identify the changes in behavior needed to become an even more likeable organization.

11

THE LIKEABLE

LEADER

In real life, for the last 5000 years, the vast majority of humans have been submissive, cringing before authority and, apart from short-lived outbursts of protest, sacrificing themselves so that a small minority could live in luxury. (Theodore Zeldin)

WHEN THE LATE JOHN GARNETT WAS DIRECTOR OF THE Industrial Society in the UK, he spent much of his time giving exceptionally entertaining and stimulating talks on leadership. On three occasions I distinctly remember him saying that "leadership is not a popularity contest". He asserted that it is impossible to be liked by everyone and that the job of a leader was to make business-like decisions, which sometimes meant making unpalatable decisions that people would not like. For example, some people would not like a decision not to promote them, others would not like it when they were being made redundant.

For 20 years this belief remained with me. I too believed that leadership was not a popularity contest, that being liked was not important. I believed that what was more important was the ability to make tough decisions to achieve business goals, even if this meant doing things that people did not like. I had developed a fixed, rigid thinking pattern on this issue that I did not even contemplate challenging.

LIKING AND PERFORMING

Thanks to Daniel Goleman's book on *Emotional Intelligence*, I did challenge this view and as a result I have totally reversed my thinking. The paradox I failed to see was that John Garnett himself was one of the most popular and likeable leaders around.

> People perform best and deliver the best customer service when they like what they do

In reflecting on my experiences throughout life and on the companies I have studied, I have come to realize that people perform best and thus deliver the best customer service when they like what they do. What they do will be affected by what their bosses, their leaders, do. Should these bosses do things that people do not like, there is a high probability that people will not like the work they do. So if a boss is always interfering, always criticizing, always refusing permission, always turning down requests, people will not like this. This will have an impact on their performance. They will personalize everything and come to the conclusion that they do not like their boss.

If anything is predictable in most organizations it is that many employees will criticize their bosses. With rare exceptions, bosses never seem to act in the way their people want. Frequently people complain about a lack of communication, a lack of consultation, a lack of involvement, a lack of trust, a lack of openness and honesty, and a lack of support. People feel bad about this and do not like their leaders for it.

In contrast, where people like their leaders there is a much higher probability of higher performance and excellent customer service. People like the fact that their bosses are fair, support them, encourage them to develop themselves and generally let them get on and do the job of which they think they are capable.

LOVE

In many of the successful organizations I studied, the word "like" seemed too weak. People seemed to love their bosses and their bosses loved them. When Paul Southworth was President of Avon Cosmetics (UK), everyone loved him and he loved them. At BT Mobile people love Richard Brimble and he loves them. At Bank Atlantic in Florida people love Alan Levan and he loves them.

Richard Branson, Anita Roddick and Herb Kelleher are three more illustrious examples of this rare breed of boss.

When you have love in an organization, the positive energy is such that there is real emotional power to connect with customers, employees and suppliers alike. The added emotional value is high.

Love in an organizational context derives from the three key attributes that are at the center of this book together with the three key internal motivators.

Likeable leaders want to do their best for their people (integrity and creativity) and they want their people to feel good working for them (added emotional value through emotional connectivity). Furthermore, likeable leaders are driven by phenomenal energy, a great deal of emotional direction and deeply rooted sets of values, beliefs and principles. Their own esprit constantly sparks an *esprit de corps*.

RESPECT

Respect is an important factor here. People love to respect their bosses. They love bosses who can make tough decisions, provided that those decisions are seen to be fair and are explained adequately.

People do not like bosses they disrespect and they disrespect bosses who are always giving in to the wildest demands of the vocal minority. In other words, doing things that people like is not the same as giving them what they want all the time. The same applies to customers. In no way is it recommended in this book that you give customers and employees everything they demand. People actually like bosses who have the ability to say "no" from time to time. This creates the necessary boundaries within which people feel comfortable in working. When bosses say "yes" all the time, the boundaries are destroyed and people do not know where they stand. The quality of the "yes" or "no" decisions made by bosses is a direct reflection of their own internal esprit and definitely not a function of a company's policies and procedures.

In a nutshell, front-line employees love bosses they respect and who they know will go out of their way to make them feel good. These are the bosses who added emotional value through effective teamworking.

THE LIKING CONTINUUM

To sustain this flow of positive, loving energy throughout an organization, with a resulting positive impact on customers, there must be a "liking continuum" (see Figure 14).

Should any of the "likes" in this continuum be displaced by a "dislike", there is a risk of a negative impact on customers, who will sense the consequent demotivation.

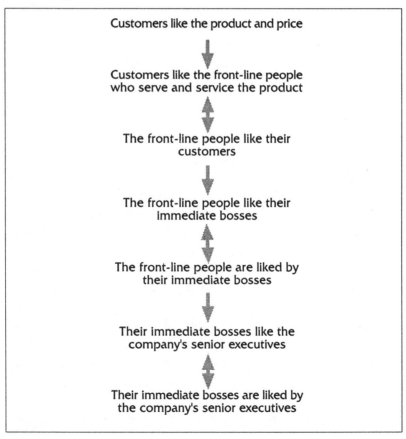

Figure 14   The liking continuum

The degree to which this happens depends on the emotional intensity of the dislike. And if the like is of high emotional intensity, there is a greater probability of excellent customer service (Figure 15).

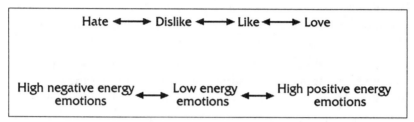

Figure 15   Emotional intensity

DISLIKEABLE LEADERS

Example 1
One person I interviewed found his boss immensely dislikeable and tried to describe why. These are his words:

> Everything he [the boss] tells me is totally rational. He has an answer for everything and seems to know it all. He is even aware of the problems of low morale in our organization. This he attributes to history and the way our organization developed before his arrival three years ago. He believes there is a long tradition of negativity in the organization which he has yet to totally eradicate. The one thing he does not know, but which everyone else does, is that no one likes him. The general view is that he is autocratic, non-listening, self-righteous, bullying, unfair, too hard a taskmaster and incredibly difficult to convince. He tells us he wants to be convinced, that he wants his senior managers to come to him with compelling business cases for change and for improvement. But this never happens because he is always issuing orders. We feel we cannot stand up to him because all he does is shout us down if he disagrees. It's impossible. He's hated around here.

I walked away from this interview convinced that the boss in question did not understand himself – if he did, he would probably not like what he found. That was why he suppressed these vital truths and as a result had become disliked.

What he had failed to do was establish a positive emotional connection with the people in his organization. As a consequence, he had drained the organization of emotional value. It was his own emotional deficiency and the potential of not liking himself that was driving the organization to despair.

Here was an organization where emotional dissonance was rife. The bottom line was that customer service throughout the company was poor. With a chief executive you do not like, how can you provide service that the customers like?

Example 2
Here is another example of a dislikeable boss, provided to me by an interviewee in Europe:

> Our director sees his job as merely issuing orders. We go to him with recommendations and he sees his job as saying "yes" or "no". He is often critical of the quality of our recommendations and accuses us openly of not having done our homework properly. We feel we can hardly move without his permission. Everything has to be approved by him. Some of my colleagues go in awe of him and are reluctant to challenge him. We told him that our company's customer service was poor. However, he did not see it that way, he saw us as being poor. He blamed us and told us to sort out the problem. We can only do this if he agrees to the budget we're asking for, but he won't.

In this case and the previous one, the senior executive had inadvertently created a negative emotional climate, full of intimidation and fear. There was a total lack of trust and risk taking, resulting in decisions being pushed up to the highest level in the organization. Customer service inevitably suffered.

LIKEABLE LEADERS

Example 1

Compare the above with Ray Shipley, who used to be managing director of Albany International, a manufacturer in Bolton, UK. He was loved by his people. He knew everybody and would take great delight in wandering around talking to people on the factory floor, or drifting into the canteen and chatting to the cleaning ladies. I visited him on one occasion when the company had just celebrated 25 years in existence. He had given each employee a watch inscribed with the company logo. As I sat with him in his office his door remained open. Suddenly, a young man in blue overalls from the factory floor knocked on the door and popped his head around. Ray Shipley invited him in with a warm, friendly smile. He greeted the young production operator by his name. "I just came up to thank you, Mr Shipley, for this watch, I really appreciate it," said the factory worker.

I was touched. This production operator had taken leave from the factory floor, walked all the way across the factory, up through the office block and then along the senior executive corridor to enter the managing director's office to thank him for a watch. The directors' floor in most companies is usually forbidden territory for people from the factory floor, but not in the case of Ray Shipley.

This simple act of giving a watch was one of many Ray Shipley had undertaken during his time with the company. As a result, he had created and reinforced a high degree of emotional connectivity throughout the organization. Employees felt valued because Ray Shipley was always demonstrating that he valued them.

Example 2

Paul Southworth is from the same mold. Until a couple of years ago he was president of Avon Cosmetics in the UK. Everyone loved him and he loved everyone.

On one occasion Avon was sponsoring a ballet at the local theater. Along with all the other local dignitaries, Paul took his wife to the opening evening. Before the ballet started, he glanced down from his seat in the circle and recognized one of his factory workers and her husband in the stalls below. He waved to her and then went down to chat to her. She was overwhelmed to have the top guy in the company come and say hello and to be able to introduce him to her husband. What was more, Paul invited them both to the VIP lounge at the interval for a glass of champagne and to meet the mayor. At the end of the ballet he invited her backstage to meet the dancers. For this factory worker it was a memorable experience. For Paul it was but one small, genuine gesture of many that he made every day to keep in touch with his people. The next morning the whole factory knew about this woman's encounter with the president at the theater. The motivation was phenomenal and when that happens customers are aware of it.

Example 3

Or take Ian Edwards, former commander of the Bedfordshire Fire and Rescue Service in the UK. He was forever encouraging his frontline fire officers to be innovative in developing their approach. As a result, they were instrumental in developing and installing some of the latest high technology on their fire tenders. The word got around of their progressive approach and Ian was invited to speak at a conference in Glasgow. He discussed this with the people involved and they agreed that a small team should go to Glasgow to do a joint presentation. He left it to them to make the arrangements.

Later, one of the team came to his office. "I presume you will be staying in a five-star hotel, sir, and that we will have our usual three-star accommodation."

"You know me better than that," he replied, "but it's your decision and you must decide what is best for the team, including me. I'll stay wherever you put me up." In the end they all stayed in the same four-star hotel.

When you achieve this degree of motivation it reflects positively on to customers. When people love their bosses they will do anything for them and that energy is normally directed towards customers, because they know that that is what the bosses really like.

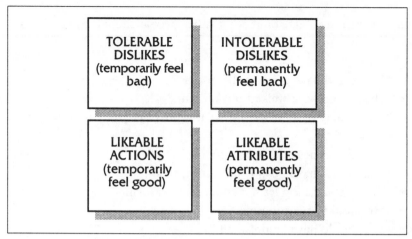

Figure 16   Likes and dislikes

TOLERANCE

Likes and dislikes can be on either a permanent or temporary basis, as indicated in Figure 16.

It is a matter of degree. We can love our kids but temporarily dislike the things they do. We can come across people who have habits (such as smoking or swearing) that we permanently dislike. We can like what a person does without liking them as a person. Occasionally we will come across people we really like because they have attributes that make us feel permanently good about them.

Nobody is perfect and even those closest to us have attributes we dislike and do things that irritate us. But we tolerate them because on balance they are people we like and love. Thus to develop a liking for people, including customers, we have to learn to tolerate those aspects of their behavior that we dislike while searching out things we like about them. The big trap into which many of us fall is that we try to change people. We try to persuade or to impose changes of behavior on others to bring them into line with our own way of thinking. In other words, we establish in our minds a model of "how to do things" and tend to dislike people who do not conform to this model. So we attempt to change people to bring them into line with our model.

We think we know best all the time. Our conversations are cluttered with assertions about what other people should do. Here are some examples:

- ➤ "He should have gone to the doctor."
- ➤ "She should have walked out on him."
- ➤ "He should have stood up to the boss and told him what he thought."
- ➤ "She should never have accepted it."
- ➤ "I shouldn't have been kept waiting so long."
- ➤ "They should have let me know what was happening."
- ➤ "He should have rung me."
- ➤ "She should have complained."

These assertions about what other people "should do" are the cause of most friction and conflict in the world. We want others to be like us, to do things our way. This applies to bosses, staff and customers. We dislike those who deviate from our way, who irritate us with what we feel is unreasonable behavior. We reason that our behavior is the best way, therefore anyone behaving differently is deemed to be unreasonable. We create expectations in our own mind of what others should do and then become disappointed when they do not do them. If they persist with these ways, our disappointment turns into permanent dislike.

Of course, we don't like to admit that we don't always practice what we preach, and that the best way we recommend to others is not always the way we take ourselves! Such is our own irrationality and self-deluding hypocrisy.

Likeable leaders don't expect to mold people in their image any more than they expect their people to mold customers in their image. Likeable leaders develop a high degree of tolerance, allowing people to do things their way provided that the agreed overall objective is achieved. Likeable leaders hold back from criticizing people who perhaps contravene company policy by making minor concessions to customers. Likeable leaders bite their tongue when they witness a front-line member of staff speaking to a customer in a different way to what they themselves would choose. Likeable leaders learn to raise their threshold of tolerance and expect their people to do the same with customers.

The focus all the time should be on what you like about your staff and what they like about their customers. Little attention should be paid to aspects of their behavior and approach that are disliked. Tolerance means that occasional bad behavior is ignored, not even noticed, while good behavior is recognized, welcomed, reinforced and appreciated. Likeable leaders advise their people not to be provoked when a customer swears or glares but instead to seek out aspects of that customer that can be liked and reflected back. Humor can be an important device for eliciting such positive responses.

DISMISSING DISLIKES

The key for any leader is to encourage people to dismiss from their minds anything they dislike about their customers (or their colleagues). This enables the team to focus on the actions and attributes they really like about other people, including themselves. It is the same as the analogy about whether the jug is half empty or half full. Focus on what you like about it, not what you dislike.

The more leaders can get their people to focus on what they like and love and to reject their dislikes and hates, the happier the team will become and the better the service it will provide to customers.

So likeable leaders are sensitive to what their people really like. They are aware of their

> Look for things you like about other people

expectations and their needs and go out of their way to try to meet them. They devote precious time to learning more about each individual in the team, to identify common ground and areas where there are similar likes. By doing so, they develop a liking for one another. They begin to see things they like about each other.

You have to look for things you like about other people. Likeable leaders are exceptionally skilled at this. If you fail to look for the things that you like, you will base your opinion on a fleeting first impression, on a look on another person's face, on a casual opening remark, on a faint body language signal. Your subconscious will compare these fleeting first impressions with the vast store of experiences deposited in your memory and automatically come up with a conclusion such as: "This person has a tattoo on his arm and therefore I don't like him" or "This person does not look me in the eye, she looks shifty to me so I don't like her." These first impressions and instinctive reactions can be dangerous. We are basing our likes and dislikes on a superficial comparison of momentary behavior with deep-rooted memories.

Janine Bensouda from the MashreqBank in Dubai told me that she had one person in her team who was totally cynical when she took over. He doubted everything about her, including her potential to improve things. She told him that she would prove him wrong and would like his support in doing so! Now they are the best of friends and he is one of her most loyal supporters.

Kesh Morjaria of Fleet Photos in London told of a situation a few years ago when everything was going wrong with his business. There was one person in his team he could just not get along with. They were not on speaking terms. Kesh was always blaming this person for getting things wrong. Ultimately, a crisis arose and Kesh had to reflect on his approach. He concluded that the problems facing the company were of his own making. He had spent too much time going around blaming other people for everything that was going wrong. So he consciously decided to change, to become more positive, to love his people including the person he hadn't previously been able to get along with. It worked! By injecting positive, loving energy into the relationship with this person, with the rest of the team, with the bank manager and with his customers, he found that he was able to turn the business around.

Likeable leaders therefore go searching for attributes they like about other people. In addition, they learn to develop attributes that the team likes and to discard those attributes (habits, body language gestures, reactions) that people dislike.

ATTRIBUTES OF LIKEABLE LEADERS

From my interviews with a large number of people about their bosses as well as studying many leaders in action, I have been able to identify many attributes that people like about their bosses. Here are 26 of them:

1   Fairness
2   Tolerance
3   Understanding
4   Prepared to listen
5   Trust
6   Enthusiasm (for what people want to achieve)
7   Support
8   Honesty
9   Treating everyone equally (no favorites)
10 Right balance between closeness (not too intimate) and distance (not too remote)
11 Mutual respect
12 Recognition and appreciation of good work
13 Communication (keeping people informed)
14 Consultation
15 Fighting for their people
16 Decisiveness
17 Positive approach
18 Happiness
19 Genuine love for people
20 Knowing exactly what they want to achieve
21 Putting themselves out for others
22 Compassion
23 Reliability (never let anyone down)
24 Rewarding people well
25 Being prepared to confront serious issues
26 Strong set of principles.

This list is far from exhaustive. I have tested these attributes with people from around the world and they are immutable. Whether you are a Christian, a Muslim, a Hindu, a Jew, a Buddhist, an atheist or anything else, the majority of people welcome these attributes in their bosses. They are equally applicable to bosses in Brazil, China, France, Saudi Arabia, South Africa, Spain, Sweden, West Africa, the UK, the USA and most other countries.

When leaders demonstrate these qualities, the same attributes become apparent in the people they lead. In turn, this is reflected on to customers.

THE HUMAN TOUCH

Another way of expressing this is to talk about a common touch, or a human touch. Touch is all to do with sensing and feeling. It is a product of emotional connectivity. A "nice touch" is one form of added emotional value. We feel touched when someone appreciates us or puts themselves out for us. Likeable leaders are "in touch" with their people and able to relate to them at their own level. There is no pretension or status barrier to get in the way of the emotional connectivity they are able to establish. In contrast, dislikeable leaders tend to be "out of touch" with their people and therefore "untouchable".

> Likeable leaders establish emotional connectivity with their people

People warm to bosses who treat them like human beings, who make real efforts to understand and support them. These bosses are able to energize people by transmitting and radiating their own positive energies. They do not treat people like numbers, like cogs in a machine. Instead, they appreciate them as real human beings with genuine interests and a forgivable set of foibles. People do not walk in fear of these bosses but instead respect them, maybe even revere them, for their wisdom, their spirit, their courage, their fairness and their help and support during difficult times.

Likeable leaders resonate positively with their people and are always in tune with them. They thus establish a high degree of emotional connectivity and add emotional value to everything they do. Conversely, leaders who are disliked create emotional dissonance and tend to be cold and indifferent towards their people.

Likeable leaders have a "feel" for people, while dislikeable leaders appear to have no feelings for them at all. Likeable leaders are people you can take your problems to and be confident that they will be sympathetic towards them. Dislikeable leaders are dismissive of people's problems and have no time for them. In turn, the staff of a likeable leader will encourage customers to bring their problems to them and will lend them a sympathetic ear. The positive emotional energy seeps all the way down from the likeable leader through the organization to each customer, who senses the warmth, the caring, the understanding and the genuine interest in them, as well as the real desire to help resolve their problems and meet their needs.

A TRANSMITTER OF POSITIVE ENERGY

So a leader is a transmitter of positive energy in the organization. This positive energy permeates every pore of the organization and vitalizes each member of the team.

None of us has consistently high energy levels. Sometimes we feel down or low. We have bad days. There are times when everything seems to go wrong and we are on the verge of despair. On these occasions, likeable leaders will sense what is happening and inject positive energy into the team. They have the ability to give people a shot in the arm to revive or even resuscitate them. They restore people's faith in their own abilities to accomplish great things.

And, of course, when the leader feels down the team will do the same for him or her.

LIKEABLE LEADERS AND SELF-AWARENESS

Likeable leaders have a high degree of self-awareness. They are sufficiently intelligent emotionally to be in touch with their own feelings and to be aware of the impact these can have on their people. They therefore know how to manage their feelings for maximum effect. They are aware of their emotional drives and direct these towards the accomplishment of incredibly challenging goals.

Similarly, likeable leaders tend be aware of their own esprit. They spend a lot of time focusing on what they believe is important in their lives and thus on developing and applying their own values and principles. To do this, they are always challenging themselves and are prepared to learn from others as well as from their own experience. They are sufficiently humble to admit their own mistakes and deficiencies and improve themselves as a result.

BUREAUCRATIC SYSTEMS

Bureaucratic systems have no place in the repertoire of likeable leaders. They will have no time for the pedantic and constraining procedures invented by the head office personnel function. They will have no need to fill in performance appraisal forms, having already given constructive feedback to members of the team on an "as and when needed" basis. They will have no need for formal briefing groups or other mechanistic approaches, having already communicated with their people on a two-way basis as and when the situation requires.

The people management approach of likeable leaders is driven by their own strong sense of personal beliefs and values (esprit), as opposed to being driven by bureaucratic edicts from head office.

THE LIKEABLE LEADER AND VISION

Likeable leaders are visionaries. They have a clear and graphic picture in their mind of the goals that they feel must be achieved and then focus all their energies on achieving them. The source of their vision derives from deep-rooted emotional desires and fundamental beliefs that they have about themselves.

Just over 10 years ago John Sculley published a book about his experience as the then chief executive of Apple Computers. Apple's fortunes have of course been on a rollercoaster ride since then. However, it is worth quoting one statement from John Sculley:

> Apple is driven by vision not policy. We aim to change the way people work, think and learn with high-tech tools. We have an uncompromising passion to make those tools more accessible, more creative. An intrinsic element of Apple's "vision" is that work should be fun.

The most significant lesson here is that the best companies are driven by vision, not policy. There is one fundamental difference between vision and policy and that is the word "passion".

Throughout my career I cannot recall a single policy I have ever been involved with that I have felt passionate, enthusiastic, excited or inspired about. Policies are two-dimensional, boring things that become encapsulated in 20 or 30 pages of typescript. However, I do remember once having a boss who took the team away for two days to create an exciting vision of future success for the company.

It is incredibly difficult to become emotionally involved with the development and implementation of a policy. But the generation of a vision can have a powerful emotional impact and be exceptionally exciting.

The following is a quote from Anita Roddick, the founder of the Body Shop:

> Vision is a key word for us, and one we believe can set a new tone for the 1990s. I think the Body Shop can be a role model for other companies. We talk about love. We talk about care. We'd rather close down than test our products on animals.

Body Shop was not founded by any of the large, corporate bureaucracies (which its competitors tend to be) but by a woman with energy, passion, drive, beliefs, values, principles and vision. When you enter a branch anywhere in the world you experience the tangible product of Anita Roddick's vision. The air

Visions must turn people on, they must create excitement and enthusiasm

is fragrant, the decor is colorful, the assistants helpful and charming and the products conform to the underlying principles of the business. They are environmentally friendly and they have not been tested on animals.

Visions can never be the product of an academic, classroom exercise. Instead, they must be a product of what you really want to achieve in life. Visions must turn people on, they must create excitement and enthusiasm. The resulting emotional energy can be used to focus people's minds and emotional energies on the pursuit of the vision.

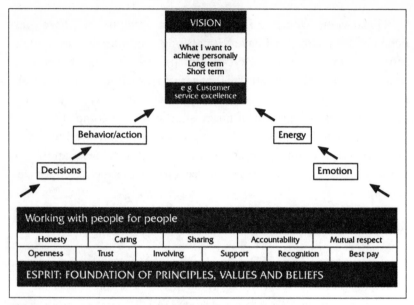

Figure 17   The approach of the likeable leader

LIKEABLE LEADERS AND ESPRIT

Leaders with no esprit will blow with the wind and tend to be reactive. They will be accused by their people as having "no mind of their own". They will make one decision one day and a different one the next. They will "move the goalposts" and "change the rules" at the slightest whim. Such leaders will have no foundation of principles on which to base their decisions and actions and this will unsettle their people and confuse them.

Their people will not know "where they stand" with them, because they do not know what they stand for themselves.

Esprit is what you stand for and sparks the emotions and energies needed to achieve your own personal goals and your vision (see Figure 17).

Thus if leaders genuinely believe in working with people for people and also in the principles of openness, honesty, trust, caring and sharing, then these principles will be sufficiently important for them to endeavor to put them into practice every moment of their working day. This means that every single decision, action and behavior will be a reflection of these leaders' personal principles.

For example, Janine Bensouda from MashreqBank in Dubai genuinely believes in working closely with her team and giving them every support. Towards the end of last year she pulled her new team together and invited them to brainstorm a set of new year's resolutions for the coming year. They did so and then prioritized the resolutions. The priority list became their vision for the new year and formed the basis of the business plan the bank had asked her to prepare.

She had turned the normally boring, bureaucratic process of business planning into an enjoyable, exciting process that incorporated a vision of what her team really wanted to achieve. She had energized the team with her creative and positive approach.

Many bosses do not have a focused vision, let alone a clear foundation of principles. As a result, they become reactive, reacting to the in-tray, the e-mail, people knocking on their door, the telephone ringing and so on.

Likeable leaders recognize and understand that there is nothing more important than the customers who pay the salaries of the people who serve them. All of their time and all of their energy are therefore geared to doing their very best for customers as well as for their people. Likeable leaders do not get diverted by financial matters, they leave these to the accountants. Likeable leaders do not get diverted by edicts from head office to generate yet another report, they leave these to their assistants. Likeable leader do not spend all their time in meetings, nor do they get distracted with the never-ending flow of paper in the in-tray.

Likeable leaders spend much of their time out with customers and at the front line with their people, supporting them, understanding them, listening to them, explaining things to them, doing things for them and giving advice when asked.

It is both the esprit and the emotion that drive likeable leaders forward towards their vision. They feel strongly for their customers and their people and the vision encapsulates this. Likeable leaders are enthusiastic if not passionate about the visions that they personally want accomplished. Through all this likeable leaders are able to inspire their people to do their very best for customers.

These positive energies, emotions and esprit enable likeable leaders to connect with customers and staff alike and thus add emotional value to every aspect of the business.

SUMMARY

To deliver service excellence it is essential that there are leaders within the organization whom the front-line staff like, if not love. These leaders will display a wide range of positive attributes that add emotional value for their people and are reflected on to customers.

Likeable leaders have both a clear vision of what they want to achieve personally and a strong esprit founded on well-established principles and beliefs. These form the basis of all the decisions they make.

The most likeable leaders love their people and their people love them. They radiate and transmit positive energy throughout the organization.

PRACTICAL STEPS

1 If you manage a team of front-line people delivering customer service, identify the attributes that they like (if not love) about you.
2 To do so, test your own reactions and identify the attributes (likes and dislikes) of your own bosses (or bosses you have previously had).
3 Try to develop the attributes that you know your people will like and love.
4 Write down in less than 50 words what your own vision of success is in relation to customer service.
5 What action have you taken over the last four weeks to make progress towards this vision?
6 Write down on one sheet of paper what your principles are in relation to people management and customer service.
7 Discuss these principles and your vision with your team and seek a consensus.
8 Be prepared to modify your principles and vision in the light of discussion with your team.
9 Be prepared to change yourself for the better and emit positive emotions and positive energy in doing so.
10 Learn to love your people.

12

RECRUITING PEOPLE YOUR CUSTOMERS LIKE

M OST COMPANIES THAT FAIL AT CUSTOMER SERVICE FALL AT THE first hurdle: they fail to recruit people that their customers like. The resulting problems often go undetected for long periods. The penalties are severe in terms of customers defecting and lost revenue.

When selecting front-line people who deal with customers, the most important criterion must be the likeability of the chosen candidate. Skills, knowledge and experience are important, but must take second place to the personal attributes of the person to be appointed.

To quote James Dyson: "Anyone can become an expert in six months." In other words, with personal drive and company support, any employee can acquire the requisite skills and experience to do any front-line job effectively over a short period. The skills and experience of employees are not the main issue when it comes to serving customers. What is more at issue is their own emotional drives and their ability to connect emotionally with customers.

Conventional methods of selection are limited and misguided when it comes to this. Too often, the priority in selecting people is technical skills and experience rather than their ability to relate emotionally to customers. The worst type of selection is that made by default, where the pay is so low, the applicants so few, that a company hires the only person who applies.

This chapter provides 14 important guidelines for adding emotional value to your recruitment process and selecting people your customers will like. Some of these guidelines may be surprising to people brought up on the conventional approach.

BE SUBJECTIVE IN MAKING SELECTION DECISIONS

It might be heresy to say this, but subjectivity is essential when selecting the right candidate. I risk sending shockwaves around the elite world of personnel practitioners in asserting that a reliance on objective selection measures will frequently lead to the wrong person being appointed. Mercifully, most selection decisions are made for subjective reasons. Recruiters just delude themselves that they are being objective!

Many personnel experts and their internal customers, line managers, have fallen into the trap of equating fairness in selection with objectivity. Can you imagine selecting a future husband or wife on the basis of objective selection criteria? If this were possible we would all select our partners using computer dating techniques.

> Subjectivity is essential to select the right candidate

The best selection decisions are made when you use a combination of "heart" and "mind" to judge a candidate. Eliminate the heart from this process and you will only select two-dimensional candidates who will have no feel for customers and therefore will not be liked by them.

The objective criteria for selecting a candidate *must* be complemented by the subjective and personal likes of the manager making that appointment. If a manager does not like the person they are hiring, then there is no hope at all of service excellence.

To quote Denille Girardat, a store manager with Nordstrom:

We like to recruit the friends of our staff. We think Frank Pizzano, for example, on our customer service desk is wonderful, therefore we feel his friends will be wonderful too. So we recruit them if we can.

Charles Dunstone of the Carphone Warehouse has the same approach:

Most of the people that come into our company are recruited by personal recommendation. We like our people and we think we will like their friends and associates.

INCREASE THE POOL OF AVAILABLE CANDIDATES

To ensure that a likeable candidate is selected, it is essential that a company creates as large a pool of available candidates as possible. This becomes increasingly difficult in a tight marketplace, but is relatively easy when there is widespread unemployment in the locality.

The pool can be increased by the following measures.

Ensure that pay levels (and associated conditions) are in the upper quartile of the marketplace for this particular type of job. To gain a leading competitive edge through service, a company has to be in the lead when it comes to the salaries it pays.

Pay is a reflection of emotional value. To be motivated, employees need to *feel* that their pay levels are fair and equitable.

Anton Najjar, for example, says that he is accused by other employers in Dubai of "spoiling" his people. The terms and conditions for people working at the J.W. Marriott hotel are definitely far better than those provided by most other employers for similar jobs.

Ensure in addition that the company has an excellent reputation as an employer. To deliver customer care it is essential that a company delivers staff care. How can an employee care for a customer when the company does not care for its employees? A positive reputation can be developed when a company does not exploit its employees through excessive hours of work and undue pressures, when excellent facilities are provided in terms of rest rooms, canteens and crèches and when managers are genuinely seen to care for their people. To quote Frank Pizzano from Nordstrom: "I had wanted to work for

Nordstrom for so long, my friends told me how great the company was."

Furthermore, if a company regularly indulges in a "hire and fire" approach to people, then its reputation will be damaged and the best candidates will avoid it. To enhance its reputation a company should be seen to protect its employees as far as possible. Making people redundant must be an absolute last resort.

Ensure that each employee receives effective and adequate training. Employees are attracted to companies that provide them with training and development opportunities. It enhances their sense of worth and provides a necessary stimulus for further improvement.

Lack of training invariably reflects badly through poor service and creating problems that make both employees and customers feel bad.

The availability pool can also be increased by excellent PR (public relations) as well as by word of mouth by employees, friends and people in the local community. Every opportunity needs to be seized to promote any positive news the company has. Creating job opportunities is excellent news in most places and local managers need to exploit this as far as possible.

CLARIFY ACCOUNTABILITY FOR THE SELECTION DECISION

The person who is finally accountable for making a selection must be the manager who will be accountable for the work of that person. The only thing the personnel experts are accountable for is the supply of a steady stream of first-class candidates, together with meaningful information and advice about them.

This was a lesson that was taught to me in my first management job at Mars, a chocolate manufacturer, where as a production manager you were totally accountable for the people in your team. In Mars and other progressive companies there is no way that a candidate can be imposed on a manager by other people who do the recruitment and selection.

In a number of companies that I studied in preparation for this book, the accountabilities for selection were very unclear. In one case, a company in the Middle East, recruitment and selection were undertaken by people in central personnel. The successful candidates were then assigned to one of the company's branches. The branch manager had no say in the process. Having taken no part in the selection process, he or she would have to work with the recruit.

In another company I looked at in the UK, a recruitment agency supplied people to work at the front line on a temporary six-month contract. Managers had no say about who would come in on these contracts. If these people proved themselves after six months then managers could give them permanent appointments. However, many of the complaints made by customers related to the service provided by these new people during their first six months while on temporary contracts.

CREATE A MENTAL MODEL OF THE SUCCESSFUL CANDIDATE

Before you embark on a recruitment and selection process, create a colorful and dynamic mental picture (or model) of the ideal candidate. Try to envisage them operating effectively at the front line, providing a "dream" service that customers love. The more you can create this picture and bring it into focus, the more likely you are to select the successful candidate.

The best way to develop this picture or model is to invite your existing team to produce it for you.

ELIMINATE PERSON SPECIFICATIONS AND JOB DESCRIPTIONS

Written person specifications and job descriptions are extremely limited when it comes to this process. They tend to be two-dimensional and essentially devoid of emotion as they strive for objectivity. They are frequently boring and border on being meaningless. The essential requirements of color, vibrancy, bright personality, esprit, positive emotion and energy are squeezed out of these uninspired documents. They provide little effective guidance to the type of person who will do a great job at the front line.

DO NOT RELY ON CAREER RESUMÉS

For the same reasons, typed career resumés yield relatively little useful information. I have seen thousands of written career resumés in my time and most of them leave me cold, telling me little about the person writing them. Most of them only give hard facts and there is scant indication of the person's capabilities, let alone personality.

There are exceptions. If the candidate is a skilled writer then they might be able to convey the essence of their spirit, emotions and energies on a blank sheet of paper. Even this, however, is impossible if you force an applicant to fill in an application form. Application forms constrain people and squeeze out essential information while distorting the rest.

Worst of all, you learn virtually nothing from most completed application forms about how a candidate interacts with customers.

DEVOTE A LOT OF TIME TO THE SELECTION PROCESS

Selection cannot be done in a hurry. If you rush an interview you will miss vital signals. A hurried decision is more likely to be a wrong decision than is a well-considered decision made after a lengthy and in-depth selection process. One interview can never be sufficient. Two meetings at least are required before committing to a chosen candidate.

So call the applicant back at least once more. Spend at least 45 minutes at each session. While you are with the candidate, try to imagine that you are a customer and how you might feel about this person.

The more time you spend with candidates, the more likely you are to discover things about them. If you confine the selection process to a half-hour interview, the impression you gain will only be skin deep. With subsequent meetings you will find that candidates increasingly reveal more about themselves. Do not miss the opportunity of obtaining such critical information.

Furthermore, you need time in a relaxed environment after the selection interviews to reflect on the decision to be made. With relaxation and reflection the mind frees up and allows other factors (such as how you feel) to come to the surface. Gradually the correct decision will appear to you. Retrospectively, you will be able to justify this decision with specific logic that explains your feelings.

USE A TEAM APPROACH TO SELECTION

The biggest selection mistakes are made when one person alone undertakes the interview and makes the selection decision. No matter how wise that person might be, they are always vulnerable to misjudging a candidate. A senior personnel person from Hewlett-Packard once told me that in his company they "interview people to death". Often a candidate might be subjected to interviews with nine different people, any one of whom could veto the appointment of that candidate.

It is a truism to say that "two heads are better than one", but this is definitely the case when it comes to selection.

> Two heads are better than one in the selection process

Likeable leaders always involve their existing team members in choosing candidates to join that team. A bad apple in the barrel can rot the others. Team members are therefore in the best position to judge whether a candidate has all the essential attributes for helping the team provide excellent service. If team members do not like the new recruit, you are going to have immense problems with motivation and the delivery of customer service.

PRIORITIZE YOUR SELECTION CRITERIA

When it comes to selecting people to undertake jobs at the customer front line, it is important to prioritize the criteria as follows:

FIRST PRIORITY – Personal attributes

➤ Customer-oriented approach
➤ Positive attitude
➤ Prepared to take initiatives

➤ Warm and friendly
➤ Kind and compassionate
➤ Has an inquiring mind
➤ Good listener
➤ Articulate
➤ Decisive
➤ Open, honest, trustworthy, sincere
➤ Genuinely interested in people
➤ Genuinely loves people
➤ Genuinely wants to help people
➤ High degree of emotional intelligence
➤ Reasonable degree of rational intelligence
➤ High degree of self-awareness
➤ Desperate desire to learn
➤ Energy
➤ Creative with a degree of flair
➤ Clearly articulated principles, beliefs and values
➤ Principles, beliefs and values that align with your own
➤ Bright, positive personality.

SECOND PRIORITY – Skills and knowledge

➤ Potential competency in using the systems required to undertake the job effectively (computers, tills, telephones etc.)
➤ Able to write a good letter
➤ Numerate (can do figure work efficiently)
➤ Literate (can read, assimilate and comprehend complex text quickly)
➤ Speaks a second language (if necessary)
➤ Able to acquire knowledge of the product and organization quickly
➤ Good memory (e.g. for past customers and their names)

THIRD PRIORITY – Experience

➤ Has a varied and interesting background

BE CREATIVE IN YOUR APPROACH TO RECRUITMENT AND SELECTION

One company that I looked at was opening a new store in New York. Its sole criterion for selecting people was "performance". It wanted good performers in the theatrical sense of the word, people who could make customers happy, who could entertain them as part of their total shopping experience. It even wanted people who could be a little outrageous at times.

The company discarded all the conventions of selection. It placed an advertisement in a newspaper and invited people to ring in. Many applicants thought they were ringing in to request an application form. What they did not realize was that they were being screened on the telephone. Those who made it to the next stage were observed as they entered the room. Did they talk to the other candidates? Did they sit at an empty table or next to other people? Did they offer to pour the coffee (which was on tap) for other people entering the room? How did they hand the coffee cup to the person? When they were asked to undertake some practical work (simulating the front-line job for which they were being selected), they thought that they were being tested for their proficiency in handling the simple tools and materials at their disposal in selling the products on offer. In fact, they were being assessed for the way they interacted with customers (simulated in turn by other candidates).

This company did not carry out any interviews but merely observed how groups of candidates conducted themselves during a one-hour session during which they were invited to undertake a series of tasks that approximated to the job they would have to do. The company had no preconceived ideas about the past experience of successful candidates. All it wanted was performers. It ended up by recruiting a psychiatric nurse, a traffic warden, an unemployed actress and many others with fascinating backgrounds.

The key to selection is not to get into a routine. It is essential that any recruiter avoids a mechanistic approach and thus eliminates detailed procedures in lengthy recruitment manuals.

The recruitment and selection process for each new job should be a creative challenge. Be creative in the way you advertise a job. Why not set a simple 50-word job-related task in the advertisement and invite people to write in with the answers? You can then take it from there.

Be creative in choosing the type of people you wish to invite to help you with selection. Have you ever thought about asking your customers to take part?

Be creative in designing the techniques you will use for the selection process. Have you ever thought about visiting a candidate at home to undertake an interview? (Ideally, an employee should treat your premises as their home, giving a warm welcome to any visitor who comes in the front door.)

TREAT ALL CANDIDATES AS HUMAN BEINGS AS WELL AS POTENTIAL CUSTOMERS

When I was appointed director of personnel at British Caledonian Airways, one of the first things to hit me was a series of written complaints in my in-tray from people who had applied for jobs but not received replies over a period of months.

The airline business is a "glamor" business and attracts many thousand unsolicited applications from people who want to fly around the world as cabin crew.

When I visited our recruitment section at British Caledonian, I was staggered to find that we had a backlog of over 4000 unsolicited applications to which we had not replied. Our team there was just overwhelmed and as a matter of routine only contacted the applicants who had been screened and selected for first interview. The rest, the large majority of unsolicited applications, were ignored.

Our recruitment team had failed to realize that each applicant was a human being and a potential customer. Instead, the recruiters just saw another piece of paper, a job application, which had to wait for eventual processing (if ever). Our challenge as managers was to get the recruitment team to see applicants as real people and even potential customers and thus treat them with the care and deference they deserved.

A company that really puts itself out for applicants is TNT (UK). Every single person who applies for a job is given an interview. Managing director Alan Jones feels this is the least the company can do.

Over the last few years I have been regaled with stories of people who have applied for jobs and not received a reply and of people who have attended for interview and not been informed of a decision (from which they easily deduced they had not been offered the job).

What customers like about you is that you treat them as human beings. The word "customer" is a mere label. You cannot differentiate between human beings. They should all be treated equally whether they are customers or job applicants.

RELY ON YOUR INTUITION (GUT FEEL) NOT LOGIC

It is essential that you collect as many relevant facts as possible about the people you are considering selecting, together with opinions of that person from other people. The more information you have about the person in relation to the job vacancy, the better placed you will be to make a considered decision. However, that decision must still take into account your feelings (gut feel) about this person. It must take into account whether or not you genuinely like them. Failure to do so will lead to immense relationship problems in the future.

Therefore you should not simply rely on objective selection criteria as a basis for making your final choice. It is a delusion that you can evaluate a person by solely using quantitative scores, numerical weightings, analytical ratings and objective rationales. Psychometric and aptitude tests, while yielding helpful information, have their limits in the selection process.

No matter how much objectivity and rationality you attempt to inject into the selection process, your ultimate decision will always be subjective. You will always choose the candidate who "feels right". You will then subsequently attempt to justify your selection decision using the objective data and rational analyses you have at hand. In other words, your rational mind will attempt to provide an objective reason for your subjective, intuitive feelings about a chosen candidate.

Remember the basic binary code of behavioral choice: people move towards what makes them feel good and away from what makes them feel bad. This definitely applies to selection. You will not appoint a candidate who makes you feel bad (whatever the reason).

The objective data you gather about a person will always be too simplistic and too limited. It will always tell you only part of the story. Everyone has a complex psychology and as a result a unique set of behaviors. Everyone thinks differently and has a different way of doing things. The minutiae of this are rarely detected by mechanical selection processes. Yet it is this minutiae that have a substantial impact on the relationship with a customer. For example, the way a person shakes hands, or speaks, or what they do with their eyes will have a substantial effect on a relationship. But these fine points of behavior go undetected in the relatively clumsy formal selection procedures that are available.

Intuitively you will be sensitive to the details of this behavior, often without realizing it. Deeply embedded in your subconscious is a software program that senses the character and capability of another person and relates them to your past experience of successful and unsuccessful people. It is, of course, important that as far as possible you raise this program to a conscious level to develop a rationale for your assessment. However, this rationale is limited to those facts you can consciously acquire. These facts themselves are subject to interpretation based on subconscious prejudices. Other key attributes will escape this conscious process, even though they will be detected by your "sixth sense" and relayed to your subconscious.

Therefore, what you must do when approaching a selection decision is to assess all the available facts and then allow your subconscious, intuitive mind to take over. Both your emotional and rational intelligence will come to the fore at this point as you analyze your own feelings about each candidate together with the assembled facts.

There is a great deal of evidence that the application of logic is severely limited in attempts to resolve intractable problems. Resolution always comes when someone applies a high degree of intuition (a combination of emotional and rational intelligence) to a problem. The same applies to a selection decision. When two or more candidates appear to be "equal on paper", you must use your intuition to guide you. Your heart is there for that very purpose.

MOVE FAST TO APPOINT THE CHOSEN CANDIDATE

As soon as you have made a selection decision, move fast to appoint the person, treating them like your best customer. You must remember that the best candidates have the best choice of who they should be employed with. You cannot take it for granted that an excellent candidate will automatically accept your offer.

When you like a candidate and wish to offer them a job, it is important that you demonstrate this and impress on them how much you want them to join your team.

The best way is to ring the chosen candidate at home during the evening immediately after the final interview. Demonstrate your enthusiasm and excitement about having this person come on board. Demonstrate your relief at having found such a high-caliber person to contribute to the excellent service that you aim to provide all your customers. Indicate that you will be making an offer that you hope they cannot refuse. You must make the person feel wanted. You must make them feel that they are of exceptionally high value to you and your team and therefore worth employing. In other words, it is critically important that you inject a high degree of emotion (added emotional value) into communicating your decision to the chosen candidate.

What you must *not* do is merely inform your personnel people of your decision and leave it to them to communicate with the chosen candidate. All they will do is write a standard letter that might take days to arrive. Such standard letters are a complete turn-off and can undermine all the hard work you have put in.

GIVE LITTLE WEIGHT TO REFERENCES

Everyone plays the reference game. We all know people we can use as referees and who will write good things about us. We all know that it is only in the most extreme circumstances that a previous boss will put into writing anything bad about a person.

References have one useful purpose – to corroborate facts. There are one or two deceitful people around who deliberately misstate facts on their applications, for example that they received a degree at the University of California in 1995 or that they were employed with XYZ Co between 1991 and 1994. All critical facts on an application should therefore be corroborated by way of written references.

However, references are of relatively little value when it comes to eliciting opinions on a candidate's character and capability. If there is an element of doubt, pick up the phone and ring the candidate's previous boss but one (you cannot ring the current boss if the person has yet to resign). Have a quiet word with a previous employer and tease out on the phone what the boss really thought about the candidate.

In relatively small industries, a network of executives and personnel professionals will already exist and be quite powerful. Use these contacts to elicit opinion and give it the weight it deserves (in your opinion!).

SUMMARY

To deliver the service customers really like, it is essential that you put an immense amount of time, energy and emotion into the recruitment and selection process. Objective selection criteria are very limited in helping you with this. To ensure the best possible appointment it is essential to use your intuition.

PRACTICAL STEPS

1 Be subjective in making selection decisions.
2 Increase the pool of available candidates.
3 Clarify accountability for the selection decision.
4 Create a mental model of the successful candidate.
5 Eliminate person specifications and job descriptions.
6 Do not rely on career resumés.
7 Devote a lot of time to the selection process.
8 Use a team approach to selection.
9 Prioritize your selection criteria.
10 Be creative in your approach to recruitment and selection.
11 Treat all candidates as human beings as well as potential customers.
12 Rely on your intuition not your logic.
13 Move fast to appoint the chosen candidate.
14 Give little weight to references.

13

TRAINING PEOPLE

TO BE LIKED BY

YOUR CUSTOMERS

T RAINING IS USELESS WITHOUT LEARNING. THE KEY TO IMPROVING relations with customers is to help front-line people learn what their customers really like. This requires helping them learn about themselves, about their own genuine likes and dislikes regarding customers as well as themselves.

Most customer-related training avoids this delicate but critical area. It concentrates on technique or attempts exhortation, but ignores the added emotional value of liking.

There is a delusion that through training you can identify and apply a few simple, practical steps that will lead to success in your relationships with customers. People are desperate for such practical techniques (rationales developed through a scientific approach to management). For example, they want to know the three easy steps for improving their telephone manner, or the four actions necessary for effective cold calling, or the five stages for closing a sale, or the seven keys to dealing with difficult customers. We seem to think that just beyond our reach is a simple technique for everything.

The gurus propagate this myth, churning out books and seminars offering quick-fix solutions and short-cuts to success. Regrettably, it is all a delusion. There is no short-cut to success. There is no simple technique for pleasing customers. And there is no one-, two- or three-day customer service training course that will give you all the answers.

Exacerbating the problem is an assumption frequently made by senior managers that out there in the organization are hordes of people who are not committed to customer service, who are not aware of the importance of it, who need to develop positive attitudes towards customers. Training programs are therefore set up to exhort people to provide better service. It is as if senior executives suddenly discover the importance of customers and therefore decide to convert all the non-believers in the organization who had previously neglected customers.

So people attend the training programs to be brainwashed in what they already know and to learn techniques they have been aware of for years (such as smiling at customers and giving them a warm welcome).

Many of these training programs are superficial and offer standard fare. The obvious is presented as a new fundamental truth, whereas it has been apparent to participants for as long as they can remember. They sit politely and lap it up – it is after all a pleasant diversion to sit in a classroom for a day or two, away from the rigors of dealing with irate and difficult customers.

THE CUSTOMER SERVICE TRAINING CHALLENGE

Everyone knows how important customer service is. Everyone thinks that they know what constitutes good service (smile at a customer, help them wherever possible, provide a warm welcome, be efficient and pleasant etc.). I have yet to meet anyone who tells me otherwise, and I have met a large number of front-line people as well as managers on my travels through 19 different countries during the last two years.

The training challenge is simple. What people say they do, they do not always do. What people know, they do not always apply.

The fundamentals of customer service are simple and could be taught to a five-year-old. Anyone can understand them and no one can fail to agree with them, let alone commit to them.

They are as simple as saying: "Smoking damages your health" or "Regular exercise keeps you healthy and fit" or "To lose weight eat less fat and sugar". Everybody knows and understands these. To live longer all we need to do is stop smoking, take regular exercise and eat less fat and sugar. Individually we will thrive as a result and our countries' economies will improve dramatically as we spend less on medical care (although there would be less tax from tobacco to pay for all this).

Isn't it amazing, therefore, that despite this simple logic, more people are dying of cancer, stress-related diseases and obesity-related illnesses?

The fundamentals of customer service taught on training programs are equally as simple. They simply say: "Excellent customer service generates more customers and therefore more profit" and "Excellent customer service is when you are nice to customers and go out of your way to help them". All you have to do is smile at customers, do more things to please them and profits will go up.

Isn't it amazing, therefore, that despite this simple logic, the public's level of satisfaction with the service provided to them is going down?

What is simple on the surface is in fact incredibly complex below. The reality is that we are dealing with perceptions, feelings, self-awareness, interpretations, expectations and a wide range of other complex psychological factors that are rarely addressed through the techniques and exhortations that set the agenda for many training programs.

> Little learning takes place on most customer service training programs

When the obvious truth is presented on a training program, people have little to learn and, as a result, little learning takes place. To tell someone it is necessary to smile at a customer is to tell them an obvious truth. The less obvious truth is that many participants do not smile at customers and furthermore are unaware of this. They actually think that they do smile, that they are friendly, that they do go out of their way to help. All they know is that it is those other people over there who do not do it, who are in need of training. What they do not know is that their customers think otherwise, that their customers do not see them smiling, nor being friendly, nor going out of their way to help them.

THE TRAINING DELUSION

We live with our delusions – our delusions that we are perfect, that we are always right, that our way is best, that it is all those other people who do it wrong, who are irrational and badly behaved. We are reluctant to admit certain unpalatable truths about ourselves and thus mount complex defense mechanisms to protect us from the pain of revelation.

We just will not admit that we are deficient in our approach to customer service. We'll absorb all the propaganda and go along with it in the classroom, but outside we will continue with our current ways because that is how we do it, and if that is how we do it we must be right. We'll learn all about the latest techniques in the classroom, but outside we will continue with our own techniques because we know they work – and what was being taught in the classroom was purely theoretical and delivered by a trainer who has no practical experience of the real thing.

FUNDAMENTALS OF CUSTOMER SERVICE TRAINING

There are two fundamental aspects of customer service in which staff require training: systems and psychology.

To improve customer service, it is essential for companies to develop systems that are more efficient and thus more effective in delivering the core service to customers. Training is essential to give people the skills to use these new systems. They might be new computer systems, new telephone systems, new delivery systems or new order-taking systems.

To train people to use new customer service systems is relatively easy. To train them in the *psychology* of customer service is much more difficult because we are dealing with people's innermost feelings and trying to modify them so that they feel good about the customer and the customer feels good about them.

It is an incredible challenge to teach a person to like a customer as well as develop the necessary attributes to be liked by a customer. To do so you have to teach people how to manage their feelings and emotions; you have to teach them to re-examine some fundamental principles relating to integrity, openness, honesty and trust; you have to teach them to be creative when many of them do not believe that they are creative. Effectively, you have to teach them to develop and apply their emotional intelligence when their whole background has been to suppress it in favor of the application of rational intelligence.

> To train people in new customer service systems is easy – to train them in the psychology of customer service is much more difficult

There are no easy steps for this. A smile is meaningless unless it is genuinely intended. It is therefore pointless teaching someone to smile at customers unless that person can reach deep down inside themselves to determine the real, genuine reason why they should smile.

Americans have a habit of saying "Have a nice day". The danger is that the phrase becomes meaningless if it is merely the result of an automatic habit or the application of action item number 36 from the training manual. "Have a nice day" only becomes meaningful when speakers actually mean it, when they genuinely want the customer to have a nice day.

Throwaway remarks have little meaning and therefore little value. Added emotional value can never be generated through programmed behavior.

INSPIRATION IN CUSTOMER SERVICE TRAINING

The key to such teaching is inspiration. The best teachers inspire their pupils to want to learn. The best teachers break open the mental boxes within which people think and demonstrate to them the exciting possibilities beyond the boundaries of these boxes. The best teachers enable people to move beyond their comfort zones into a exhilarating world full of creative new opportunities. The best teachers demonstrate that beyond the roads of everyday routine is a rich reservoir of immensely satisfying wisdom that anyone can acquire.

A smile is but a surface reflection of the complex psychological makeup of any one individual. There are a thousand different types of smile – false, contrived, warm, wry, inviting, rejecting, welcoming, dismissive, compassionate, cold, threatening and understanding.

To instruct a front-line person in a classroom to smile is equivalent to instructing them to breathe. But there are many different ways of breathing, some more effective than others. There is deep breathing for relaxation, there is sighing, there is snorting, there is the type of breathing that opera singers must master.

To smile effectively you must know yourself well and know why you are smiling. When the smile becomes genuine it conveys a message that you want to convey to a customer. When the smile is false it is a mere façade hiding what you really think.

The key to customer service training therefore is to spark an interest in participants to learn more about themselves and how they relate to customers. It means encouraging them to hold up a mirror to themselves and see themselves for what they are, and more importantly how customers might see them.

Unless there is a high degree of trust, it is too dangerous to get other members of the class to pass comment on how they see each individual. The pain of revelation can be too shattering. The safest course is to spark individuals to look at themselves without the fear of exposure to others.

BENCHMARKS IN CUSTOMER SERVICE TRAINING

One way of doing this is to encourage comparison. By providing benchmarks, either in the classroom or elsewhere, individuals are able to see the best and the worst and compare themselves with this. They will see John Cleese shouting at guests in his hotel and say to themselves: "Am I like this?" They will examine the case studies presented to them and relate themselves to the examples provided. They will come across instances that spark their interest and trigger a learning process motivated by a simple thought: "Perhaps I could be like that" (good example) or "I hope I'm not like that" (bad example).

Such training need not be confined to the classroom. Learning is an ongoing process that can take place during regular team meetings or even during daily work activities.

Two companies I looked at actively encourage their people to get out and about to observe excellent customer service elsewhere. For example, WPA in Taunton, UK, will from time to time send front-line people off site for an hour or two to experience the customer service in other local establishments. They come back and report on their experiences and compare themselves with it. In this way they learn what is good and what is bad and compare themselves with it.

Nando's in South Africa believes that its front-line people will be unable to deliver outstanding customer service unless they have some experience of what it is. So it too sends it people out to search for this elsewhere.

Once you find excellent customer service you know it. You know it is different from the mediocre service you normally experience. Having found it, having experienced it, you can relate it to your own performance and ask yourself the question: "Why not me?" and "What do I have to do to deliver such excellent service?"

STUDY TOURS

At management level there are always a variety of ways of learning about improving customer service. Quite a few business schools arrange "study tours" where executives are taken on a one- or two-week tour of organizations that provide exceptional service. While they can be helpful, these study tours can prove exceptionally expensive. My advice to clients is to arrange their own – it is much more cost effective. Instead of spending $20,000 on a business school study tour for an individual, why not give that executive $4000 to go off for a week on their own study tour, to seek out the best in a certain country or locality?

The great thing about learning about different companies' approaches to dealing with customers is that you can experience them and learn from them every day of the week. Every time we make a business call, every time we write to a company, every time we venture out of our homes to go shopping or visit a restaurant, we will encounter a customer service situation and can benefit from our experience. We are steeped every day in learning opportunities about customer service.

THE MOTIVATION TO LEARN

The key is that each one of us must *want* to learn. Because of the dependency culture that exists in many organizations, there is a mindset that associates learning with classroom training only. People in these organizations expect to receive training on a plate and to be spoon-fed with learning.

I am forever surprised in the seminars I run around the world how few people are desperate to improve themselves. They attend training seminars because their bosses tell them to. Relatively few of them have inquiring minds and the tendency is not to ask questions. Few of them study books, or journals, or go out of their way (beyond the classroom) to learn more about the subject at hand. They tend to see training as something external to themselves, something their employer wants of them to help them improve in their jobs. So they acquiesce to the training and sit through days of it, deploying minimal energy to soak up the available lessons.

Learning is an active process that requires an immense amount of discipline and hard work

I am a student of success. I love successful organizations and successful people. One of the key traits of successful people is their desperate desire for continuous improvement. Successful people are avid students of life. They study books, read journals and search out and grill the experts to milk them of their experience and knowledge. They have a continual thirst for learning. They are hungry for new insights into their chosen profession. They work hard at improvement, knowing that their learning will set them apart from the competition and give them a leading edge.

These people have learnt that learning is not a passive activity where you sit in a classroom and soak it all up. It is an active process that requires an immense amount of discipline and hard work as you practice and practice the lessons acquired from all around. You cannot learn a language by sitting in a classroom for two days. Learning a language requires not only classroom lessons, but tuition and a grueling schedule of practice. Customer service and relationships are no different. Customer service is language requiring not only classroom lessons, but also tuition and an extensive amount of practice. To improve at a language you have to be incredibly motivated and determined. The same applies to customer service.

To improve at customer service you have to examine your every move, question your every thought, become aware of every single feeling and challenge yourself continually to develop an even more effective approach. Without such a challenge we slip back into the comforts of routine and potentially bad habits. We forget to say "thank you", we forget to call customers by their names, we forget to smile, we make excuses, become defensive, avoid difficult customers and generally drift towards low-energy, non-threatening activities. Customer service is hard work and so is learning about customer service.

THE NEED FOR CHALLENGE

The best teachers of customer service recognize this and challenge their students to examine their own approach. They inspire people to find new ways, to identify improvements and to be creative with every single transaction. They provide helpful feedback using a high degree of constructive honesty. The best teachers have their students' interests at heart. They want them to succeed and to help them seek out ways of succeeding.

Parroting a training manual can never accomplish this. Too many trainers become clones of the person who designed the training package. Mechanistically they plough through the training manual without questioning its efficacy. Their *raison d'être* is to apply a training methodology encapsulated in the prescribed training material, rather than starting from where students are and working from their needs.

THE NEED FOR FLEXIBILITY

Training and learning require a high degree of flexibility as opposed to a rigid format that can be purchased off the shelf.

To ensure that the learning takes place, a trainer must spark people's thinking about what they do and how to identify ways of improving this. They must then go off and practice until they are virtually perfect in this new approach. To get people to think what they do they have to become aware of the deep-seated reasons for doing it their current way. This requires a high degree of self-awareness about one's own deep-seated thoughts and feelings, as well as a high degree of awareness of both the organization's and the customer's requirements.

Furthermore, a trainer must help students dig deep to discover the basis of their core motivations in terms of energy, emotion and esprit. Unmotivated students will not learn. They might pretend to learn in a classroom, but unless there is genuine motivation no real learning will take place and there will be no improvement in practice.

The trainer must motivate participants to answer for themselves questions such as: "Why should I, a front-line person, improve my approach to customer service? What is in it for me? Why should I bother to do more for customers?"

THE ALL-IMPORTANT PHILOSOPHICAL FOUNDATION

These are deeply philosophical questions, the answers to which underpin the essential psychology of customer service. An employee's attitude will reflect their own values, which in turn are based on their philosophy of life (whether or not it is articulated as such).

To improve customer service, to become liked by customers, an individual must develop a high degree of self-awareness, not only about their own feelings and thoughts but also about what they stand for as an individual.

The successful teacher will challenge the students' core philosophy to discover why they want to learn more about the subject. It is totally unacceptable to reply: "Because my boss told me I must attend this course."

Customer service is all about serving people, it is all about giving something special to other people. Without that recognition and desire to do so, little learning will take place and customer service training will become ineffective. Giving is the basis of love. We need to learn to love!

The successful teacher will excite students about the immense satisfactions to be gained from pleasing other people, from giving yourself to others, from putting other people's interests before your own and from loving people. These core principles are at the center of most religions, yet are denied in the selfish pursuit of everyday pleasures.

Customer service training can be a precious voyage of self-discovery, during which we are jolted out of our comfortable mental boxes of everyday routine to become aware of the great opportunities for further personal satisfaction through pleasing others. A manual can never achieve this, but an inspired teacher can.

> Customer service training can be a precious voyage of self-discovery

At times we all lose sight of what we are about, we cannot see the wood for the trees, we become trapped in our own minds. We all need the opportunity to see things differently, to learn of better ways. Effective training can provide the answer by offering learning opportunities.

I offer no prescription for a customer service training program other than a set of questions and challenges that each student of customer service must answer for themselves.

Sean, a customer service agent with BT Mobile, told me an interesting story. When he joined the team, Richard Brimble told him: "You have nothing to do for the next three weeks except learn about how we operate. Now off you go!" Sean was given no structured training, no material to read. He was left completely to his own devices. So he wandered around and chatted to people. He sat by them, watched them work, asked them questions. He learnt about the systems and the methods they used. But the most important thing he learnt was that everyone in the team really put themselves out to help him.

SUMMARY

Customer serving training is all about learning about oneself, about rediscovering and reapplying one's own basic philosophy of human relationships, as well as about our own essential psychology. Conventional customer service training will only state the obvious and prescribe superficial answers to what are in fact complex issues.

PRACTICAL STEPS

1 What did you learn from the last customer service training course you attended?
2 What did you learn about yourself and how you relate to customers?
3 When did you last consciously seek to learn something about customer service beyond the boundaries of the classroom?
4 Take an hour off work today and go and learn something about customer service. Seek out the best customer service in your locality and learn from it.
5 Write down on a piece of paper what you are all about as a person.
6 Write down on a piece of paper your innermost feelings about customers and the people you work with.
7 Seek out the most inspirational customer service trainer around and invite him or her to run a one- or two-day session for you and your team.
8 Start getting into the habit of reading books and journals to learn about how other people and other organizations go about making improvements.
9 Run a customer service training seminar for your own team and see how much you learn.
10 Get your team to run some customer service training sessions and see how much they learn.

14

DEALING WITH CUSTOMERS YOU DISLIKE

I CAN PREDICT ONE THING. WHEN I INVITE MY AUDIENCES TO highlight issues that trouble them, they will invariably mention "dealing with difficult customers".

It seems that many people at the front line are plagued by difficult customers – customers who shout, give abuse, are potentially violent, are unreasonable, are offensive, swear, are demanding and are nigh on impossible.

The instinctive reaction is to dislike these people. Nobody denies that they exist, in fact go into a front-line environment and you will soon come across examples of these so-called difficult customers.

HOW CAN YOU LIKE DIFFICULT CUSTOMERS?

The challenge frequently put to me when I assert that it is essential that you like customers is that it is impossible to like everyone, especially difficult customers.

The real question is: "Who assigns the 'difficult' label?" The answer is that it is rarely the "difficult" customer. The solution is to change the label or, to be exact, to change the way you see these people. Instead of seeing them as difficult, try to see them as human beings who, like everyone else, want to be liked.

Very few people set out to be difficult

With one or two rare exceptions (I'll come on to these later), very few people set out to be difficult. They appear to be difficult because of the difficulties they encounter in the world. These so-called difficult people are not that much different from you and me, in that they want to feel good about the things they do in their everyday life. They become difficult because they are frequently frustrated in their pursuit of feeling good and therefore they feel bad.

Their frustration often arises because of different opinions about what constitutes reasonable conduct. We are all in danger of making the gross and erroneous assumption that our way is right and that those who do not conform to it are wrong. Therefore customers who do not conform to our requirements we perceive to be "difficult". We generate routines to handle customers and expect our customers to comply with these routines. We therefore tend to dislike customers who object to the routines we have devised for them.

Thus a customer who complains that nobody served him when it was obvious that all the front-line staff were busy is described as difficult. A customer who asks for non-standard items is perceived as difficult. A customer who frequently draws the manager's attention to minor variances or discrepancies in the company's approach is seen as difficult. A regular customer who was upgraded last time, is refused it this time and now complains is called difficult.

There is plenty of evidence that those customers who shout loudest achieve most. It often pays to be difficult. Front-line employees and their supervisors will tend to make concessions in the face of customers' extreme demands – just in order to obtain some peace and quiet.

THE FRONT-LINE EMPLOYEE WHO NEVER HAD A DIFFICULT CUSTOMER

Two years ago I was running a seminar in the USA and the debate inevitably got round, once again, to how to handle difficult customers. A number of participants related some vivid anecdotes about problems that they had faced with customers. Suddenly one young woman, Natasha Keal, put up her hand and waited patiently to be invited to speak.

"I find this very strange," she said quietly. "I can't recall the last time I had a difficult customer. All my customers are very nice to me and I never have a problem with them."

Natasha smiled as she spoke. She had a soft, warm voice with a trace of an Irish accent. I invited her to explain why this could be so. Why was it that all her colleagues in other branches seemed to have problems while she did not?

"I just treat my customers like friends," she explained, "all of them. If I get a mother coming in stressed out with a screaming baby in a buggy, I do my best to help. If I get an old lady coming in grumbling about our charges, then I listen to her, explain as best I can and try to be nice to her. If I get some bum coming in drunk then I'll crack a joke, process the transaction quickly and guide him quietly out the door before he annoys other customers."

I talked to Natasha at the break. "I love my job, I love my customers," she told me. "It would be boring if they were all the same. If they have a problem I think: 'Great – I'm set up with up a real challenge now – this is what it's all about.' I don't make it personal with them and they don't make it personal with me. I tell them: 'You gotta problem then you bring it here, I'll do my damnest to fix for you.' I don't hold it against them if they don't smile, if they complain, if they're angry. I try to get to understand and to help. That's what it's all about."

> If my customers have a problem I think: "Great, I'm set up with a real challenge now!"

Natasha was a lovely woman, who liked everybody and whom everyone would like. She took an interest in everything and had a totally positive outlook on life. Later, over lunch, she told me the story of her life, of how her father had been killed in Vietnam, how her mother had died of cancer five years previously, how she had been scalded with hot oil when she was three (she still had the scars), how her first husband had gotten in debt, become an alcoholic and regularly beaten her up. She was now very happily married second time around with two young sons aspiring to become baseball stars.

"I learn from life, that's my school," she told me. "I learnt that most people make things difficult for themselves. So I make it easy for myself by making it easy for my family and my customers. We're all humans, aren't we? I guess I feel bad at times but then I tell myself it could be much worse. That way I make myself feel better. I really look forward to coming into work every morning. I just can't wait to see my customers. Some are regulars and some are new but they're all great people. That's the secret. You gotta discover what's great about them. Once you recognize it they'll love you!"

EMPLOYEES WITH DIFFICULTIES

The more I spoke to Natasha and the more I studied this subject, the more I began to realize that those front-line employees who complain about difficult customers in fact have difficulties with themselves. The same applies to those managers who complain about difficult employees.

When an employee complains about a difficult customer, what they are really saying is: "I personally have a difficulty with handling this type of customer."

Therefore the key is to look at yourself rather than at the customer, to raise to the subconscious those fears that cause a negative reaction when a certain person (a customer) behaves in a way that we ascribe as difficult.

The question is: "What is my difficulty with this customer?" as opposed to: "What is it that makes this customer difficult?"

As soon as these fears can be identified, it is relatively easy to address them. It is our own suppressed fears that create the difficulties.

A few years ago I was traveling in a train from London to Leeds. I was lucky enough to have four seats and a table to myself. I had spread my files out on the table and was enjoying a coffee while I worked at my papers. Suddenly two uniformed conductors crossed paths in the aisle by my table. I overheard one tell the other: "We have a problem, there is a passenger down the back who is going berserk. He's jumping up and down and shouting at everyone."

My initial reaction was one of relief, that the passenger was not in my carriage and therefore it was not my problem.

Two minutes later a man swaggered along the aisle and sat down opposite me. He seemed drunk but did not smell of alcohol. He stared at me with wide eyes. His demeanor was threatening and totally unpredictable. My first instinct was to get up and walk away, but then I realized that there were some older people sitting nearby and this man might descend on them.

This was the man who had allegedly gone berserk in another carriage. He was now sitting opposite me and smoking, although we were in a non-smoking compartment. He stared at me and then stubbed his cigarette end out in my empty coffee cup. He picked up one of my documents and pretended to study it. His manner was aggressive and for a minute or two I was not sure what to do. Suddenly he began talking to me.

"Where you going?" he demanded, eyeing me angrily.

"Leeds," I replied politely.

"What you doing there?" he asked, almost shouting.

"I'm on business," I told him.

He hammered the table and shook his fist at me. "How dare you talk to me like that!"

"Excuse me?" I asked coolly. "What did I say?"

"How dare you tell me to mind my own business!"

I explained to him what I planned to do in Leeds. I decided to set my papers aside, forget about my own selfish interests and take a total interest in this man. I got him talking about himself. Apparently he was going to Doncaster, where he told me he lived in a giant red palace and he was having a wonderful party that night. "Lots of beautiful girls," he whispered to me. "You should come along. Just mention my name."

This person lived in some sort of fantasy world. For the rest of the journey I encouraged him to talk. Much of what he said was not coherent and made no sense. But he had calmed down – much to the relief of the other passengers and the conductors on the train. At Don-caster he held up the train while he searched for his case that he had left in some other carriage, but he couldn't remember which one.

I learnt a lot from that situation. When people appear difficult, take a genuine interest in them. Treat them equally, with respect, and try to get inside their thinking and understand their feelings.

Wendy Tan from the Prudential Bank in the UK says:

> The only place that problems exist is in our minds. We can solve problems by changing our thinking. A disabled person only has a problem if he *thinks* he has and we think he has.

We all have limitations, but limitations are not the same as problems and difficulties unless we think they are.

PEOPLE WHO FEEL REJECTED

Many people feel rejected by the society in which they live. They have no one who will take an interest in them. These people do not feel valued and feel that they have little, if anything, to offer. So instinctively, as a defense mechanism, they develop antisocial behaviors to protect the remaining vestiges of their self-esteem. They delude themselves that threatening words, aggressive behavior, occasional violence, even going berserk, will create for them a mode of respect among those whom they perceive as rejecting them.

While the secret is to take an interest in these people, many front-line people resist this as they feel it poses a risk for them. They do not want to form relationships with people who exhibit deviant behaviors. There-fore they avoid these difficult people, they look the other way or mini-mize their contact with them. These reactions are often subconscious, but even so are sufficient for the so-called difficult customer to sense rejection. Because they feel rejected, their deviant behaviors are rein-forced and repeated as a form of protection against further rejection.

Natasha Keal had learnt that by befriending a person they are less likely to harm you than if you reject them. This is the paradox. We steer clear of people whom we do not like and whom we fear, but in doing so, we put them in a position where they are more likely to cause us trouble than if we had taken an interest in them and tried to build some form of relationship with them.

PERSONAL GOALS AND INTERESTS

We all have personal goals. Difficult customers are those people who get in the way of us accomplishing these goals. These goals are applications of our own selfish interests, whether it be striving for a quiet life, the next coffee break or a chat with our friends. It could be getting away punctually when the branch shuts or avoiding getting into trouble with our bosses. These goals and interests frequently go unarticulated and become part of our innate, day-to-day driving

> **Dealing with difficult customers is all to do with your state of mind**

forces. Many of them can be exceptionally positive (as in the case of Natasha Keal). However, there is always a danger that we drift towards low-energy routines in which our goals and interests become self-centered and focused away from the people we should be aiming to serve.

If our goals and interests are to help customers, then their problems become our problems, their difficulties become our difficulties, their solutions become our solutions. We need to discipline our mind (and our subconscious) not to label a customer as a difficult because they have a difficulty. The secret is to see this person as someone in need of help whose difficulty we can help resolve. By describing the customer as "difficult" we are in great danger of rejecting that person rather than resolving the difficulty.

Dealing with difficult customers is all to do with your state of mind. The mental discipline that we need to get into is therefore as follows:

➤ Stop seeing specific customers as difficult and begin seeing them as human beings who have difficulties with which we can help.
➤ Learn to accept that every human being has a different way of expressing themselves as well as behaving.
➤ Concentrate on helping the person overcome the problem rather than on that person's negative personal attributes.

➤ In doing so, try to identify the positive attributes of that person and reflect these positives back to them ("While I'm really sorry you've experienced all this hassle, I must say that you were absolutely right in bringing it to our attention. The points you make about our shortfalls are very important and will help us a lot when we're looking at ways of improving our service.")

➤ Try to examine the difficulty from the customer's viewpoint. Try to identify the rationale on which they are raising this problem, as well as to understand the feelings that have been generated as a result.

➤ In dealing with customers who have difficulties, avoid trying to persuade them of the correctness of your own (or your company's) viewpoint. This might cause further conflict. Instead, try to empathize by displaying emotions that connect with the customer's (for example, compassion, kindness, frustration etc.) The key is to avoid attempting to convince the customer that they were wrong, that they did not understand, but to help the customer develop a set of positive feelings about the way you are going to address their difficulty. The company's position is unimportant in the customer's eyes. What is much more important is to resolve the problem.

➤ Eliminate any negative feelings you might have towards the customer. Discipline yourself to find as much as you can that you like about customers with difficulties. The more you find, the more capable you will be of resolving the difficulty.

➤ See difficulties and problems as welcome challenges that you will really enjoy resolving. Develop an attitude of mind whereby you think: "The bigger the problem the customer puts in front of me, the better it is."

➤ Always remember that all customers are human beings. They all want to be liked, to be respected, to be valued, to have people take an interest in them. Many customers cover this up with a set of surface behaviors that others find difficult. Your challenge is to get under the surface and discover each customer for what he or she really is.

VALUE JUDGEMENTS

What you must avoid doing in dealing with difficult customers is making value judgements about them as people. Any hint of disapproval on your part will exacerbate the problem. Any suggestion that the customer might be wrong will risk provoking another outburst. It is critical when dealing with difficult customers that you demonstrate that you have respect for them, that their opinion is valued, that their point of view is worthy of consideration.

Often customers who are difficult are those who struggle to express themselves, to articulate their feelings. You can help here if necessary by trying to paraphrase what they say. In this way you will come across as understanding and they will feel valued as a result.

Of course, there is an exception to the discipline of not making value judgements about customers. There will be rare occasions when a customer's language is so foul and their behavior so abusive that you have to draw the line between tolerance and intolerance. There will always come a point when you say to yourself: "Enough is enough, I have to put my foot down now." When that point is reached, you have to speak in a firm and fair way to tell the customer that their behavior, despite the frustrations of their case, is not acceptable and that you cannot proceed with helping them resolve their problem if they continue this way. It normally works!

DEALING WITH UNREASONABLE CUSTOMERS

Now for the bad news! A difficult customer is not always synonymous with an unreasonable customer. As mentioned above, it is possible to develop a mindset where you begin to see a difficult customer as a customer with difficulties. However, no matter how hard you try to be understanding and empathic, no matter how hard you try to overcome a customer's difficulties, there will always be an extremely small minority of customers (say one in a thousand) who are totally unreasonable with their demands on you and your organization.

These are either customers who have developed expectations that are way beyond your capability of meeting, or customers who are plainly "trying it on" to extort as much out of your organization as possible. The world is far from perfect and regrettably we have to accept that rogues do exist – even among your customers!

The skill at the front line is to differentiate between customers with genuine difficulties and those who deliberately set out to create difficulties in order to further their own cause.

Those with genuine difficulties are often unable to cope with their difficulties and therefore behave in a difficult way. They become aggressive, bad tempered, irritable and appear to be unreasonable.

Those who create difficulties often appear to be more rational, having contrived a logic to place excessive demands on the organization. The logic frequently goes like this:

➤ "You failed me, now you owe me the earth."
➤ "My vacation was spoiled because there was no sea view as promised and we were a long way from the beach, while the brochure said it was a short distance. I therefore want full recompense."
➤ "You sold me a quarter-page advertisement. What you didn't tell me was that it would be located in the worst possible position in the magazine where no one would see it. Therefore I want my money back."
➤ "You promised me delivery yesterday, it still hasn't arrived. If I don't receive it by 5 o'clock tomorrow, I will be suing your company for the lost business I have incurred."
➤ "My new computer crashed within two days of installation and it took a further two days for your engineer to come and fix it. This has cost my company thousands in lost orders. I demand compensation for this."

WHEN TO SAY "NO"

The harsh reality of life is that there is a finite limit to what you can do to please a customer. There is a fine line in judging whether a customer's demands are genuine or contrived. Ideally, you can extend as much goodwill to a customer as possible, but in practice the art of the possible requires a well-defined boundary beyond which a creative resolution should not stray.

Most companies define and confine their boundaries through excessive regulation and policy. Front-line employees find themselves severely restricted in their room for maneuver to satisfy a customer's extraordinary demands. Policies are laid down and employees are expected to comply with them strictly, even if their application appears unreasonable. Poor customer service and alienation of customers inevitably result.

The more progressive companies allow their front-line employees to define their own boundaries. TNT, for example, allows front-line employees total discretion in resolving customers' problems. However, this does not mean throwing money away. It means trusting front-line employees to define boundaries of reasonableness when dealing with customers who place unreasonable demands on them.

The final judgement about what constitutes a "reasonable" response to an unreasonable demand must lie with the front-line people who represent the company.

USING COMMON SENSE

In the end, common sense must prevail. A front-line employee faced with a customer demanding a replacement for a product that was obviously damaged by the customer must use their own common sense in responding to that customer. The decision could go either way depending on the circumstances, but it is the front-line employee who must be in a position to decide how to handle this apparently unreasonable customer.

The separation of a genuine difficulty from a contrived difficulty is not easy. The line is frequently blurred and subject to many different interpretations based on varying rationales. It depends on where you are coming from. It depends on how you see things. It depends on what both you and the customer are really seeking to achieve. Policy and regulation can be increasingly cumbersome and blunt-edged in dealing with the finer points of meeting the extreme demands of unreasonable customers. Common sense, savvy and *savoir-faire* are effectively the only recourse. Front-line employees who are well endowed with common sense will have no problem dealing with unreasonable customers, while those who lack it will tend to see these customers as extremely difficult.

Much as we would like to, we cannot say "yes" to customers all the time. There comes a point when we have to say "no" to demands for a discount or an upgrade or special treatment or compensation or to jump the queue or a special favor.

There is a limit to everything and the skill is in exercising this limit without alienating the customer. Natasha Keal had these skills, that is why she never experienced difficult customers. She told me she would often have to say "no" to customers, but they would leave the branch full of respect for her, having fully understood the explanation she had given for not meeting their demands and, what's more, liking her for her straight talk.

NOT COMPROMISING YOURSELF

Common sense, savvy and *savoir-faire* can only be developed when an individual has a strong set of principles and beliefs on which to base decisions and actions. When you know yourself well, when you know what you stand for, it is easy to take a stand against people seeking excesses – you know that compliance with these excessive demands would compromise your own principles. If, for example, you believe totally in fairness, then you would not allow your best friend to jump the queue. If you believe totally in honesty, you would not agree to a request from a customer to overstate the amount on the receipt so that they can claim more expenses. If you believe in dignity, you would not allow a customer to abuse a colleague, although the way in which you would stop the abuse would be with dignity rather than reactive abuse.

There is a limit to everything. Customers who go well beyond the limit of your principles should not be tolerated, but having said that, the method of restricting their excesses should be tolerable and honorable rather than excessive on your part. With good care, kindness and humor a drunk should be escorted off the premises. With sincerity and respect, a customer demanding excessive compensation for a failure should receive a reasonable explanation as to the limit being applied.

THE IMPORTANCE OF PRINCIPLES

The key is to challenge your own principles, your own rationales and, before coming to a conclusion, to attempt to see the situation from the customer's viewpoint. It could just be that on reflection the customer who first appeared unreasonable is actually being reasonable. It could just be that on reflection the customer who seems to be difficult is no more difficult than you – in fact, it could be you who is being difficult.

We must not close ourselves in and limit ourselves to an increasingly narrow interpretation of what are in fact common-sense principles. The most important principle is to please the customer wherever possible. In an ideal world, these possibilities are infinite. In the real world there is a limit, but this limit should never be too narrow.

It is important to push back the limits, the boundaries, the borders at every available opportunity. If the store is scheduled to open at 8.30 am, then it might be reasonable and not too difficult to open it at 8.25 am if a customer demands it. Refusing to do so might create a difficult customer. If a customer returns with a defective product one week after the warranty has expired, it is not unreasonable to give the customer the benefit of the doubt rather than strictly adhere to the time limit, thereby creating a difficult customer.

One icy cold morning in Cardiff, Wales, I checked out of the Post House hotel to find that my car would not start. I had an urgent meeting to drive to. I returned to reception, asked for a taxi and then gave the receptionist my car keys and asked her to arrange for my car to be fixed. She did. She rose to the challenge. Other people might have perceived my request as being difficult or unreasonable.

At a record store in Johannesburg I selected four different CDs. On approaching the till I found a long line of customers waiting to pay for their purchases. I caught the eye of a member of staff and asked him whether he would mind opening a second till. He shook his head and told me I would have to wait. As far as he was concerned, I was being unreasonable and difficult.

On a British Airways flight from Jeddah, Saudi Arabia, to London I wanted to purchase some duty-free perfume for my wife and daughters. However, the flight didn't depart till 2 am and I knew that by the time the bar trolley had been around and the meal served it would be an hour or so after take-off before the duty-free trolley appeared. I wanted to sleep immediately after take-off and not wait more than an hour for the duty-free service. So I caught the eye of a flight attendant before take-off and explained my problem. It was no problem to her. Rather than insist I comply with her routine, she met my demand, remembering to put aside my duty free and to give it to me on waking. She could have seen me as an unreasonable and difficult customer who was trying to buck the system.

SUMMARY

Customers can be unreasonable and difficult. However, it is more probable that it is the company and its front-line employees who are being unreasonable and difficult in meeting customers' specific demands.

The interpretation of difficulty and unreasonableness depends on common sense or *savoir faire*.

PRACTICAL STEPS

1 When you come across a difficult customer, stop yourself in your tracks and ask yourself: "Is it really the customer who is being difficult, or is it me?"
2 Try to distinguish a customer who is being unreasonable and a customer who has a difficulty.
3 Try to develop a frame of mind where you really do welcome the difficulties that customers present to you. Try to see these as challenges rather than ordeals.
4 Use common sense in dealing with unreasonable customers.
5 Do not compromise your principles by caving in to the unreasonable demands of customers.

15

FINDING OUT WHAT YOUR CUSTOMERS LIKE

R ECENT RESEARCH IN THE UK INDICATED THAT THE NUMBER OF customers complaining about the service they receive has increased dramatically. Another piece of research showed that the overall level of satisfaction among customers in the USA about the service they receive has declined by a full percentage point. A third piece of research showed that 73 percent of customers surveyed had cause to complain to one organization or another during the previous year.

COMMON CAUSES OF COMPLAINT

Among the most common causes of complaint were:

➤ Failing to do something when promised
➤ Inefficiency
➤ Rudeness
➤ Delays

➤ Failing to keep customers informed of changes
➤ Inflexibility
➤ Faulty products.

A lack of emotional connectivity shows through in rudeness, a lack of integrity shows through in failing to do something when promised and in failing to keep customers informed of changes. A lack of creativity leads to inflexibility. A lack of emotional connectivity, integrity and creativity can also lead to delays and inefficiency.

It is not difficult to deduce from the above what customers really like.

Before we look at the role that measurement has to play in customer service, it is perhaps worth devoting a few paragraphs to why measurement, used in the right way, is so important.

WHY MEASURE?

Measurement for measurement's sake is a waste of time. The *only* valid reason for having a measure is that it helps us take action that will make ourselves and others feel good. The measurement process must help us do things we and others like. The measure itself normally gauges the gap between the current situation and a benchmark standard that we like and that makes us feel good. Measurement of the gap enables us to take remedial action and make improvements.

So if losing weight will make us feel good, we will measure our weight. If we like a certain room temperature, we will use a thermostat to measure temperature and adjust it accordingly. If we like to drive safely we will measure our speed and moderate it accordingly.

In business terms, we like our companies to do well and thus we measure their financial performance and take the appropriate action when revenues fall, costs increase and profit declines.

While measurement is a rational process, used in the right way it is very much geared to the emotional aspect of moving towards what we like. Measurement is a formal sensing process, sensing deviations from the required standard and giving information to help close the gap.

Measurement is synonymous with change, improvement and a sense of potential well-being. So good measurement is vital in customer service. From my studies around the world, it is evident that most companies make substantial efforts to measure customer satisfaction.

MEASURES, RATINGS AND FEELINGS

In examining customer service measures, it is important to differentiate between an actual measure, a rating and a feeling. Often the three become hopelessly confused, for example when a rating is in effect no more than a feeling.

A measure is an absolute. Weight, height and volume are absolute measures, for example. There is no dispute about them. It can be proved that this package weighs one kilo, that that gate is two meters high and this bottle contains three liters.

A rating is a comparison and can also be absolute. We rate a football team highly because it wins frequently and is better than most, we rate this player highly because he is always scoring goals. We rate this car because it can out-accelerate most others in its class.

Both measures and ratings are objective and can be validated scientifically using quantitative equivalents.

However, most of us do not use objective measures and ratings when arriving at a judgment. We tend to use subjective measures based on our feelings. But because our culture tends not to permit this, we prefer to rename our feelings as ratings. "How do you feel about this hotel?" becomes "How do you rate this hotel on a scale of 1 to 5?" Similarly, we tend to ask "How do you rate this interviewee?" as opposed to "How do you feel about this interviewee?"

With sleight of hand we have magically converted subjective measures into illusory objective measures.

DELUSIONS ABOUT CUSTOMER SERVICE MEASURES

The paradox therefore is that many companies are deluding themselves that they are measuring customer satisfaction when in fact they have no real measure of what influences customer choice – and that is the feelings of customers (what they like and dislike). By converting data from tick-boxes into analyses to create these illusory objective measures, companies effectively lose all feel for how their customers see the company and the services it provides. They are measuring what *they think* is important to the customer rather than what the *customer feels* is important and what they like. Senior executives and customer service experts sit in their offices and determine measures that their common sense dictates are important, for example telephone response times, on-time deliveries and levels of customer satisfaction (based on tick-box surveys). What they do not realize is that customers are often judging them on other factors that bear little relationship to the quantitative service standards the company has so rationally developed. Customers measure you in relation to their own expectations of your service and their feelings about it. These expectations and feelings are based on past experience and reputation.

> Too many companies measure what they think is important rather than what the customer feels is important and what they like

Much of what you measure the customer will take for granted. This relates specifically to the routine operation of your business. The customer will take it for granted that things will work (this is their expectation) and give no further thought to it. In other words, when you are at your best in the mechanistic delivery of a product or a service, the customer will form no other judgement than that you are "OK" or "satisfactory" or "meet expectations".

Similarly, if you consistently perform badly and a customer stays with you (because they have no choice), then the customer will take it for granted that things will *not* work (this is their expectation) and give no further thought to it. The customer will form a judgement that "you are useless, as always" and put up with you during each attempted transaction.

DEVIATING FROM EXPECTATIONS

It is when you deviate from their expectations that customers begin to feel positive or negative about your service. When you meet their expectations (good or bad) they will have little feeling for what happens, since they see this as routine. People reserve their emotional energies for the exceptional, not wanting to waste them on predictable, everyday encounters. It is these exceptional emotional energies that determine whether a customer defects from you or conversely reinforces their view that they have made the right decision to give you their custom. It is these exceptions that customers like (if positive) and dislike (if negative).

While it is vitally important for companies to measure the service they routinely provide their customers, they should not be under the illusion that this is what customers are measuring them by. The whole purpose of measuring the routine is to ensure that a high standard of service is consistently provided according to your own definition (for example, telephone responses within five seconds, claims answered in seven days, deliveries within 48 hours etc.).

Customers like you when you exceed their expectations and therefore go beyond the routine. Regrettably, such excess can never be routine. The act of giving a small gift on one occasion might exceed a customer's expectation, but if the gift is given on every occasion then it becomes a routine, is taken for granted and ceases to invoke a positive emotional response. This is why creativity is so important in customer service. New ways of exceeding expectations must be found on as many occasions as possible.

Creativity is the antithesis of routine, it adds emotional value and as such can invoke a positive emotional response from a customer. The key to ascertaining and measuring what your customers really like must therefore focus on their feelings about the creative responses provided by everyone they are in contact with in your company.

As mentioned earlier, many customers are fed up with completing customer comment cards, because these fail to detect their real feelings and furthermore they rarely see any action as a result.

A MEASUREMENT STRATEGY

There are eight essential steps to measuring what customers like about you:

1 Measure how customers feel about the service you currently provide them. Do they like it? What would they like in the future?
2 Based on the above research, create a service promise that guarantees the service they would like and then publicise and communicate this service as widely as possible. The service promise provides the foundation benchmark for your measurement process.
3 Establish a set of routine measures relating to each item in the service promise.
4 Put in place the necessary systems and resources to measure the levels attained in relation to the service promise benchmark.
5 Train your staff not only in using the systems to deliver the promised service but also to create opportunities to exceed the service promise. The benchmark (the service promise) in fact becomes a challenging minimum that must frequently be exceeded.
6 Measure the quantity and quality of all these creative initiatives and obtain feedback from customers in relation to them.
7 Obtain feedback from customers in relation to these initiatives.
8 Make more promises and increase the level of the benchmark.

MEASURING WHAT CUSTOMERS LIKE AND HOW THEY FEEL

All possible means should be used to measure how customers feel about the service they receive and whether or not they like it. The measure itself should take the form of an "overview" picture compiled using detailed feedback from the following sources:

➤ Letters from customers, including complaints and compliments.
➤ Feedback from front-line staff who regularly deal with customers (such feedback should be encouraged and utilized).

➤ Senior executives should regularly set out to meet customers who have just undertaken transactions at the front line.

➤ Customer focus groups, ideally facilitated by an outside expert who can dig deep into a customer's mind to ascertain how they really feel about the service provided.

➤ In-depth, one-to-one interviews with customers.

The picture should also include suggestions from customers about the steps that need to be taken to improve service.

I suggest that companies minimize the use of questionnaires, surveys and telephone research, as the information they yield can be relatively superficial if not too general and meaningless. While they are easy to quantify and analyze, such "remote" forms of research are not too helpful in identifying the precise steps that need to be taken to improve service. All questionnaires, surveys and telephone research do is measure what the customer takes for granted. They rarely pick up the exceptions on which customers make their judgements.

The best form of research, albeit expensive, is based on face-to-face interviews with random samples of customers. Only in this way can you create a climate in which a customer will reveal their true feelings. Tick-box surveys are useless for this purpose as they railroad customers down a line of thought that often bears little relationship to their real feelings.

CREATE A SERVICE PROMISE

In terms of integrity, it is vitally important that you make a commitment to customers concerning the service you will deliver. The example overleaf is a hybrid of a number of service promises from companies I have studied.

This formal service promise could be made by most companies to their customers. As such, the promise reflects the increasing levels of expectations that customers have of companies with which they deal.

It should be emphasized that this typical service promise should act as a minimum benchmark. It should create in your customers' minds an expectation that you will fulfill on the large majority of occasions and that customers will therefore take for granted.

A TYPICAL SERVICE PROMISE

➤ We will deliver and install the equipment within two working days.

➤ We will provide you with a 24-hour freephone helpline 365 days a year.

➤ In the event of any problem with the product, we promise next-day service at your home or office, provided that we are notified by 4 pm.

➤ We will give you a full refund or exchange, no questions asked, if you wish to return the product within seven days of purchase.

➤ You will receive one year's free warranty for the purchased product, with an option to purchase an extension of this warranty for an additional two years.

➤ We will endeavor to answer all telephone calls within 20 seconds.

➤ If the expert you require to help you is not immediately available, we commit to arranging a call-back from this person within one hour.

➤ We will answer all correspondence you send us within two working days of receipt.

➤ We pride ourselves in extending the highest standards of courtesy and friendliness towards our customers and promise to keep to these standards every time you are in contact with us.

➤ We trust our customers to be honest with us and in the same way we promise to be honest with them in every dealing we have with them. Thus we will never oversell to our customers or mislead them in any way.

➤ Overall, we guarantee that every single person in our organization will do their very best for you when you require help.

DEVELOP A SET OF ROUTINE MEASURES

There must be a measurement process relating to each item in the service promise. Thus if the promise is to deliver and install within two working days, it is essential that you have a measure of how many times this actually occurs. The more you fall below this standard, the more you know that customers are going to feel bad.

If you promise that a customer will be able to speak to an expert within one hour of calling, it is essential that you have a measure of the number of times this occurs.

Too many organizations develop measures that do not relate to the service promise. If you want to achieve something for the customer on a regular basis, then declare it and measure the degree to which it is accomplished. There is no simpler set of criteria for measurement.

> Too many organizations develop measures that do not relate to their service promise

I have come across companies that have hundreds of customer service measures but no service promise. The measures become meaningless in the absence of any commitment. Integrity requires a front-end commitment together with open and honest feedback measures that relate to it.

PUT IN PLACE THE NECESSARY SYSTEMS AND RESOURCES

Before making the commitment (service promise) to customers to achieve a high level of service (the benchmark), it is essential that there is a front-end investment in the systems and resources necessary to deliver on these promises and to measure the levels attained in relation to the benchmark. This might mean improved telephone systems, improved computer systems (for example with instant access on screens to customer information) and improved tracking procedures.

It also requires ongoing training of staff in the use of these systems.

TRAIN YOUR STAFF

Having established the service promise and put in place the systems, resources and measures, it is important to train your staff in two areas:

> ➤ The use of the systems (the essential routines).
> ➤ Creating opportunities to exceed the formal promise (the non-routine).

Proficiency in the use of systems is essential for a number of reasons. It maximizes the probability that the service promise will be kept, but it also enables you to receive feedback from the front-line experts who use these systems on how they can be developed and improved.

All the above relates to the routines of measuring the standard service that a customer expects to receive and therefore takes for granted. However, it is essential that your front-line staff seize every conceivable opportunity to exceed your formal service promise by taking initiatives that customers do not expect and that they are really going to like. Training has a vital role in this, as does the development of a management style and organization culture that encourages such initiative.

This training will encourage people to make even more promises to customers, to improve on the declared standard measures and to create "added emotional value" extras that will make customers feel really good. This added emotional value can be as simple as an extra smile, some unsolicited but helpful information, or a friendly call when least expected to find out how things are going.

The additional promises that staff make to customers will effectively be informal promises over and above the formal promise. For example, it might be to courier some key documents to the customer within three hours, or to research some additional information that the customer requires and fax it to them within the hour. It might be to drop by and see a customer next time a member of staff is in the area.

MEASURE THE QUANTITY AND QUALITY OF ALL THESE CREATIVE INITIATIVES

This is the most exciting part of the measurement process. As mentioned throughout this book, customers like it when you go beyond the routine and do something extra for them. To encourage the whole organization to focus on creating these opportunities (in addition to being proficient in the routines), there must be some measure of the initiatives that have taken place. These measures can then be used as basis for promoting visibly higher levels of performance.

For example, at the TGI Friday's restaurant in Covent Garden in London, letters from customers congratulating staff on various endeavors are posted on a noticeboard near the rest-rooms. The positive measure is as follows: "How many letters do we receive from customers each month congratulating staff on their excellent service?"

As mentioned in Chapter 6, at BT Mobile one of the customer service agents has introduced "customer service bubbles" to capture comments that customers make about the service. Staff are also encouraged to write ideas up on flipcharts. Points are awarded for each speech bubble and every idea put up. At the end of the week the supervisor, Louise, awards a bottle of champagne (paid for out of her own pocket) for the customer service agent with the most points.

These measures are in addition to the routine ones of measuring complaints, response times and percentage of calls answered.

However, not all customers write complimentary letters and often small initiatives by staff (such as the extra smile, the extra-special welcome) might well go unnoticed by managers unless some way of measuring this is found. Mystery shopping is one way of detecting the minor but all-important initiatives that need to be encouraged. Additionally, senior executives and staff should spend a fair amount of time walking around observing the levels of service at the front line and providing positive feedback when they see someone taking the initiative.

Bigger initiatives should be recorded by the staff themselves and a log kept in order to maintain a record of their own achievements.

Obtain feedback from customers in relation to these initiatives

The most effective way of measuring what customers feel about the service is through customer focus groups. All other methods tend to scratch at the surface and at best provide one-off snapshots of what customers think and feel about your service.

I have developed a special "three-tier" approach to customer focus groups that has been used successfully with a number of organizations to dig deep into the minds of their customers.

Tier 1
Open-ended, non-loaded questions about how the customers view their experiences with the company.

Tier 2
More searching questions about how customers feel about the company and what factors influence their decision making.

Tier 3
Targeted questions based on a subtext relating to the company's own specific agenda (that might not have been covered in the previous questioning).

Obtaining a measure of what customers really like, think and feel about a company and the service it provides is not easily done when customers are given a survey form or comments card which promises it will only take a few seconds of their time to complete. At best, all the company will see is the tip of the iceberg. Customer focus groups enable researchers to get below the surface and explore in depth what customers really think and feel about a company.

Even more effective than customer focus groups are in-depth, one-to-one interviews with customers. While these are incredibly expensive to undertake, the investment in time and money pays dividends in discovering what customers really like. With skilled interviewing it is possible to dig deep into customers' minds and extract how they truly think and feel about a company's approach.

MAKE MORE PROMISES AND INCREASE
THE LEVEL OF THE BENCHMARK

In order to remain ahead of the competition, it is essential that a company continually increases its standards and raises the benchmarks against which it measures its performance.

The most progressive companies are always striving for new ways to make promises to their customers, promises that only the company can keep and no competitor has a chance of meeting. This relates to both formal promises (the service offer) and the everyday informal promises made by staff.

Take for example Progressive Insurance based in Ohio. Its benchmark is to promise an immediate response when making a claim. Its aim to make insurance hassle free and provide a local claims service 24 hours a day, seven days a week. Its intention is to get people who insure their automobiles with the company back on the road as quickly as possible after an accident.

EXAMPLES OF MEASURING CUSTOMER
SERVICE

The following are just a few outline examples of the approach of different companies to measuring customer service.

LLOYDS TSB

Lloyds TSB is one of the largest banks in the UK with approximately 350 different banking services, 16 million customers, 3000 branches, 82,500 employees (of which 52,000 are in retail) and generating over $5 billion in profit before tax.

Various surveys show that Lloyds TSB has the highest rating for service of all banks in the UK. For example, a survey by the Forum of Private Business showed that out of 18 key measures Lloyds TSB came first in fifteen. These included:

➤ Best bank managers
➤ Highest degree of trust

➤ Best knowledge
➤ Best advice
➤ Best range of services
➤ Best speed of decision
➤ Best efficiency
➤ Best reliability
➤ Most friendly staff
➤ Most helpfulness.

To achieve such high standards, the bank has a comprehensive set of measurement methods based on:

➤ Customer focus groups
➤ Informal meetings of staff and customers
➤ Customer suggestion forms
➤ Hundreds of thousands of questionnaires sent to customers annually
➤ Market research
➤ Mystery shopping.

These measures have enabled the bank continually to make improvements in pursuit of its vision of customer service excellence. For example, the service improvement initiatives include:

➤ Free customer relations phone line
➤ Staff can make up to $500 ex gratia payments to customers (if things go wrong)
➤ All complaints replied to within 48 hours
➤ Customer comment cards
➤ A series of customer service training initiatives, including "Delivering Service Excellence" which extended to all branches
➤ Empathy audits
➤ Establishment of a "service challenge" to all branches
➤ Management training in "Outstanding Leadership" to help them become emotionally connected leaders.

For the service challenge, all branches are measured regularly against a number of key customer service parameters. These include:

➤ Queuing
➤ Privacy
➤ Friendliness
➤ Courtesy
➤ Product knowledge
➤ Ownership of problems
➤ Telephone responses
➤ Correspondence
➤ ATM (automated teller machine) reliability
➤ Complaints.

SUN MICROSYSTEMS

Senior managers at Sun Microsystems, headquartered in the USA, are obsessed with attaining the highest possible standards of customer service. Their focus for this is a Sun Quality Index (SQI).

The SQI is a key factor in salary determination for the company's managers. Like many other progressive companies, individual rewards relate to the attainment of critical non-financial targets. This is so important to Sun Microsystems that a substantial percentage of salary is at stake should managers fail to achieve the SQI target.

The SQI has three main components:

➤ ESI Employee satisfaction index
➤ CLI Customer satisfaction/loyalty index (retention)
➤ CQI Customer quality index (key business drivers).

The ESI relates to how employees feel about the company and its managers. Employees are surveyed regularly to determine the degree to which they are satisfied with what is going on in the company.

The CLI relates to how customers feel about the company and the service it provides. Again, regular research is conducted to ascertain the degree of satisfaction. The focus here is on retention and what makes a customer stay with the company.

The CQI relates to a number of key business drivers, such as response times and first-time fixes.

A critical factor in striving for an ever-improving SQI is the motivation throughout Sun Microsystems to innovate and improve the service provided.

The approach is based on the concept of "Sun Teams". Employees are encouraged to come up with creative new ideas and pursue them through to implementation. Anyone with such an idea will find a sponsor from within the organization (not necessarily their boss) and then work with a team of interested people to ensure that the idea is evaluated, developed and implemented.

There are approximately 200 Sun Teams around the world. Every year their innovations are evaluated by a panel and country winners go to San Francisco with their partners, where awards are made to gold, silver and bronze winners.

DIXONS STORES GROUP

Dixons is one of the most successful retail operations in the UK. Its chains include Currys, PC World, The Link and Dixons itself. At its Hemel Hempstead head office there is a call center operation to take questions from retail customers and branch staff.

The manager of the call center, Ann Harley, has established a simple measurement process to ensure the highest standard of response. Calls are regularly monitored by team leaders in relation to specific criteria, including:

➤ Open greeting
➤ Correct information provided
➤ Customer's name used
➤ Correct call transfer decision
➤ Confirmation of action
➤ Apologizing if necessary
➤ Questioning skills
➤ No drinking and eating while taking call
➤ Call closure.

On the correspondence side, letters to customers are regularly audited against the following criteria:

➤ Customer complaint correctly identified
➤ Appropriateness of response
➤ Punctuation, spelling and grammar
➤ Construction of letter.

To inject some fun into achieving high standards, there are frequent innovative competitions, for example the "Customer Service Olympics" in which call center teams can compete for gold, silver and bronze medals. Teams are allowed to give themselves names such as the "Lunchbox Sprinters" (for performance over the lunch period) and the "Mega Correspondence Marathon Runners".

On a broader basis, the Dixons Stores Group regularly monitors customer service performance on a wide range of factors, including punctual delivery, staff attitude, staff knowledge, keeping promises made to customers and speed of response.

SUMMARY

Many companies measure the wrong thing. They measure what the company thinks is important as opposed to what customers really like about its service. The best way of measuring the latter is to undertake customer focus groups.

In measuring customer service it is important to differentiate between routine, steady-state services that customers take for granted and non-routine exceptions by which customers judge you.

PRACTICAL STEPS

1 Review and challenge the measures currently used by your company in relation to customer service.
2 Ensure that these measures reflect what customers genuinely feel about your company.
3 As appropriate, develop and implement a new strategy for measurement.
4 Differentiate between the routine service that customers take for granted and the non-routine exceptions by which customers judge you.

5 Undertake some customer focus groups to find out what your customers really think and feel about the service your company provides.
6 Establish a clear "service promise" to customers that can be used as a high-level benchmark for all aspects of the customer service operation.

16

THE ONE-HOUR COURSE FOR ADDING EMOTIONAL VALUE

THIS CHAPTER CONTAINS A SERIES OF 10 SIMPLE, PRACTICAL EXERCISES that you can use to help you add emotional value and get your customers to like you. If you are a manager, these exercises can also be used with your team.

The first nine exercises should take no longer than one hour in total. The tenth exercise involves a review of this book and will take longer.

EXERCISE 1
LIKING CUSTOMERS: ESSENTIAL OR UNIMPORTANT?

I have run this exercise for many groups around the world and it is aimed at getting both the emotional and intellectual juices flowing.

Answer this simple question:

How important is it to like your customers?

ESSENTIAL   ☐

UNIMPORTANT   ☐

Give reasons for your decision.

The general response across the world has been that approximately 60 percent of people think it is essential, while 40 percent think it unimportant.

Some of the more vocal of my audience members stick up their hands and tell me that I have asked the wrong question. It should be: "How important is it to respect your customers?"

My response is as follows: "It is essential to like your customers. If you don't like them they will definitely not like you."

I go on to argue that most people I know want to be liked. Therefore the key challenge in customer service is to find something you like about your customers.

EXERCISE 2
PREPARE YOUR FRAME OF MIND

The more you like your customers, the better you will be able to relate to them and the better service you will provide. You therefore have to prepare a "frame of mind" each morning for liking your customers.

This means becoming totally focused on your customers and allowing nothing else to distract you.

As you wake up tomorrow morning, think about the day facing you and the work you have to do. Then consider the following statement and indicate whether you agree or disagree. (At this stage you do not have to define who your customers are.)

"The most important aspect of my work relates to customers."

AGREE   ☐

DISAGREE   ☐

Most people agree with this statement.

However, when people analyze how they spend this time at work, they soon discover that what they do rarely reflects the importance they ascribe to customers. They become distracted with issues relating to their colleagues, with bureaucracy and with meetings. Most admit that they spend much less time than necessary on matters relating to customers. Reverse that today!

If you really mean it, do it! Here is a suggested mental exercise.

MENTAL EXERCISE

Prepare a customer-focused frame of mind:

➤ Focus all your attention all day on your customers.
➤ Everything you do today should be geared to improving your relationships with customers and your service to them, thus reflecting the importance you place on them.
➤ Put aside any action and any decisions that are not geared specifically to helping your customers.
➤ Think only of your customers.
➤ At the end of the day, review what you have achieved for (given to) your customers.

Really look forward to dealing with your customers.

EXERCISE 3
IDENTIFY YOUR CUSTOMERS AND DEFINE YOUR PERSONAL INTERACTIONS WITH THEM

Before you can apply the three most important attributes for adding emotional value and gaining competitive advantage, you must not only be in the right frame of mind for liking customers, but you also have to identify who your customers are and have identified your interactions with them.

Review the day ahead and make a list of the customers you expect to have contact with and the types of interaction you will have with them. These could include internal customers.

CUSTOMERS	TYPE OF INTERACTION
example:	
1 A.N. Other	Anticipated complaint
2 Jeff Woods (sales rep)	Enquiry about new product literature
3 Jill Baker (buyer at XYZ)	Call about new product launch
4	
5	
6	
7	
8	
9	
10.........	

Be as rigorous as possible in forecasting your day. You need to focus on each customer with a view to adding emotional value in each interaction and so reinforcing if not improving your relationship with them.

Any other non-customer-related activities that cannot be fitted into the list you have made should be discarded.

EXERCISE 4
DEFINE YOUR FEELINGS ABOUT THESE CUSTOMERS

Now be scrupulously honest with yourself and write down your immediate thoughts about the feelings you have for each of the customers specified on the previous list. What do you like about them? What do you dislike about them?

Here are some examples.

CUSTOMERS	MY FEELINGS ABOUT THESE CUSTOMERS
example:	
1 A.N. Other	"Not another complaint! Don't these customers understand that even we make mistakes!"
2 Jeff Woods (sales rep)	"He's an aggressive, pushy sales guy who never seems satisfied with the information we provide him."
3 Jill Baker (buyer at XYZ)	"She's pompous, arrogant and gives the impression she always knows best. I'll waste a lot of time trying to get hold of her."
4	
5	
6	
7	
8	
9	
10	

Of course, these examples are all negative.

The risk is that if you feel negative about customers they will sense it, not matter how clever you are at disguising it. They will sense that you dislike them and that you see their behavior as irritating. This will therefore be reflected in their relationship with you.

EXERCISE 5
TURN ALL YOUR NEGATIVE FEELINGS ABOUT CUSTOMERS INTO POSITIVE ONES

Review the previous exercise and discard your negative feelings.

You will need to apply a large amount of positive emotional energy to eliminate these negative feelings. It is a discipline to be applied every day, one that repels all negative thoughts about customers before they arise.

Now go out of your way to find something positive about each customer, something that will make you feel good about them.

CUSTOMERS	NEW POSITIVE FEELINGS ABOUT CUSTOMERS
example:	
1 A.N. Other	"I'm delighted that this customer has taken the trouble to give us some feedback."
2 Jeff Woods (sales rep)	"It's great to have colleagues who are ambitious and really put themselves out to learn more about what's going on."
3 Jill Baker (buyer at XYZ)	"She has always been fair and reasonable in all her dealings with me. She always gives me a hearing and when a buying decision goes against us she always has the courtesy to inform me."
4	
5	
6	
7	
8	
9	
10.........	

The key is to go on searching your mind for things you genuinely like about your customers, rather than allowing things you dislike about them to dominate your thoughts.

As soon as you feel good about your customers you will be able to communicate this effectively and create a much more positive relationship. They will like you more because you like them more.

EXERCISE 6
OPPORTUNITY ONE: CREATE OPPORTUNITIES TO DO POSITIVE THINGS FOR YOUR CUSTOMERS

Here is your opportunity to apply the three most important attributes in adding emotional value.

Just to recap, the three most important attributes are:

➤ Connect emotionally with your customers.
➤ Demonstrate integrity.
➤ Be creative in meeting their needs.

In creating opportunities to be positive, examine your previous routine and try to develop some new, likeable responses. There is an example overleaf.

The key is to connect with the complaining customer as quickly and effectively as possible, as opposed to distancing yourself from the customer by using a mechanized, standardized response. The opportunity should also be seized to make a commitment to the customer that you can subsequently honor, thus showing your integrity. Finally, take a creative opportunity to ring the customer a few weeks later (or write if appropriate).

CUSTOMER/INTERACTION PREVIOUS ROUTINE RESPONSE

example:

1 A.N. Other
(letter of complaint)

Read letter quickly. Detect yet another complaint about a product quality defect. Pass letter to customer service department with an instruction to send out standard letter no. 31 (relating to quality defects).

NEW "LIKEABLE" RESPONSE (TO ADD EMOTIONAL VALUE)

Ring customer immediately and express concern about complaint received. (emotional connectivity) Listen carefully, taking notes. Promise to follow up with an in-depth reply and do so. (integrity) Further follow-up call after in-depth reply has gone out. (creativity)

EXERCISE 7
OPPORTUNITY TWO: CREATE MORE OPPORTUNITIES TO DO POSITIVE THINGS FOR YOUR CUSTOMERS

Opposite is a second example of doing positive things for customers.

A front-line sales representative is a classic internal customer whose effectiveness depends to a high degree on support from the center. The key here is to shift thinking patterns away from seeing such representatives as "nuisances" who make "unnecessary demands on the center" to "essential activists at the front line" who need a constant stream of emotional support from the center and creative responses to their needs.

CUSTOMER/INTERACTION example:	PREVIOUS ROUTINE RESPONSE
2 Jeff Woods (message enquiring about product literature)	Divert to sales administrator and ask her to ring Jeff Woods to sort out the problem and get for him the literature he needs.

NEW "LIKEABLE" RESPONSE (TO ADD EMOTIONAL VALUE)
Ring Jeff Woods direct and tell him it was good to hear from him. Have a chat about his weekend. Did he go sailing? (emotional connectivity) Clarify his needs for product literature and make a promise that you will follow up with the sales administration people to ensure that he gets what he wants. Then follow up. (integrity)
Offer to go out on the road with Jeff in a couple of weeks' time to give him some support with customers and to learn a little more about his needs and how he can be helped from the center. (creativity)

EXERCISE 8
OPPORTUNITY THREE: CREATE EVEN MORE OPPORTUNITIES TO DO POSITIVE THINGS FOR YOUR CUSTOMERS

Overleaf is a third example. We tend to avoid customers we dislike and if not careful will deal with them in a mechanistic, routine way. By finding things you like about these customers, you open up new avenues for dealing with them. These make them a delight to do business with.

CUSTOMER/INTERACTION	PREVIOUS ROUTINE RESPONSE
example: 3 Jill Baker (action to call her about new product launch)	Try to call her and fail to get through. Prepare a fax with the new information. Send the fax together with a terse note saying that you tried to ring. Wait for her to call.
	NEW "LIKEABLE" RESPONSE (TO **ADD EMOTIONAL VALUE)** Ring and chat to Jill's secretary. (emotional connectivity) Find out when Jill is available this week. (creativity) Arrange to drop by and see her, promising to bring some new samples with you. (integrity) Confirm arrangements with a friendly fax or e-mail indicating that you are looking forward very much to seeing her again. (emotional connectivity)

EXERCISE 9
REVIEW PROGRESS DURING THE DAY

Find a quiet corner at the end of the afternoon and sit down and review your experiences with your various customers during the day.

PART ONE

Make a list like the one opposite.

THINGS I LIKED ABOUT MY CUSTOMERS TODAY	THINGS I DIDN'T LIKE ABOUT WHAT I DID TODAY
The complaining customer was overwhelmed by my quick response and was almost apologetic for having complained. I felt for her.	I don't think I was sensitive enough to the customer's immediate embarrassment. While she was impressed and appreciated my call, I don't think I did enough to put her at her ease.
Jeff Woods was very grateful for my call. He's been having a difficult time with a continuing shortage of supply of the latest product literature. He was excited about the prospect of me going on the road with him.	I should have apologized for having neglected him so much recently. Instead I made lame excuses about how busy I had been. I must learn not to talk badly of Jeff when with my colleagues at lunch. I've tended to run him down in the past.
Jill Baker faxed me back offering to take me to lunch on my visit next Friday. She told me she had quite a few issues she wanted to discuss with me as XYZ was planning to expand its business with 10 more store openings.	I must learn not to be put off by Jill's accent and personal style. I think in the past she had inadvertently made me feel inferior and this influenced my "stand-offish" behavior towards her. I think a little of it showed today.

The emotionally intelligent approach is to identify and analyze what you like about other people and also to dig deep inside yourself to identify and eliminate any negative feelings you have about them. It means keeping a continual focus on the positive – positively identifying what you like about others and trying to behave in a way that others will like.

PART TWO

Make a list of the things you've achieved for (given to) your customers today.

Here are some examples.

TODAY'S GIFTS TO MY CUSTOMERS

1 Expressing concern about the complaint and promising to follow through.
2 Calling Jeff Woods immediately.
3 Promising to get sales literature problem sorted out for Jeff Woods.
4 Promising to go out on the road with Jeff Woods.
5 Promising to go and see Jill Baker and to take some free samples with me.

EXERCISE 10
REVIEW OF THIS BOOK

Working with your team, review each chapter of this book, perhaps taking one chapter a week.

Discuss with your team the practical steps at the end of each chapter with a view to implementing them.

Undertake any additional exercises in the chapter.

APPENDIX I

EMOTIONALLY

CONNECTED STARS

THE FOLLOWING ARE JUST A FEW EXAMPLES OF PEOPLE I HAVE COME ACROSS IN preparation for this book and who have provided valuable input as a source of inspiration. Without exception I found each person's approach enthralling.

Regrettably, space does not permit me to mention the names of everyone in their teams.

Since the initial encounters for this research, some of the people mentioned have moved on to bigger and better things or, in one or two cases, have retired.

JOHN BARNES, HARRY RAMSDEN'S, LEEDS, UK

Has succeeded in putting passion, fun and service as well as an international dimension into the traditional English habit of eating fish and chips.

UWE BECK, EYE AFRICA, JOHANNESBURG, SOUTH AFRICA

Uwe has successfully built up an executive taxi service by being reliable, creative and emotionally connected with his customers.

JANINE BENSOUDA, MASHREQBANK, DUBAI, UAE

Janine has immense reservoirs of positive energy and deep wisdom that have enabled her to get her people on side in the call center and provide remarkably innnovative customer service.

MICHAEL BICHARD, DEPARTMENT OF EDUCATION AND EMPLOYMENT, UK

Previously Chief Executive of the Benefits Agency, Michael has had a major influence on the provision of government services in the UK. Clear thinking, deeply principled and an excellent leader.

LISA BRIGHT, SMITHKLINE BEECHAM, WELWYN GARDEN CITY, UK

Dynamic, positive, an inspiration to all, Lisa and her team at Welwyn Garden City are an incredibly impressive group of people.

RICHARD BRIMBLE, BT MOBILE, LEEDS, UK

Richard just believes in giving people their head to do whatever is necessary for the customer. The people I met in his team are as motivated and positive as you will find anywhere in the world. They are true believers in the approach to customer service advocated in this book. (Richard has now moved on.)

DEBBIE BUANO, BARNES & NOBLE, PLANTATION BRANCH, FLORIDA, USA

In my opinion, Debbie runs the best bookstore in the world. She has a team of people who really do get involved in providing the best service to their customers.

CHARLES DUNSTONE, THE CARPHONE WAREHOUSE, UK

Has built up a dynamic business by concentrating on integrity and the application of an emotional proposition to customers.

IAN EDWARDS, BEDFORDSHIRE FIRE AND RESCUE SERVICE, UK

Another stalwart of the common-sense school of management. An expert on motivation, empowerment and real leadership.

ARNOLD EKPE, ECOBANK, WEST AFRICA

Arnold believes that to differentiate his bank from all the competitors, he and every single person in the bank has to get one thing right, and that is service. He has therefore embarked on a major initiative to motivate people in this direction.

FIONNUALA FRENCH, MORTGAGE EXPRESS, NEW BARNET, UK

Fionnuala has succeeded in developing a very progressive approach to customer service and team motivation at Mortgage Express.

RICH GALLITELLI AND DENILLE GIRARDAT, NORDSTROM, SHORT HILLS SHOPPING MALL, NEW JERSEY, USA

Rich is one of the best store assistants I have come across in a long while. He really knows how to please customers and provide the service they like. Denille Girardat, his boss, is the epitome of a likeable leader.

TERRY GOULD, ROYAL BOROUGH OF WINDSOR AND MAIDENHEAD, UK

Terry has succeeded with his team in obtaining the prestigious Charter Mark award twice for their pioneering approach, providing excellent customer service to the community.

DEBBIE HARDIMAN, YELLOW PAGES, READING, UK

Debbie runs one of the most motivated customer service teams I have come across.

ANN HARLEY, DIXONS STORES GROUP, HEMEL HEMPSTEAD, UK

Ann Harley is another call center manager who has done remarkable things to motivate her people and provide the very best service.

THOMAS HUTH, MARRIOTT BEACH RESORT, MARBELLA, SPAIN

Friendly, helpful and professional, Thomas Huth is the epitome of everything that Marriott stands for.

ALAN JONES, TNT (UK), ATHERSTONE, UK

Alan believes that service is everything and that his people can be "better than the best". TNT has won award after award for its quality approach. It truly has a pioneering attitude to empowered customer service.

ALAN LEVAN, BANK ATLANTIC, FORT LAUDERDALE, FLORIDA, USA

Alan Levan is an inspiration to everyone. They all love him and he loves them. Bank Atlantic can provide innumerable examples of incredibly innovative customer service, often initiated by front-line people.

LLOYDS TSB, UK

Lloyds TSB is perhaps the most customer service-oriented bank in the UK. It has many pioneering people on the customer service front, including Colin Fisher, Peter Ayliffe, Harold Russell, Jacey Graham, Sue Kurnaz, John Wilson and Clive Kenyon.

ROGER MAHARAJ, PRINT DYNAMICS, FORT LAUDERDALE, USA

Roger is a brilliant front-line guy who remembers all his customers, has an immense amount of positive energy and knows all about service. An inspiration to his colleagues in one of the fastest-growing print companies in the US.

JULIAN METCALFE, PRET A MANGER, LONDON, UK

Julian is so obsessed with service that he puts his own telephone number on the packaging of his company's food products.

KESH MORJARIA, FLEET PHOTOS, LONDON, UK

Deeply philosophical and incredibly creative, Kesh Morjaria has succeeded in turning an ailing business around by concentrating solely on people and customers.

ANTON NAJJAR, J.W. MARRIOTT, DUBAI, UAE

Anton has a passion for service and believes he has an outstanding team of people (400 in number). He has a simple mission that everyone shares: "To have each guest leave the hotel completely satisfied!"

PAUL NICHOLSON, MOUNT ALVERNIA HOSPITAL, GUILDFORD, UK

Paul and his team have developed and applied a total philosophy of care throughout the hospital. Care is everything and permeates every aspect of how the hospital operates.

JOLONE OKORODUDU, ECOBANK, COTE D'IVOIRE

Jolone is one of the most passionate and pioneering people I have come across in West Africa when it comes to customer service. A true believer!

KIM OLANDER, SANDVIC CORODANT, SWEDEN

Kim and his colleagues in this Swedish manufacturing company have undertaken some pioneering work in connecting emotionally with customers through partnership working.

FEARGAL QUINN, SUPERQUINN, IRELAND

Feargal, an author himself, has one of the most innovative approaches to customer service I have come across for a long time. If you are looking for bright, whacky ideas, then this is the place to go.

MIKE ROBERTS, SUN MICROSYSTEMS, BAGSHOT, UK

Mike has been instrumental in developing and applying a highly focused approach to customer service in this high-tech company.

ANDREW SCARVELIS, ROYAL HOTEL, PARIS

Andrew believes in a totally positive approach to customer service. His hotel is immaculate in keeping to the highest standards. At the same time his staff are incredibly motivated to provide their very best. This is reflected in a consistently high level of positive feedback from customers.

RAY SHIPLEY, ALBANY INTERNATIONAL, BOLTON, UK

Down to earth, salt of the earth, here is a man loved by all but very progressive in his approach, especially with regard to customer service. Ray is now retired.

PAUL SOUTHWORTH, AVON COSMETICS, NORTHAMPTON, UK

A hero among his people at Northampton. Well loved, dynamic, respected and a friend to all. He knows how to please customers. Paul has now moved on.

JULIAN STAINTON, WPA, TAUNTON, UK

Julian is totally obsessed with customer service and so are his people. It shows through in every aspect of this healthcare insurance operation. Staff are given their head and they deliver. The bottom-line results are there to show it.

PHIL STONE, EQUITABLE LIFE, UK

Phil and his team are really switched on to adding emotional value.

WILF WALSH, HMV, LONDON, UK

Wilf is one of the most progressive retailers I've come across. He gets out and about and gives his staff their head. The end result can be felt when you approach any of his staff in one of their music stores.

Other "stars" to look out for:

➤ ASDA, UK (as progressive a retail chain as you will get).
➤ Ben & Jerry's, USA (a values-driven company).
➤ Body Shop, UK (as values driven as any company can be).
➤ British Airways, UK (in-flight cabin staff consistently good).
➤ Dyson Appliances, UK (incredibly innovative).
➤ Multichoice, South Africa (is developing an incredibly progressive approach).
➤ Nando's, South Africa (it dares its staff to make the customer a friend).
➤ National Bank of Abu Dhabi, UAE (has a highly progressive approach to customer service).
➤ Progressive Insurance, USA (one of the best when it comes to speedy and responsive service).
➤ Richer Sounds, UK (an inspirational leader).
➤ Ritz Carlton Group (high reputation for empowered approach).
➤ South West Airlines, USA (Herb Kelleher has pioneered the unusual and some say he is "Nuts" – the title of his book).
➤ TGI Friday's (always a pleasure to meet their staff).
➤ Virgin, UK (all the companies in Richard Branson's group, always fun, always exciting).

APPENDIX II

SUGGESTED

FURTHER READING

IN PREPARATION FOR THIS BOOK I HAVE READ, DIPPED INTO OR REFERRED TO the following books. Each will prove helpful to readers wishing to extend their interest in emotions and related subjects. Not all of these are management books and some only deal indirectly with emotions. A shortlist of journals I regularly find helpful in my studies on this subject is also provided.

Faking It by Digby Anderson and Peter Mulen (The Social Affairs Unit, 1998).

Gestures by Roger Axtell (Wiley, 1998).

How Brains Think by William H. Calvin (Weidenfeld & Nicolson, 1996).

Moments of Truth by Jan Carlzon (Ballinger, 1987).

Ben & Jerry's Double Dip by Ben Cohen and Jerry Greenfield (Simon & Schuster, 1997).

Executive EQ by Robert Cooper and Ayman Sawaf (Orion, 1997).

Descartes' Error: Emotion, Reason and the Human Brain by Antonio R. Damasio (Avon, 1994).

Practical Intuition by Laura Day (Vermilion, 1996).

Social Psychology in the 90s by Kay Deaux, Francis C. Dane and Lawrence S. Wrightsman (Brooks/Cole, 1988).

The Three Faces of Mind by Elaine de Beauport (Quest, 1996).

Serious Creativity by Edward de Bono (HarperCollins, 1992).

Kinds of Minds by Daniel C. Dennett (Weidenfeld & Nicolson, 1996).

On the Psychology of Military Incompetence by Norman E. Dixon (Cape, 1976).

Against the Odds by James Dyson (Orion, 1997).

Cognitive Psychology by Michael W. Eysenck and Mark T. Keane (Psychology Press, 1995).

Emotion in Organizations, edited by Stephen Fineman (Sage, 1993).

Bury Me Standing by Isabel Fonseca (Vintage, 1995).

Emotion and Social Judgements, edited by Joseph P. Forgas (Pergamon Press, 1991).

Emotional Blackmail by Susan Forward (Bantam, 1997).

Nuts by Kevin and Jackie Freiberg (Bard Press, 1996).

Interaction Ritual by Erving Goffman (Penguin, 1967).

Vital Lies, Simple Truths by Daniel Goleman (Touchstone, 1985).

Emotional Intelligence by Daniel Goleman (Bantam, 1995).

The Age of Unreason by Charles Handy (Hutchinson, 1989).

The Empty Raincoat by Charles Handy (Hutchinson, 1993).

Virgin King by Tim Jackson (HarperCollins, 1994).

The Emotional Computer by José Antonio Jáuregui (Blackwell, 1995).

The Neurotic Organization by Manfred F.R. Kets de Vries and Danny Miller (Harper, 1984).

Corporate Religion by Jesper Kunde (Børsens Forlag, 1997).

Mindfulness by Ellen J. Langer (Addison-Wesley, 1989).

The Power of Mindful Learning by Ellen J. Langer (Addison-Wesley, 1997).

The Nordstrom Way by Robert Spector and Patrick D. McCarthy (Wiley, 1995).

Emotional Confidence by Gael Lindenfield (Thorsons, 1997).

Stop and Sell the Roses by Jim McCann (Ballantine, 1998).

The Paradox of Success by John R. O'Neil (Tarcher Putnam, 1993).

Love and Survival by Dean Ornish (HarperCollins, 1998).

The Cognitive Structure of Emotions by Andrew Ortony, Gerald L. Clore and Allan Collins (Cambridge, 1988).

Changing Moods by Brian Parkinson, Peter Totterdell, Rob B. Briner and Shirley Reynolds (Addison-Wesley, 1996).

The Heart's Code by Paul Pearsall (Broadway, 1998).

The Molecules of Emotion: Why You Feel the Way You Feel by Candace B. Pert (Scribner, 1997).

Thriving on Chaos by Tom Peters (Macmillan, 1988).

Liberation Management by Tom Peters (Knopf, 1992).

The Pursuit of WOW! by Tom Peters (Pan, 1994).

In Search of Excellence by Tom Peters and Robert Waterman (Harper & Row, 1982).

How the Mind Works by Steven Pinker (W.W. Norton, 1997).

Crowning the Customer by Feargal Quinn (O'Brien, 1990).

Shadow Syndromes by John H. Ratey and Catherine Johnson (Bantam, 1997).

The Richer Way by Julian Richer (EMAP, 1995).

Corporate Creativity by Alan G. Robinson and Sam Stern (Berrett-Koehler, 1997).

Body and Soul by Anita Roddick (Ebury, 1991).

Emotional Clearing by John Ruskan (Rider, 1998).

The Pscychology of Facial Expression, edited by James A. Russell and José Miguel Fernández-Dols (Cambridge University Press, 1997).

Company Man by Anthony Sampson (HarperCollins, 1995).

Maverick! by Ricardo Semler (Century, 1993).

The Fifth Discipline by Peter Senge (Doubleday, 1990).

Hystories by Elaine Showalter (Picador, 1997).

Measuring Emotional Intelligence by Steve Simmons and John Simmons (Summit, 1997).

The Passions by Robert C. Solomon (Hackett, 1993).

Becoming Emotionally Whole by Charles Stanley (Thomas Nelson, 1996).

Figments of Reality by Ian Stewart and Jack Cohen (Cambridge University Press, 1997).

Irrationality by Stuart Sutherland (Constable, 1992).

The Passion of the Western Mind by Richard Tarnas (Pimlico, 1991).

Maximum Achievement by Brian Tracy (Fireside, 1993).

For Shame: the Loss of Common Decency in American Culture by James B. Twitchell (St Martins Press, 1997).

Emotional Intelligence at Work by Hendrie Weisinger (Jossey-Bass, 1998).

An Intimate History of Humanity by Theodore Zeldin (Sinclair-Stevenson, 1994).

RECOMMENDED JOURNALS

➤ Harvard Business Review
➤ Sloan Management Review
➤ Psychology Today
➤ Business Age
➤ Fortune
➤ Forbes
➤ The Economist
➤ Time Magazine
➤ Customer Service Management
➤ Customer First

APPENDIX III

CLUSTERS

THESE ARE CLUSTERS OF WORDS THAT BEGIN WITH THE SAME LETTER AND fall into a loose generic category. No two words in any cluster should have the same root.

a is for answer

answer	announcement
ask	analogy
ascertain	analysis
assert	anticipation
abstract	axiom
appraise	attribution
assessment	allegation

b is for book

book
biography
blueprint
bible
binder
browse
bibliography

c is for cluster

cluster	chelate
crowd	crystal
combination	chemical
colloid	congeal
colony	clan
chapter	congregation
chord	chorus

c is for church

church
Christian
cross
carol
communion
Catholic
conversion

c is for calamity

calamity
catastrophe
chaos
collision
crisis
Chernobyl
crash

f is for fiction

fiction
fantasy
futuristic
fabrication
falsehood
folly
fortune-teller

g is for great

great
giant
gigantic
gargantuan
galactic
gorilla
grand

g is for good

good
god-like
gentle
gracious
gallant
giving
generous

h is for home

home
house
hut
hovel
hotel
haven
hospitality

k is for kindness

kindness
kindle
kiss
kinship
kindred
knight-errant
kitten

l is for lesson

lesson
learner
lecturer
luminary
leader
lexicon
legend

m is for murder

murder
machine gun
mutilate
massacre
menace
maniac
mow down

m is for mother

mother
maternal
milk
mum
midwife
mama
mollycoddle

n is for negative	n is for nought	p is for purposeful	q is for question	s is for speed
negative	nought	purposeful	question	speed
never	nothing	position	quiz	streamline
nuisance	neutralize	pride	quote	sprint
naughty	nobody	prime	quantify	supersonic
nasty	naked	principle	quibble	scoot
null	nude	positive	qualify	slick
no	nihilistic	power	quarrel	streak

t is for transport	v is for victim	w is for worst	w is for weird
transport	victim	worst	weird
train	vice	woeful	wizard
ticket	vicious	wicked	wonder
travel	vengeance	wretched	wild
truck	violate	witch	way-out
trunk-route	vandal	washout	whacky
trolley-car	vanquish	war	whizzkid

APPENDIX IV

EMOTIONS

Sadness
dejection
depression
despair
despondency
dispirited
downhearted
gloom
grief
loneliness
melancholy
misery
self-pity
sorrow
sympathy
unhappiness

Enjoyment
affability
amusement
bliss
contentment
delight
happiness
indulgence
joy
pride
relief
satisfaction
thrill
elation

Fear
alarm
anxiety
apprehension
concern
consternation
dread
insecurity
horror
panic
terror
troubled

Anger
animosity
annoyance
exasperation
fury
hatred
hostility
indignation
outrage
rage
resentment

Disgust
abhorrence
contempt
derision
disdain
distaste
loathing
revulsion
scorn
slight

Shame
chagrin
compunction
embarrassment
humiliation
guilt
mortification
regret
remorse

Love
adoration
caring
devotion
fondness
generosity
infatuation
intimacy
protection

Acceptance
affinity
closeness
friendliness
harmony
kindness
trust
warmth

Negativity
coldness
distance
distrust
envy
jealousy
possessiveness
rejection

Surprise
amazement
astonishment
awe
dismay
shock
wonder

Others
curiosity
interest
empathy
understanding
compassion
complacency
enchantment

THE EMOTIONS OF BUSINESS (EXAMPLES)

Why do people buy insurance?
> Because it makes them *feel* secure.

Why do executives fly Concorde?
> Because it makes them *feel* important.

Why do people go to restaurants when it is cheaper to eat at home?
> Because it make them *feel* good.

Why do people read newspapers?
> Because it makes them *feel* up-to-date and knowledgeable about what is happening in the world.

Why do people deposit their money in banks?
> Because they *feel* it is safe there.

Why do people go to watch sports events?
> Because of the excitement and their *feel* for their team.

Why do people spend so much money on fashionable clothes?
> Because it makes them *feel* smart.

Why do people visit doctors?
> Because it makes them *feel* better.

Why do people buy expensive mineral water?
> Because they *feel* it is the thing to do.

APPENDIX V

EMOTIONAL RANGE

Outrage	that the customer should have been treated so badly
Concern	that the customer isn't feeling too well
Anxiety	that the customer hasn't received the urgent ticket that was mailed yesterday
Relief	that everything went well for the customer after the initial problem
Amusement	when the customer's child refuses to let go of a toy the mother doesn't want to purchase
Pride	that the customer won the tournament using the equipment purchased from you
Kindness	when you went out of your way to help a blind person make a purchase
Astonishment	that the product failed to work first time
Revulsion	when the customer drew your attention to the filthy conditions in the rest rooms
Regret	that the customer has had cause to make a complaint a second time within a few days

APPENDIX VI

CUSTOMER SERVICE

INTEGRITY TESTS

All my answers below are worthy of further debate. They are not absolutes!

1 *In your opinion, one of your company's products is inferior to that of a competitor. A customer asks your opinion about this product. She wants to know in what way it is better than the competitive product. What should be your response?*

Author's answer
Your opinion could be wrong. Your response to the customer should be: "This product has many positive attributes that customers like. I can point these out to you. However, I am not an expert on our competitor's products and I would be loathe to give you a comparison. To be honest I am biased and therefore I must leave you to weigh up the pros and cons about which product is best for you."

2 *A customer returns a product, complaining it is faulty. You replace it without question. You subsequently check the product but cannot find the fault. Your manager instructs you to repackage the product as new and put it back on the shelf. What should you do?*

Author's answer
Do as you are told. For all you know the product is as good as new. However, raise the subject at the next team meeting and propose that returns which are "as good as new" be offered to customers as specials at a discounted price.

3 *A customer approaches the counter and offers to pay the full amount for a product, not having noticed that there is a substantial discount on all products purchased from that section. The customer appears quite happy to pay the full amount. You are on a profit-related bonus. Do you take the full money or draw the customer's attention to the discount?*

Author's answer
Inform the customer of the discount and charge the lower price.

4   *A newspaper article has highlighted major deficiencies in the services provided by your company to its customers. Privately you agree, as you know the company has been cutting back on staff. However, your company has issued a PR statement refuting the allegations. What action do you take when a customer asks you directly your opinion about these deficiencies?*

Author's answer
Your job is to represent the company. You should therefore reiterate the company line (as per the PR statement). If you feel you are in a position where you have to misrepresent either the company or your own principles, then you should take this up with the company first, not the customer.

5   *A customer contacts you and places a large and important order that he insists must be delivered within seven days. You know personally that the factory is running at full capacity and it is unlikely that the order will be met in time. You consult your boss, who tells you to take the order and promise delivery in seven days. He hints that you can fob off the customer with excuses on the seventh day. What do you do in the circumstances?*

Author's answer
Be honest. Say there is a small risk of a delay but you will take personal accountability to ensure that every effort is made to deliver on time. Then do your very best to achieve this.

6   *A customer is being abusive to one of your colleagues and is demanding to see the manager. You know that your manager is up to her eyes in work and is fed up with seeing this customer, who has been in many times before to complain. She has therefore told everyone that if this customer comes in she does not want to see him. Your colleague tells the customer that the manager is out. What would you do in the circumstance?*

Author's answer
Think laterally. Tell the person you are accountable for solving this type of problem. Then invite the customer to a quiet corner, offer him a cup of tea and then sit down and listen, agreeing wherever possible. Show as much interest in the customer as possible. If pressured, state that your manager is not in a position to help as she has assigned total accountability to you for this.

7   *It is 5.25 pm and you are about to close up. On this occasion you are particularly keen to leave on time at 5.30 pm as you have planned to visit your children's school for a concert and you do not wish to disappoint your children by being late. Just as you are thinking about putting your coat on, a customer walks through the door. It is 5.27 pm. You sense that the customer is going to take a lot of time to look at the product range before making a decision. What do you do?*

Author's answer
Be honest with the customer. Explain that normally you would stay on to help but on this occasion you have to be away on time. Invite the customer back at the earliest possible opportunity and offer a special discount for this inconvenience. Obtain the customer's name and telephone number and ring her up the following morning to apologize once again and to repeat your offer of a special discount.

INDEX

The author would be delighted to receive comments from any reader about this book. He can be contacted as follows:

Dr David Freemantle
Superboss Ltd
PO Box 813
Windsor SL4 2XU
UK
Fax: +44 (0)1753 863412
E-mail: team@superboss.co.uk
Internet: www.superboss.co.uk